GROWING UP AND ~~GROWING OLD~~

Life Course Studies

A Theory, Culture & Society series

Life Course Studies relates issues of ageing, human embodiment and the life cycle to the broader questions of social and cultural change. The series will focus attention on the cultural and social contexts in which various theorizations and images of the life course are formed and maintained. Individual titles will cover different aspects of the life course, including childhood, adult life and old age.

Theory, Culture & Society caters for the resurgence of interest in culture within contemporary social science and the humanities. Building on the heritage of classical social theory, the book series examines ways in which this tradition has been reshaped by a new generation of theorists. It will also publish theoretically informed analyses of everyday life, popular culture, and new intellectual movements.

GROWING UP AND GROWING OLD

Ageing and Dependency in the Life Course

Jenny Hockey and Allison James

SAGE Publications
London • Newbury Park • New Delhi

First published 1993

SAGE Publications Ltd
6 Bonhill Street
London EC2A 4PU

SAGE Publications Inc
2455 Teller Road
Newbury Park, California 91320

SAGE Publications India Pvt Ltd
32, M-Block Market
Greater Kailash – I
New Delhi 110 048

Published in association with *Theory, Culture & Society*, School of Health, Social and Policy Studies, University of Teesside

British Library Cataloguing in Publication Data

Hockey, Jennifer Lorna
 Growing Up and Growing Old: Ageing and Dependency in the Life Course. – (Life Course Studies: Theory, Culture & Society Series)
 I. Title   II. James, Allison   III. Series
 305.26

 ISBN 0–8039–8559–2
 ISBN 0–8039–8833–8 Pbk

Library of Congress catalog card number 92–50901

Typeset by Mayhew Typesetting, Rhayader, Powys
Printed in Great Britain by Biddles Ltd, Guildford, Surrey

For David who made sure we would take it further, and in affectionate memory of Marianne, his wife.

CONTENTS

ACKNOWLEDGEMENTS

The authors and publishers thank the following for permission to reproduce material:

Butterworth Heinemann for the poem 'Ellipse' from Averil Stedeford, *Facing Death* (1984), Heinemann Medical Books;

David Higham Associates for an extract from Dylan Thomas, *Under Milk Wood* (1954);

John Johnson (Authors' Agent) Ltd for 'Warning', © Jenny Joseph. From *Selected Poems*, Bloodaxe Books (1992);

Maggie Ling for the cartoon on page 12;

The Sutcliffe Gallery for the photograph on page 20;

G.E. Company (USA) for the advertisement on page 22.

INTRODUCTION

Since the 1970s there has been an increasing interest from the social sciences in studies of the life course, and in this book we explore the conceptual system framing the life course in contemporary Western societies.[1] In particular, we focus upon the ways in which it contextualizes the life experiences of children and elderly people, considering both its symbolic import and practical effects in terms of discourses of dependency. By using the term *life course*, rather than *life cycle*, we wish both to reflect and explore changes in the way life within Western societies is divided up. Rather than a predictable passage through fixed stages, there is now more variation in the way society's members pass through life, with the emergence of new social categories such as 'neo-nates', 'young old', and 'old old' registering this increasing diversity (Bryman et al., 1987). Understanding this process of age categorization through the life course – its symbolic import and social consequences – is a central concern of this volume.

Partly in response to such changing demographic patterns, 'old age' appeared as a new section on both the library shelves of educational institutions and in high street book shops, as the increasing numbers of elderly people began to be seen as a new 'problem' for politicians and researchers alike. In 1951, out of a population of 50.3 million people in the United Kingdom, 1.8 million were aged 75 years and over. By 1981, whilst the total population had only increased to 56.4 million, those aged 75 years and over now numbered 3.3 million (*Social Trends*, 1988). This 'problem' of the increasing numbers of very elderly people led to the development of theoretical approaches to ageing, in addition to the well-established body of literature about the care of elderly people. During the same period there were the beginnings of another new area of research interest. Though the study of childhood had been a focus for developmental psychologists since the early twentieth century, the 1970s saw a greater breadth of interest developing within a range of social science disciplines. Social historians, sociologists and anthropologists all addressed the topic and, through their work, produced a significant shift in focus towards seeing children as social actors rather than simply as adults in the making (James and Prout, 1990b).

It is perhaps not surprising then, that the early 1980s should find both of us engaged in research in these areas: growing up and growing old. Jenny was finishing her participant observation research amongst elderly people for a PhD thesis on attitudes towards death, whilst Allison was completing her doctoral work which focused on childhood and socialization.[2] We had both trained as social anthropologists at Durham University and, although this was at different times, as postgraduates both of us chose David H.M. Brooks as a supervisor. Later, and somewhat uncannily, we were living as near neighbours to one another, just one house apart. Inevitably we shared much common ground and gradually our friendship developed. Living so close to each other and often despairing of the solitary nature of research work we would frequently meet together over morning coffee or drop in for a cup of tea.

Out of these neighbourly encounters came the groundwork for this book. During conversation, as we bounced ideas off one another or wrestled with dense field material, it became increasingly apparent that the life experiences of elderly people in residential homes and those of children were strikingly similar. There were a number of parallels in the limitations and restrictions placed upon them and in the opinions expressed about them by their 'carers'. It became clear, for example, that elderly people in residential homes and children in their family homes were both subject to regimes of control which, while masked by loving care, effectively denied them much active choice or say in the direction of their own lives. We noticed, too, many similarities in the way both elderly people and children were made dependent through the particular strategies employed by independent adults (mothers, fathers, teachers, nurses, care assistants) in their roles as carers. The strategies of resistance used by elderly people and children to circumvent or obstruct the controls placed upon their actions were also remarkably similar: feigning deafness or refusing food allowed elderly residents and children fleeting autonomy and control over their own bodies, an experience which was often denied to them. For children, such acts of resistance marked a move towards greater independence; for very elderly people, these same acts temporarily halted or symbolically reversed the threat of encroaching dependency.

Soon we began to think more carefully about these parallels in experience and came to the provisional conclusion that the practices carried out in the residential home mirrored the socializing processes of the children's family home. There was, in effect, a process of infantilization occurring. Parents' care for their children was registered in their explicit control of children's behaviour and actions. By contrast, care workers with frail, elderly people exerted a more subtle and implicit system of control within the regime of care itself. Through overt and hidden social practices, whether of caring control or controlling care, both elderly people and young children were being denied full personhood for, if personhood in Western society is symbolized through ideas of autonomy, self-determination and choice, then these were the very options being edited out by those caring for the very young and the very old. We suspected that there might be more to this than sets of interesting parallels. Indeed, we knew that others had already identified them and drawn attention to their emotional and social consequences (Gresham, 1976). We were also aware that such metaphoric linkage of the life course is by no means a recent phenomenon. In the fourth century BC the metaphor of childhood for old age was already well established through Aristophanes's suggestion that old age is but a second childhood. From the medieval period till the end of the sixteenth century an individual's life was visualized as being in seven distinct stages – 'one man in his time plays many parts, his acts being seven ages' – and, as described by Shakespeare, old age was again seen as child-like:

. . . The sixth age shifts
Into the lean and slipper'd pantaloon,
With spectacles on nose, and pouch on side;
His youthful hose well sav'd, a world too wide
For his shrunk shank; and his big manly voice,
Turning again towards childish treble, pipes
And whistles in his sound. Last scene of all,
That ends this strange and eventful history.
Its second childishness and mere oblivion;
Sans teeth, sans eyes, sans taste, sans everything.

(*As You Like It*, II. vii)

However, as yet, all this remained untheorized in the literature and, as our work progressed, we began to think how this might be done. The infantilization practices we had noted and the use of metaphors of childhood in descriptions of old age could, we thought, in both cases be seen to soften the approach of death which confronted very elderly people and their carers on a daily basis. Through time this initial hunch developed into a more theoretical understanding of the metaphoric role of childhood in framing dependency in a whole variety of forms. There was then a shift in our thinking: we moved on from merely noting and remarking on parallels in social experience between children and frail, elderly people to accounting for them as metaphoric transformations being played out through the life course in a systematic and oppressive manner. We were beginning to piece together and comprehend a continuum of behaviour in social practice, from the casual 'let me help you, dear' through to the babying of spoon-fed, cot-bound elderly people. We also began to see this as a continuum through time, as elderly people moved from the independence of the 'young old' through to the encroaching dependency of the 'old old'.

Though our careers and our domestic ties led both of us away from Durham we continued to maintain close links, as friends and colleagues, both of us committed to pursuing the connections that had been the focus for many of our early conversations. Allison's experience of becoming a parent for the first time and Jenny's of her children growing up and becoming independent fuelled this desire. In 1988 we took the opportunity to formulate our ideas more concretely by writing a joint paper (with the same title as this book) for the Association of Social Anthropologists conference on ageing (Hockey and James, 1988).[3]

In this brief history, then, are located the major themes of this book and an indication of the style of its presentation which makes no separation between the personal and professional. For example, what, for us, started as a 'professional' interest is for many people, carers and cared for alike, of intense personal concern. At the same time, working together on this book has caused us both to draw upon and reconsider our roles as mothers, as daughters of retired parents and as ageing women. Our experiences as carers of dependent children and independent men, our possible future role in caring for elderly parents, make the concerns of this book most personal for us.

Our central concern, then, is to explore some of the issues surrounding concepts of dependency, personhood and power in Western societies through people's everyday experiences of them. We endeavour to make sense of the ways in which, through metaphors of childhood, many elderly people, and others who are dependent, risk becoming socially marginalized. We ask why it is that this form of oppressive discrimination often passes unremarked in everyday life. Our focus on the metaphoric use of language does not mean, however, that we ignore social practices for it is clear that the cognitive system which sustains linguistic metaphors of childhood is also played out non-verbally through social practice. In Geertz's terms, it is one of the 'socially established structures of meaning' which inform people's actions (1975: 12).

The arguments which we are developing in this book to understand dependency during childhood and deep old age can be extended to include other forms and ways of oppressive discrimination – such as those experienced by some younger disabled people who cannot live independently. Through parallels in everyday experiences their similarity of social position is revealed. Thus it would seem that those who lack, or who are denied autonomy, are often made to share a space on society's fringe, whether permanently or temporarily. Although some people are able to withstand the ideological, moral, economic and social pressures which, as we shall see, insidiously impinge on their everyday activities, many others are forced to retreat. People with disabilities or those who are chronically sick may, like very elderly people, experience feelings of deep and personal humiliation as the subjects of the unthinking practice of infantilizing actions. Therefore, although our main focus in this volume is on the ways in which metaphors of childhood are used to structure conceptions of old age, these parallels will also be noted.

Central to our argument is the cultural specificity of this apparently unremarkable practice of infantilization in Western cultures. Whilst not denying the biological realities of old age or its distressing aspect when, for example, senility or total paralysis overtake the physical body, we do suggest that the Western framing of such dependency as 'childish' is just one version, just one vision of old age. There are alternative ways of seeing and understanding; indeed, there are some encouraging signs that in Western cultures this vision may be changing both politically and economically. For example, the passivity often imputed to very elderly people through assertions of their 'child-like' and marginal social status masks an increasing politicization. Older people are beginning to assert their citizenship rights to independence and are challenging those structures of power which have for so long maintained their dependent status. Economic changes have also provided sections of the elderly population with a powerful role in consumer society. A parallel process of politicization is also evidenced in the increasing vocality of people with disabilities who, rejecting charity, are demanding their right to work and adequate support for independent living (Oliver, 1990). Technological advances have opened up more opportunities for work and leisure for some disabled people. However, despite new social movements such as these, a great deal of both overt and subtle discrimination still persists, as it does for elderly people.

Through detailing the many different ways in which attitudes and beliefs structure personal everyday encounters and also sustain wider acts of discrimination at the level of social structure we offer, then, the kind of analysis which Söder has recently pleaded for. It is one which relates 'the ideological and structural moral dilemmas to the dilemmas individuals try to handle in daily encounters' (1990: 238). In this way we establish 'the links between public attitudes and prevailing ideologies and social structures in society' as we unravel the logical cognitive structure which sustains practices of infantilization (1990: 238).

Our social material for this book is enormously varied. Metaphors of childhood are widespread, a common discourse of Western cultures, located in slips of the tongue as much as the grand soliloquy, in the quality press as well as the sensational reporting of the tabloids. At one extreme, they can be discovered enacted through legislation, whilst at the other they take shape through the form and quality of interpersonal encounters between carer and cared for. This book draws therefore on a wide body of source material: published accounts are placed alongside our own and other people's field experiences, press cuttings accompany more literary works, popular culture sits with high art. To restore the balance of power which infantilizing practices disrupt through the denial of personhood and independence, we have also drawn upon autobiographical and personal accounts. In all of these a consistent set of ideas about dependency and autonomy are to be found writ large.

Alongside this body of 'ethnographic' texts we have placed material which relates to non-Western societies. Drawing on an anthropological perspective these provide points of comparison and reveal the many other ways in which childhood, ageing and impairment can be culturally perceived. This use of the comparative method makes our approach part of an 'interpretive humanity concerned with cultural specificity and diversity rather than a generalizing science concerned with cultural and social universals' (Holy, 1987: 12). It is not, however, without certain limitations: in particular, the uneven availability of source material. For example, the number of autobiographical accounts of childhood, ageing and impairment in Western societies is relatively small and fewer still are available to us from non-Western contexts. Thus the works of Winifred Foly (1986) and Rose Gamble (1979) on childhood hardships, Gladys Elder (1977) and Ellen Newton (1980) on old age and Christy Brown (1990) on growing up disabled have become well known, memorable almost by virtue of their scarcity as examples of this form of account. Furthermore, whilst powerfully revealing, they leave us ignorant of all those other individuals who failed to develop a publishable degree of literacy in both Western and non-Western cultures. Ethnographic accounts, whilst more plentiful, are still relatively uncommon and, in particular, accounts of disability outside Western societies are very rare indeed (Oliver, 1990; Reynolds-Whyte, 1990). However, this paucity of material is itself significant. It supports the argument that children, elderly people and those with disabilities may, like women, be a 'muted' group in society, denied a representative voice (Hardman, 1973; Ardener, 1975). Furthermore, it suggests that in societies where disabilities are more common and more visible, where life expectancy is reduced and where children are not so separated from adult life, perceptions of these issues as noteworthy or significant may be less marked. These twin themes will be drawn out through the volume.

In that we are concerned to reveal the logic by which infantilizing practices in Western cultures are sustained we are, inevitably, drawn into a great deal of theoretical discussion of the ways in which metaphor works. An important starting point is Lakoff and Johnson's proposition that 'our ordinary conceptual system, in terms of which we think and act, is fundamentally metaphorical in nature' (1980: 3). We therefore offer an analysis of how metaphor shapes our understanding of reality, of how it is that a particular ideology of old age is sustained at the expense of others, of the kinds of rituals and social processes which maintain children and elderly people in marginal places on society's fringe and of the ways in which their personhood is denied. However, rather than presenting an abstracted theoretical perspective at the outset, we have chosen, instead, to address these themes through particular substantive issues and the detailing of field studies and auto-biographical accounts. As Geertz has argued, it is through such illustrative material that the 'mega-concepts' of social sciences 'can be given the sort of sensible actuality that makes it possible to think not only realistically and concretely *about* them, but, what is more important, creatively and imaginatively *with* them' (1975: 23).

In Chapter 1, we introduce the idea that there is a specific cultural repertoire of figurative language associated with ageing in British and other Western contexts, which can be used to empower and centre independent adulthood at the expense of childhood and dependent old age. This theme patterns a wide diversity of social contexts and experiences, including people of all ages who are made dependent. In discussing the ideological role which this plays in shaping a particular construction of the ageing process we are drawn into a discussion of the way in which metaphors work. How is it that the perception of dependency in old age as 'child-like' is authenticated in social discourse? Chapter 2 opens discussion of this question by exploring the meaning of the concept of personhood in

Western cultures, relating it to the historical construction of individualism and the development of modern conceptions of children as non-persons. As human beings, predominantly thought of as a group apart, dependent and helpless children came to be dominant symbols for the dependency of others. In Chapter 3, we explore the precise ways in which dependency is understood as 'childish' by focusing upon the physical body and examining the ways in which the bodies of elderly people are socially constructed through metonym as child-like: that is, certain features predominate as meaningful, whilst others are dismissed. Thus it is that incontinence, for example, may mark an elderly person as a non-person, as child-like, despite his or her obvious physical maturity in other aspects of the body. Chapter 4 continues to explore the resonance of the metaphor of the child in constructing the nature of dependency by considering the powerful role of a familialist ideology in Western cultures. This reveals that the model of care which the family provides may mask a quite rigid system of control, which sustains dependency at the expense of independence. In Chapter 5 we draw upon Turner's concept (1974) of ritual liminality in order to explore the exclusion of children and elderly people from the world of adult work and leisure and show how this not only sustains the dependency of these social categories but also contributes to their marginal social status. Finally, Chapter 6 explores some of the possible ways in which a liminal or marginal social status can become a source of strength for those so classed, a position from which resistance, struggle and change may be embarked upon.

Notes

1 Whilst recognizing the enormous diversity of cultures encompassed within the term 'Western society', we use it to refer to themes and issues common to many societies within the West, combining with this more general level of discussion specific examples from within the West. Britain and the United States will provide the main source of these.

2 In those studies and throughout this book the names of all institutions and individuals have been changed in order to maintain confidentiality.

3 Our thanks are due to all who have offered criticisms and comments on this and later papers which have formed the basis of this book. Allison James is also grateful to the British Academy for a Postdoctoral Fellowship which provided financial support during the writing.

1

INFANTILIZATION AS SOCIAL DISCOURSE

This book explores the cognitive structures through which human beings create and manage the idea and the experience of dependency. In particular, it focuses upon the ways in which conceptions of children and childhood are used to structure metaphorically the experience of old age and other contexts of dependency in many Western societies. Using Britain and the United States as our primary case studies, a number of themes run through the discussion: first, a recognition of the interdependence of people in everyday life which is, however, disguised and re-presented through a cognitive system working to maintain dependence and independence as binary oppositions; secondly, an acknowledgement that power in society is contestable despite its apparent fixity in the hands of a few; thirdly, a challenge to the stigmatizing role which categorical stereotypes can play in the lives of particular groups of people; fourthly, a realization of the ways in which ideas about personhood, individualism, gender and the life course are embedded within particular socio-historic contexts and cultures;[1] lastly, a depiction of the powerful role which metaphors can play in structuring and shaping people's personal and public lives. The following chapters detail the precise ways in which the metaphoric use of childhood as a mode of thought impacts upon and unravels through the daily lives of those who are very old and others who are dependent. In doing this we neither condone nor justify such infantilizing practices. Instead, we lay bare the logic which sustains them in order that change might better be effected. As Lakoff and Johnson have remarked, exploring such metaphors of living is important for 'what is at issue is not the truth or falsity of a metaphor but the perceptions and inferences that follow from it and the actions that are sanctioned by it' (1980: 158).

In considering the life course as a source of metaphors for dependency we ask why it is that in the Western context confused elderly people may be described by their carers as being in their second childhood. How is it that the onset of a disabling physical condition, whether in old age or earlier in life, is often accompanied by a reduction or loss of social status if dependency ensues? We ask what is the semantic resonance and source of this common framing of dependency, so vividly depicted in Arber's recollection of his early experiences of becoming disabled:

> The first time I went out in the chair I said I would never go out again. It wasn't only that people stared, old ladies offered me sweets, and patted me on the head. My wife was asked if she was taking her baby for a walk. (1991: 56)

Such casual remarks or careless gestures may not be intentionally humiliating, designed to demoralize. But this is their effect. What interests us and offers us a challenge to understand is why such involuntary actions seem to be a somehow 'natural' response to dependency, and are often construed as kindly meant. Infantilization processes can have a powerful and potent role in shaping many dependent people's everyday experiences, engendering feelings of social marginalization, personal humiliation and emotional vulnerability. How is it, then, that for some elderly people this same process may occur as a mutually negotiated form of social interaction which takes place between themselves and younger adults (Coupland, 1991)?

Examples of such infantilizing practices – the treatment of elderly or disabled people as if they were children – were first held up for critical attention by practitioners and clients involved in the health and welfare services in the 1950s (Gresham, 1976). Condemned as degrading and humiliating, infantilization is, contemporarily, seen largely as a practical problem, to be effaced by geriatricians and social workers in particular, through scrutiny of care practices. But, as this volume argues, malpractices such as 'babytalk', pet naming and child-like 'play' activities are not confined to the care regimes of certain hospitals or residential homes. Rather, these are but specific examples of a more diffuse and more powerful mode of thought, and a continuum of practice. It is one which is so exceedingly common as to pass as an unremarkable aspect of everyday discourse within Western cultures. Infantilization, then, is not just an issue for those directly involved in the giving and receiving of care in Western society. It touches us all. Metaphors of childhood permeate the very language we use and images we draw on, providing implicit frames of reference for everyday social interactions and encounters. What this volume seeks to do is explore both how and why they do so as, in this first chapter, we lay out the broad sweep of their semantic power.

Examples abound. Two readers' letters were published in a quality British newspaper in 1991 written by people in their seventies who argued a spirited *defence* of active, independent and autonomous old age, assertively rejecting the ageism to be found within many Western cultures.

> I am a 73-year-old 'wrinkly' who, determined not to become a cabbage after retirement, took up the piano at the age of 70. . . . Three days a week I work for an international trading company. My shorthand is still 120 plus and touch typing is second nature to me.
>
> 'Wrinkly', when used to designate an old person, is not amusing – it is semantically incorrect, rude and unkind. After all, we old people do not describe our teenage friends as 'the spotties' . . . (*Observer*, 7 July 1991)

These letters were, however, positioned in the newspaper under a cartoon sketch of an old man – thinning hair and wrinkled face, half spectacles, and sports jacket – juggling with a tube of anti-wrinkle cream, a typewriter, a cabbage, a musical treble clef and a document in French. The caption 'Wrinkle, wrinkle, little star' was placed beneath. What purpose did this image serve? Why did it seem appropriate? Whatever the explicit intention of this gratuitous parodying of a children's nursery rhyme – wrinkle replaced twinkle – combined with the jocular cartoon, the immediate effect was conceptually to link old age with childhood. Through poking fun, was the sentiment expressed in the letter – that it is never too late to learn – reinforced or, conversely, trivialized? Did it reframe these letters as 'amusing comments' rather than serious critiques? Whatever the effect, it is significant that a childish rhyme seemed culturally appropriate as a fitting caption for a discussion of old age.

The drawing of such analogies between old age and childhood are commonplace, appearing frequently in press reports:

> Twin sisters . . . celebrated their 90th birthday. The birthday girls celebrated on Tuesday with sherry and birthday cake. (*Post Midweek*, 7 October 1982)

This reference to 'girls' may seem unproblematic in the context of newspaper reports of local events; like the pat on the head and the offer of sweets, the association with childhood is a purely figurative expression of affection. But, as we shall see, the figurative often becomes literal and, whilst these particular examples may seem trivial, this volume argues that they are symptomatic of more damaging and embedded practices of infantilization. Played out in a diversity of social practices and ideologies, these range from everyday experiences at the doctor's surgery or in the family home, through to state legislation in the political and economic spheres. The cumulative effect is thus far from trivial.

In recent years critical attention has been drawn to the problems

and implications raised by these practices for both the recipients
and givers of care (Gresham, 1976; Dolinsky, 1984). The often
patronizing attitudes of nurses involved in the care of elderly
patients is condemned and it is argued that infantilizing practices
constitute a form of psychological abuse which may exacerbate
their helplessness. Knowles, for example, sees that treating very
elderly people as if they were children may 'start a slow and
insidious process of institutionalization through smothering' (1987:
59). Suggestions have also been made of ways in which changes in
working practices can ameliorate the everyday relationships
between carers and cared for in an attempt to restore the dignity
of those who are physically dependent (Crump, 1991).

   Although welcome, acknowledgement of the issues and suggestions of measures for improvement in the care of dependent elderly
people may not in themselves be sufficient to effect wider changes

in social practice. As will become clear, there is a more fundamental and intractable issue: the cultural pervasiveness and embeddedness of metaphors of childhood within the discourses surrounding ageing and dependency. In effect, in a Western culture such as Britain or the United States, where the ideology of childhood is most intimately entwined with that of dependency, the infantilizing of those who are dependent but who are not children has become 'naturalized'. It is seen as somehow inevitable, as the way things are. Attitudes and practices seen as appropriate to the care of dependent minors may in this way be unquestioningly and 'naturally' transferred to other dependent groups under the auspices of care. This makes them therefore very resistant to change. As we shall show, they derive their meaning and substance from an exceedingly powerful cognitive model which denies full personhood to those who, in the way that children are, are perceived to be dependent. Through this culturally constructed model of dependency, many of those in deep old age and others who are dependent – some people who are chronically sick or disabled – may be made to take a conceptual position alongside children on the margins of society. The following chapters detail some of the ways in which this occurs.

It is our contention, then, that the 'babytalk' sometimes used by nurses with their sick or geriatric patients *and* the state legislation which often effectively excludes elderly people from paid work in mainstream economic life are both manifestations of a key logical cognitive structure through which human dependency is created and re-created in Western cultures. Traceable in a series of shared concepts and models, the metaphor of the child provides one important vehicle for and structure within which human dependency of whatever kind is understood. It is a mode of thought which, whilst perhaps softening the emotional impact of deep old age or physical dependency during adulthood, is experienced as socially marginalizing and personally humiliating by people who are themselves dependent. Moreover, it is a way of thinking about dependency which is in fact far from 'natural'. Through the course of this volume its historical emergence within British culture will be both demonstrated and compared with a whole range of other cultural models of dependency and old age. Thus it is, we suggest, only by understanding and exploring the ways in which the language and ideology of childhood works to structure ideas of dependency, that is by historically and culturally locating its imagery and meanings, that any long term and effective change in social practices can be set in motion. That is to say, we need to explore why it is that infantilizing practices often pass unremarked and why it is that those who are no longer able to look after themselves should so readily remind us of children. Only then can suggestions for improvements in social practice be made.

Our twin aims, then, are to demonstrate the far reaching nature of this systematic mode of thought, and to account for both its conceptual basis and practical realization within society. We address the ways in which broad social categories – such as 'the elderly' and 'the young' – are, through the workings of this conceptual system, mobilized as reference points for individual elderly people or children. But in doing so we do not seek to ignore the reality that some human beings are physically and mentally impaired either throughout life or during certain periods of it; neither do we fail to recognize that certain of life's intrinsic biological stages – infancy and deep old age for example – make human survival impossible without the periodic care and dedicated support of others. On the contrary, what interests us is how these intrinsic and inescapable aspects of human life are subject to a particular and culturally specific conceptual framing and why it is that this framing, often pursued through acts of great warmth and consideration, may nevertheless be experienced as deeply humiliating by those receiving care. This book thus establishes an arena for discussion, as well as generating agendas for change, by drawing upon a large and varied body of illustrative and theoretical material from a broad range of historical eras and cultural contexts. In this way it becomes possible to trace out the social construction of dependence (Barnes, 1990; Oliver, 1990).

Images and metaphors of dependency in the life course

By situating our discussion of ageing within a life course, rather than a life cycle, perspective it becomes possible to emphasize the variations and continuities in social status and position which people experience as they mature (Bryman et al., 1987). It also permits us to see the ways in which the apparent 'naturalness' with which metaphors of childhood are invoked by the carers of dependent elderly people are shaped by the broader categories and social values through which ageing and the life course are commonly described. That is to say, they are not random, aberrant features of language use and social practice but instead are constitutive of the conceptual systems through which the life course is thought about in Western cultures. To show some of the ways in which these conceptual systems are maintained and reproduced we shall focus on popular depictions of ageing, although a similar exercise could be carried out exploring images of disability (Longmore,

1985; Hadley and Brodwin, 1988). Drawing on anthropological work on life cycle rituals (Van Gennep, 1960; Turner, 1974), we suggest that the biological process of ageing in societies such as those of Britain and the United States is conceived in terms of a positive to negative *rite de passage*: childhood and youth provide a positively perceived preparation for the centrality of independent adult life which, gradually, gives way to the negativity of deep old age. It is an elliptical movement, portrayed in numerous ways in everyday life – through language, visual images and the use of stereotypes. But, as we shall see, at the core of each is the assumption that dependent old age is an unwelcome aspect of adulthood for, as Featherstone and Hepworth (1986) suggest, there is a stigma associated with the loss of bodily competence.[2] Indeed, a survey commissioned by Age Concern in 1992 revealed that four out of every five young adults in Britain feared old age, with two-thirds citing either loss of independence or poor health in old age as a predominant concern (*Guardian*, 22 January 1992). The questions we ask then are: first, how do these attitudes manifest themselves in everyday life and, secondly, why should this be?

Verbal imagery

The qualitative movement through the life course, depicted above as a positive to negative passage in many Western cultures, is embodied in numerous colloquial phrases and everyday observations. 'Growing up', for example, is understood as a more positive experience than 'growing old'. Such is the power of metaphoric language that this emphasis upon an 'upwards' movement not only acknowledges accumulating height but also resonates with other metaphors which literally 'high'light positively perceived aspects of life (Lakoff and Johnson, 1980). When we are on the 'up and up', we often feel 'elated' or 'high'; we look 'up' to those we respect, but look 'down' on those who are 'beneath' contempt, 'down and out' or 'down at heel'. We may be 'downcast' when things are going badly and feel 'down in the dumps' and 'down in the mouth'. Those who are growing old, literally shrinking and losing height as old bones bend their frames, and those nearing death, are both described as 'going downhill fast', poised, as it were, to enter the 'valley' of death. Such examples demonstrate the powerful compass of metaphoric language which gives a logic and consistency to the metaphors we live by and, in particular, to the passage from childhood through to old age.

The 'up'/'down' orientational metaphors (Lakoff and Johnson, 1980) through which passage through the life course is conceptualized are paralleled by another set. A group of spatial metaphors reflect a positive to negative, centre to periphery movement. In Highfield House, a residential home for elderly people, those who were 'going downhill fast' were also seen to be 'on their way out', to be moving towards the margins of life itself (Hockey, 1990). Thus it is that the combining of these two related metaphoric systems, in other contexts, produces the 'down-and-out', that is, the most marginal of society's members.

Other examples reinforce, through their semantic resonance, how a particular and negative perception of old age is 'naturalized' in language in a Western culture: in Britain, for example, 'over the hill', 'past it' and 'one foot in the grave', spring easily to mind as common descriptions of old age. Although many of these verbal images are polysemic – perhaps entailing a range of subtly different meanings for those who encounter them – they embody, nevertheless, an implicit 'ageism' and frame a particular ideology. This, as we shall see, has a powerful influence upon social practice. Following Thompson (1984), we would argue, then, that

> in using language we are constantly engaged in a creative imaginative activity. We are constantly involved in extending the meaning of words, in producing new meanings through metaphor, word-play and interpretation; and we are thereby also involved, knowingly or not, in altering, undermining or reinforcing our relations with others and with the world. To study ideology is to study, in part, the ways in which these creative imaginary activities serve to sustain social relations which are asymmetrical with regard to the organization of power. (1984: 6)

The potential range and potency of metaphors of childhood for dependency are highlighted by considering the example of the sensitizing experience of feminism and black consciousness to language use. The strides towards equal opportunities made by the feminist movement during the 1960s and 1970s were, in part, a result of a recognition of the deep-seated and ingrained nature of sexist attitudes in Western cultures. Tinkering with systems for equal pay was recognized as inadequate when perceptions of and access to opportunities for work were already unequally weighted through language and social imagery. As feminists pointed out, the well-worn language of sexism which is repeated endlessly in mundane day-to-day encounters between women and men, is both generated by and serves to reproduce sets of discriminatory attitudes which favour men's interests to the cost of women's. Only by change at this fundamental level of social discourse and practice would equal opportunities become truly equal. Hence, in Britain and the United States, an insistence on the terms 'Ms', rather than

'Miss' or 'Mrs', 'chair' or 'chairperson' rather than 'chairman' was no frivolous demand. It revealed the very embeddedness of sexist attitudes in language itself (Spender, 1980). In the same way, the raising of consciousness about race has shown how prejudice operates in subtle and implicit ways to 'naturalize' discriminatory attitudes based on skin colour. While 'nigger' and 'blackie' are now used only as terms of intentional abuse, the negative and thence racist associations which the colour black has in Western (and indeed other) cultures remain (Milner, 1983). Black, traditionally, is perceived to be far from beautiful; it is associated with evil (black magic), depression (black moods), dirt ('black as the ace of spades'). White, by contrast, has connotations of virtue ('pure as the driven snow') and cleanliness (snowy white) which is next to godliness. When the language of ageing is subjected to the same scrutiny it becomes apparent that similar subtle discriminatory practices operate conceptually to marginalize and diminish the social status of elderly people. A similar case can be made for the language associated with disability (Shearer, 1981).

Differential evaluations of stages in the life course are commonly to be found in everyday language use and their import should be considered. For example, very old people may jokingly be described as entering their 'second childhood', or as going 'ga-ga' when their memories falter. This use of the term 'ga-ga' to describe aspects of old age is echoed by the babbling baby who utters 'goo goo ga ga'. Through this mutual referencing, old age is drawn into alignment with the dependency of early childhood. 'Ga-ga' refers to the utterances of two voices – those of the very old and of the very young – in that language, for both these categories of people, may be absent. Not yet learnt or now scrambled, 'ga-ga' stands for two kinds of nonsense. However, it is only babies who are recognized as having the potential to change. Only they will learn to talk sense; amongst very elderly people speech patterns may disintegrate. Those who are not so old, whose minds although not their bodies remain active, may be described as 'young at heart'. Welcomed, and therefore perhaps not questioned, the phrase 'young at heart' asserts the ascendancy of youth, making it a desirable condition to hold on to despite an ageing exterior. At their very core, beneath the wrinkled skin and inside the arthritic frame, such elderly people are applauded for their retention of a youthful outlook.

The metaphoric linkage of both ends of the life course is evident in the work of Dylan Thomas (1954) in his striking account of life in a small Welsh town:

First voice
All over the town, babies and old men are cleaned and
put into their broken prams and wheeled on to the
sunlit cockled cobbles or out into the backyards under
the dancing underclothes, and left.
A baby cries.

Old man
I want my pipe and he wants his bottle.

(Dylan Thomas, *Under Milk Wood*, 1954: 36)

These lines offer an amply fleshed image of the start of the day
in the lives of the very young and the very old. The first voice
speaks and the old man calls out and through this discourse we
are led to understand as similar the circumstances of those whose
lives have barely begun and those whose lives are almost over.
Both are imaged as helpless and dependent, with little else to do
but slumber in the sunshine. From dust to dust the life cycle
completes itself.

Does the continued affirmation of metaphors of childhood for
dependent old age thus represent one way in which the finality of
life in death is culturally managed? Deteriorating speech patterns
amongst very elderly people is feared to presage the disintegration
of the mind and body and its ultimate outcome, death. Might it be
then, that through the childish term 'ga-ga' the rambling incon-
sistencies of senility are softened in their emotional impact? Is
hope, promise of a future, held out through comparisons with the
growing child or are the very elderly simply mocked for their
forgetfulness or idiosyncrasy?

The consequences of such a mode of thought have, as we shall
see, considerable social significance for, as one recent development
confirms, such sentiments are not merely the stuff of literary allu-
sion or device. A newspaper article from 1990 reports the establish-
ment of America's first day-care centre for both children and
elderly people, and echoes the themes of Dylan Thomas's poem:

> the company hoped working parents could drop off their children and
> elderly relatives in the morning, knowing they would have been fed,
> entertained, educated and cared for when they collected them in the
> evening. (*Daily Telegraph*, 7 March 1990)

Visual imagery

The conceptual pairing of the very young with the very old in
language use, reflects, we suggest, a particular framing of ageing
in Western cultures. But what purpose might it serve, what ideas
are conveyed? Examples of its manifestation in visual imagery

indicate some of the meanings which may be conveyed. The cover of one of the Open University key set books about ageing, *An Ageing Population* by Carver and Liddiard (1978), depicts in photographic form an old man and a young child standing together at a garden gate. The old and young are pictured in safe companionship, engaged in hands-in-pocket scrutiny of the outside world within which they themselves have no part. It is a poignant image which conceptually brings together the extreme ends of the life course, old age and youth. In their mutual social marginalization, life appears to be going on without them over the garden wall. Sepia tinted, albeit contemporary in content, the image evokes a bygone Golden Age. A temporal distance is established, one which implicitly connotes the social distance between the innocent haven of old age/childhood and the demanding public world of adulthood.

Two interpretations are possible. First, this image may remind us that 'childhood is the happiest days of one's life', just as retirement is now advertised as a time of (p)leisure in magazines for elderly people such as *Choices* (Phillipson, 1982; Young, 1990). Secondly, the imagery of the photograph may work figuratively to deny the life course its logical conclusion. Is death perhaps being conceptually avoided or softened through the cyclical restructuring of time?

The second theme is the more culturally explicit. It appears, for example, in a photograph taken by Frank Meadow Sutcliffe (1853–1941), one of the first to work within what later became known as the tradition of English pictorial photography. The sepia photograph, taken on Tate Hill Pier, Whitby in 1884, depicts an old man smoking a clay pipe cuddling a small boy. They are in fact grand-nephew and great-uncle. The old man, an arm encircling his nephew's shoulder and a hand enclosing his small bare feet, draws him into a shared intimacy. The photograph is entitled, significantly, 'Morning and Evening'. Through its association with the daily temporal cycle old age and childhood are located side by side at either end of the day; as day turns into night, so each eve is followed by a new morn. Contemporarily, this theme of social marginality, as experienced by both elderly people and children, finds echoes elsewhere. It is, for example, made central to the early 1990s film *Cinema Paradiso*. An old man and young boy find a common purpose and trust in one another through the cinema. They become united as outsiders, escapees – one imaginary, one real – from the stifled and closed atmosphere of a small Italian community. Old and young are depicted bound together through adversity and through their distance from the centres of social power.

Arluke and Levin (1984) have drawn attention to similar juxtapositions of the old and the young in US advertisements. The pairing appears in diverse contexts, from advertisements for incontinence pads through to those for restaurants. These, they suggest, situate old people in a 'second childhood' by ascribing to them the moods, personalities, appearance, physical problems and social life of children:

A prescription drug ad for a stool-softener features a smiling bifocaled older woman. The text reads: 'Minnie moved her bowels today. The day started right for Minnie. That young doctor feller gave her a stool softener to take last night. And it worked! . . . Minnie figures she's got the smartest doctor in town.' It is not too farfetched to imagine that Minnie's smile not only expresses her physical relief but also her pride at being told she moved her bowels. (Arluke and Levin, 1984: 9)

Is Minnie positioned as child-like to make the physical deterioration of old bodies seem somehow more acceptable or the impact of
ageing upon the body less severe?
An advertisement for a medical care system in the *Guardian*
newspaper (19 April 1989) provides a comparable British example.
Depicted in a fine line drawing are the faces of an old man and
young girl. Pressed close together, in loving proximity, they both
gaze into the distance. The slogan reads: 'We bring technology to
life.' Why was this particular image used? Both children and
elderly people have a potential need for medical care, as do
independent adults. Is it that the old man's perhaps uncertain and
limited future (illness and death) becomes somehow more certain
and assured through association with the child's future (wellness
and life), thereby emphasizing the ability of the medical care
system to prolong life through the application of technology?
Whilst it may not be possible to detail the precise way in which
these infantilized images work upon the imagination, their
cumulative effect is clear: they perpetuate the paternalistic treatment of elderly people as 'dependent inferiors' (Arluke and Levin,
1984: 10).

> The 'Kiddies Menu' of a popular Massachusetts ice cream parlour
> portrays an older man walking hand-in-hand with a young boy. As
> clearly stated on the face of the menu, 'for all kids under 10 and over
> 65' the bill of fare consists of a 'hot doggie', 'kiddie burger' and a
> 'peanut butter and jelly samwich' (*sic*). (1984: 9-10)

The visual images and adoption of childish terms (hot doggie,
kiddie burger, and samwich) connote the 'natural' mutuality of the
young and the old, a shared social position and shared dependency
on the caring of others.
    The cyclical linking of the broad age-based social categories
'childhood' and 'old age' is often given a more concrete form
through the evocation of a particular social relationship: the affectionate kinship tie that ideally exists between grandparent and
grandchild. As in the previous examples, this may be depicted
through close physical contact, the clasped hands and shared
touch. An advertisement for the Royal Air Force Benevolent Fund,
which appeared in the *Daily Telegraph* (29 March 1990) in Britain,
draws upon this theme. In the advertisement an old man – grey-
haired and bespectacled – and a young girl are depicted. He gazes,
half smiling, out of the frame, whilst the child looks adoringly at
the man. We can tell the man's age through his appearance: sports
jacket, casual checked shirt and woven tie. A military photograph,

We bring technology to life

Everywhere in Europe, our focus is on life.

I.G.E. Medical Systems and the European associates of General Electric CGR have teamed up with the medical community throughout Europe.

We bring world-class expertise to technology in x-ray, mammography, computed tomography, magnetic resonance, nuclear medicine, ultrasound and radiotherapy...the advanced techniques that help to diagnose and treat patients with speed and accuracy.

Throughout our sales and service organisation, research laboratories and manufacturing facilities, some 6,000 Europeans are dedicated to the future of medicine.

Working closely with physicians and medical researchers to develop tomorrow's advances...today.

Our vision and capability span the globe, but our commitment is local. Wherever we are our focus is on life.

I.G.E. Medical Systems

 I.G.E. Medical Systems is an affiliate of General Electric Company (USA) and not connected with the English company of a similar name.

I.G.E. Medical Systems Ltd., Coolidge House, 352 Buckingham Avenue, Slough, Berks SL1 4ER. Tel: 0753 874000.

depicting the man's past successful career, hangs on the wall behind them. The caption is 'spoken' by the child on the old man's behalf: 'Grandpa was admired for many brave acts, but he won his DFM for his part in the Battle of Britain. Now he's been in the wars himself he says its the RAF Benevolent Fund that really deserves a medal.' Why does not the man speak for himself? This apparent silence and passivity positions him in old age as lacking effective power, a social position made all the more poignant by his former prominent rank in society.

Stereotypes of ageing

The themes of physical decline, dependency, marginality and passivity and of the natural affinity between elderly people and those who are young, which commonly appear in both verbal and visual imagery, help to sustain certain cultural stereotypes of ageing. According to Cohen, stereotypes, whilst rarely having 'validity as accounts of how people see themselves' do nevertheless act as powerful symbolic markers of identity which are used to attribute characteristics to others: 'in the "public" face internal variety disappears or coalesces into a simple symbolic statement' (Cohen, 1986: 13). A problem arises, then, when those so caricatured are not empowered to respond to or reject the labels others put on them through asserting their personal and individual differences from the stereotypical. Here, a range of stereotypes of elderly people is considered.

Roald Dahl's portrayal of the young George's hostile relationship with his grandmother (*George's Marvellous Medicine*, 1982) seems, at first sight, daringly heretical in rejecting the 'natural' affinity of grandparents with their grandchildren. In this children's story George's grandmother is described as a 'selfish grumpy old woman', 'a grizzly old grunion of a Grandma'. Their relationship is far from loving and mutually rewarding:

> Most grandmothers are lovely, kind, helpful old ladies, but not this one. She spent all day and every day sitting in her chair by the window, and she was always complaining, grousing, grouching, grumbling, griping about something or other. Never once, even on her best days, had she smiled at George and said, 'Well, how are you this morning, George?' or 'Why don't you and I have a game of Snakes and Ladders?' or 'How was school today?' (1981: 8)

That George successfully endeavours to rid himself of his grandmother sharply contradicts the stereotypical images of the grandparental relationship, somehow 'naturalized' in Western cultures.

But, whilst debunking the myth of 'natural' empathy between the very young and very old, Dahl's portrayal of old age is, at the same time, also extremely conformist in playing on other gender-specific stereotypes of old age. On the one hand elderly women are popularly depicted as 'harmless little old ladies', 'old dears' and 'old biddies', having no power, being literally 'biddable' and of little social consequence; on the other, like George's grandmother, they are also depicted as crones, dragons, hags, bags and, traditionally in fairy tales, as witches. But, whether positive or negative, both stereotypes work conceptually to marginalize elderly women.

Whilst the negative image of old women as witches has long placed them permanently outside society's boundaries in what Victor Turner (1974) describes as a liminal social position,[3] the other stereotypical image – 'little old lady' – at first sight appears more positive. Less stress appears to be placed on the social marginality of old age. However, the emphasis upon 'little', as already indicated, presages a downward and inferior movement, a diminishing rather than augmenting of social position (Lakoff and Johnson, 1980). The combination of 'little' with 'old' distances her further, makes her appear vulnerable and frail. In the tabloid press banner headlines announce the rape, murder or mugging of 'pensioners' and 'war widows'. Public outrage at the vulnerability of elderly people to the world outside their own front door is fed by enlarged photographs showing heavily wrinkled faces distorted by black eyes and bruises. In this way the 'little old lady', helpless and dependent, is opposed to the 'old woman', the scheming harridan, the wicked witch.

Passive in her gentleness, the 'little old lady' is, by contrast, white-haired in her virtue, but lacks a position of power from which to defend herself. She may also be depicted as marginal or eccentric, a source of ridicule and mild amusement, as can be seen in the following headlines from British newspapers:

Zap! Old lady with brolly KO's Batman. (*Sun*, 13 December 1989)

SAS defences are breached by grandmother with hedge trimmers. (*The Times*, 11 January 1990)

The first caption heads a report of how an old lady, opening her door to a courier dressed as the Cape Crusader, 'promptly set upon him thinking he was a masked mugger' (*Sun*, 13 December 1989). Here an old woman's act of self defence is represented as idiosyncrasy: 'she was like a woman possessed' the courier claimed. The second headline covered a report about a 59-year-old woman who cut a hole in the perimeter fence surrounding an army training ground. Believing security at the camp to be poor, she took this action to demonstrate the risk of terrorist attack. For the readers of the newspaper report, however, this political message is distanced through its framing. Her age is used to both explain and diminish her action, reference to her use of hedge trimmers evoking the cosy domestic worlds of 'home' and 'garden'. Reports of the activities of younger adult campaigners are rarely given such jocular treatment.

Whether through conforming to or subverting the image of the 'little old lady' elderly women can become newsworthy and, through being brought to public attention, the stereotypes of ageing are both reinforced and perpetuated. One Sunday newspaper (*Observer*, 30 June 1991) carried two stories in the same issue about elderly women. The first confirmed their dim-wittedness. Centering on the inordinate amount of rain which had fallen during the first week of the Wimbledon Tennis championship, the story opened with the following sentence: 'Silly questions are part and parcel of Wimbledon.' And, as an exemplary case, the authors of the report chose to focus upon an elderly woman:

> One commissionaire whose day job is the more serious business of soldiering in Ulster, could only smile mutely when set an unanswerable poser by a bewildered and sodden little old lady. Umbrella in hand, she asked him, straight-faced: 'Could you please tell me, officer, what time the rain will stop?'

The elderly woman is here portrayed as 'bewildered', childish perhaps, verging on the confused and senile; her question is reported for sentinent adult amusement. An amusing tension is created between the commissionaire's 'real' masculine world of 'serious soldiering' and the marginal world of the little old lady. This parallels the way in which children's misperceptions and comments are quoted in women's magazines. Both are seen as beguiling in their silliness, charming in their naivety.

The second story from the *Observer* is one which radically reverses expectations of the 'little old lady' role. Here, she is surprising – newsworthy – for her acuity. A gardener who opened his gardens to the public is described as now being 'wary of little old ladies with bad colds':

> When he last opened his Peterborough garden to the public, he noticed just such an old dear get out her hankie, blow her nose, drop the hankie conveniently over a flowering plant, pick it up, and hey presto, the plant was gone. By the end of the day he had lost 700 plants. 'Little old ladies who smile and compliment you on your lovely garden are just as much a danger as professional thieves', he says . . . 'Usually good gardeners will ask if they can take cuttings, but I was so impressed by the way this old lady operated that I didn't have the heart to accost her,' he said.

The thief and the 'little old lady' are as seemingly opposed a pair as the thief and the child; they are, as it were, mutually exclusive social categories. Neither elderly people nor young children are held to be fully accountable for their actions, being figuratively or literally above and below the age of criminal responsibility. Punishment may thus fall outside the legal system, an affair 'of the heart'; and the gardener 'didn't have the heart to accost her'. Hence our horror at children involved in petrol bombing in Northern Ireland (Fraser, 1973) or reports of children involved in violence as, for example, the story of a nine-year-old and six-year-old boy involved in the assault of a woman reported in the *Guardian* (13 April 1989).

Similarly, with respect to old men, both positive and negative stereotypes exist. The latter, exemplified in the phrase 'dirty old man', derives its semantic power through what Lakoff (1987) describes as a process of metaphoric chaining. By this he means that colloquial expressions are not randomly derived, a mixed bag flung together. They are, instead, connected by logic, 'structured in terms of an elaborate cognitive model that is implicit in the semantics of the language' (1987: 408). In this instance the 'man' derives his negative association through dirt, which as Douglas (1966) has suggested is conceptually 'matter out of place'. Old age, in this way, becomes imaged as both tainted and disordered. The phrase 'dirty old man' therefore metaphorically refers to a disordered person and is applied literally to the man who makes inappropriate sexual advances. The deviancy is all the more dramatic because, as we show in Chapter 3, elderly people are, like children, widely perceived to be sexually *inactive*. Those who, in old age, display their sexuality thus risk being stigmatized, ridiculed and condemned. The literal 'dirty old man' would thus become doubly marginal.

He contrasts strongly with the 'old boy', who represents a much more positive stereotype of male gender in old age. Despite the association with childhood, 'boyhood' can lend male ageing an acceptable face, expressed most prestigiously in the 'old boy network'. We shall explore later, through more detailed examples in Chapters 3–5, how such metaphors work to position individual elderly men and women within and around what Fernandez (1970) has termed a 'quality space' concerned with the body, the family and a working life and how gender may shape the social relations of infantilizing practices within these domains. It suffices here to note how the economic and political power which must be relinquished at retirement by most men is, for those who retain it, disguised and made socially acceptable through phrasing the social networks made during their working lives in terms of childhood rather than those of old age. In this way there is a gendered aspect to the metaphoric linkage established between childhood and old age: elderly women are more positively stereotyped through a *reduction* of their *adult* status – 'little old lady' – whilst elderly men are so viewed by *augmentation* of their *child* status as 'grand old boys'.

As Dolinsky notes, stereotypes such as these may be used indiscriminately, 'applied to everyone classified as elderly regardless of their health, status and race' (1984: 13). Once unpacked, however, these apparently trivial examples of the framing of old age reveal a persistent recourse to oppositional thinking. Embedded within each everyday example are metaphoric strategies which create distances and make distinctions between the worlds of adulthood and old age, worlds which, viewed from another perspective, could be seen instead as related points within a shared continuum.

The life course as a 'cycle of life'

Implicit within many of the metaphors of childhood used for the ageing process is a restructuring of time and status in the life course (Myerhoff, 1984). The metaphoric transformation which turns an old man into an 'old boy', for example, works through drawing on the temporality of human existence, through merging two different points in the life course, boyhood and old age. Other metaphors draw on the cycles of the natural world for their referents. The temporal structure of the day and the seasons are used to re-represent the linearity of human life from birth to death as a cyclical process. Through such imagery the finality of death in old age is masked by the metaphors of life embodied in the idea of the child: a new life is begun, as an old one has ended. The young are green striplings, who are burgeoning, blossoming forth in the springtime of their youth, Rousseau's children of nature full of budding hope and bursting with life. Fieldwork that explored the experience of bereavement reveals the use of this image on a condolence card sent on the death of a child:

'In loving memory of Patsy, a beautiful flower who came to bud on earth and to bloom in heaven.' Nearby baskets and bunches of rosebuds provided a literal representation of this imagery. (Hockey, unpublished data)

By contrast, the old are shrivelled sticks, who overripen to face the autumn of their days. The old belong to the 'Evergreen' club, a metaphor invoking for elderly people a safe passage through the winter of their lives. Just as surely, those who pass their twilight years in Eventide homes, who are at the eleventh hour, are assured the prospect of a new dawn through their association with the daily temporal sequencing of dawn and dusk. (See Figure 1.)

Lakoff and Johnson argue that the Western metaphor 'time is money' makes of time a precious commodity, 'a limited resource that we use to accomplish our goals' (1980: 8). Time can be 'wasted, budgeted, invested wisely or poorly, saved or squandered' and of all times it is a life-time which has most invested in it (1980: 8). Lives can be lost, wasted, ended and too short; they must be supported, spared, re-animated and provided for. Death, the end of life, must come at the appropriate time, but when it comes it is still negatively perceived. Does the cultural strategy of restructuring time then serve conceptually to avert ageing and re-frame dependency? Are birth and death made to sit side by side, rather than at opposite ends of a line of finite length? If so, then there is no end point, no finality and our ideal of temporal progress – upward and onward, striving forward, achieving more – need no longer be contravened by the awkward biological facts of life/death. As metaphoric children, very elderly people can share a child's position on the curve of upward growth whose high point is, as we shall show later, that of adulthood, the time of maximal achievement. 'Growing up' leads inevitably to the time for 'growing old', the downward spiral, but through the metaphoric restructuring of time, the wheel turns and death is seemingly subverted. What metaphors of childhood disguise is the failure of science to increase longevity or overcome human impairment, to mitigate dependency.

For this reason then, the language and imagery of childhood which is used to describe the predicament of very elderly people may, as already suggested, also touch those who are disabled and dependent. It conceptually repositions them in a strategic move which avoids directly addressing and confronting the distressing consequences of old age or disease. But, whilst this may make caring easier, it may be of little comfort for those who are receiving care. Being made into metaphoric children does not curtail their experience of social and economic marginalization nor enable them to participate more fully in social life. It simply exacerbates it.

The elliptical path traced in Figure 1 summarizes the movement around 'quality space' which metaphors of childhood and infantilizing practices accomplish and which we will be concerned to trace out through the course of this book (Fernandez, 1970). It is a schematic representation of different qualitative experiences during the life course as an individual moves from childhood, through the adult years to old age. It emphasizes the centrality of adult life, in contrast to the relatively weaker and more marginal social positions of being a child and an elderly person. This idea

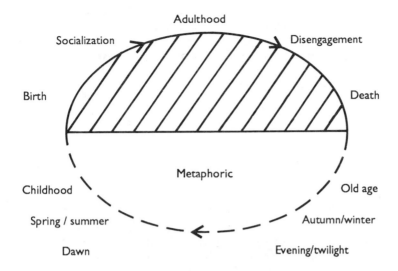

Figure 1 Schematic representation of the life course

is echoed by other social theorists (see Leach, 1966; Martin et al., 1974; Turner, 1989). Jung, for example, uses the passage of the sun through the heavens to image the human life course. Describing the onset of old age he therefore uses orientational metaphors:

> at the stroke of noon the descent begins. And the descent means the reversal of all the ideals and values that we cherished in the morning . . . light and warmth decline and are at last extinguished . . . There is something sunlike within us, and to speak of the morning and spring, of the evening and autumn of life is not mere sentimental jargon. (In Campbell, 1971: 15)

The image of an elliptical movement also encompasses the particular ideologies of old age and childhood that are embraced by the psychological and gerontological literature. For example, socialization can be seen as the upward curve to adulthood, disengagement, the downward path to old age (Cumming, 1963). This is the literal linearity of the life course which, through the dynamics of metaphor, becomes transmuted. The circle is completed and its transformative potential unleashed: dust to dust, ashes to ashes and old heads can continue to be placed on young shoulders.[4]

Some of the perceptions and actions which follow from this image of the life course and from the role which metaphor plays

within it have already been indicated, but field studies by Gresham
(1976), Hazan (1980), Hockey (1990) and Jones (1975) provide
further detailed examples. Gresham (1976) reports clinical observations from institutions for the care of elderly people in the United
States:

> An elderly woman (age 82), who has just finished her breakfast, which
> was fed to her by a practical nurse, gets a patronizing pat on the arm
> from the nurse, who says, 'Good girl! you ate all your breakfast.'
>
> Nurses making change of shift rounds stop at the bedside of Mr John
> Jones (age 66). One nurse pats Mr Jones on the head and asks, 'How
> are you this morning, Johnny?' Mr Jones does not answer. (1976: 205)

As Gresham describes, reprimands and punishments may be
common and elderly dependent people may find themselves being
treated explicitly as children:

> 'Little old men' are left unshaven for days until the whiskers need
> scissors before a razor would help. The implication seems to be they no
> longer need to shave or be shaved every day, just as young boys usually
> don't have to shave every day. 'Cute little old ladies' who are unable
> to fix their own hair, find themselves with 'pigtails' and bows. It seems
> that some enjoy 'dressing up' these 'little ladies' as if they were dolls.
> (1976: 207)

In a later study Hazan describes how, in the very fabric of life at
a Jewish day centre for elderly people in London, analogies were
constantly being drawn between the elderly members and children:

> the first suggestion to boost activities amongst participants made by a
> new administrator introduced to the Centre was to arrange documentary
> and Walt Disney film shows 'like they used to do in my old school'. The
> bingo organized by outside volunteers was opened by the well-known
> phrase used to children 'Are you sitting comfortably? Then we'll begin.'
> On another occasion – a Sunday tea arranged by outsiders – small gifts
> in birthday-like packets were distributed amongst those attending.
> (1980: 31)

Such practices, although by no means uncommon, are not
deliberately chosen as part of a caring strategy. Instead they appear
to be 'natural' ways of behaving towards those who are very old
or senile, a way of coping with people who, like children, are
physically unable to take care of themselves.
Hockey's field material, gathered during work in a residential
home for the elderly in Britain, reveals similar processes of subtle
infantilization and the loss of many attributes of independent
adulthood.

> A new resident must, for example, hand over their pension book,
> valuables and medicine to the Matron. Control of possessions is placed

in 'adult' rather than 'elderly' hands. Medicines, labelled 'Keep out of reach of children' are doled out to them at set times by care staff: £5 of their pension is returned to them as 'pocket money'. The use of alcohol and nicotine is also to be moderated and residents, like guilty children faced with parental wrath, are forced to hide their spirits in the bottom of their wardrobes and tell lies about the stale cigarette smoke lingering in their rooms. Food is consumed from sterilised plastic crockery. Occasionally a 'surprise' gift of chocolates or cigarettes is set beside each resident's morning cereal bowl. For adults, hygiene takes precedence over aesthetics where both elderly people and children are concerned and, indeed, it is sweets and 'goodies', rather than fine china, which are seen as a source of pleasure for them. Whilst the guide issued to prospective residents promises adult leisure pursuits such as 'concerts, socials, table games and library service', residents in fact find themselves decorating hard-boiled eggs for the Easter competition under the guidance of the local cub troupe. (Hockey and James, 1988: 6)

Parallels can be drawn with the experiences of some disabled people who meet with disempowering practices in their relationships with the able bodied, where the metaphor of childhood is an implicit frame. Merry Cross describes such an incident.

When I was in a wheelchair for three weeks, I was appalled. People patted me on the head and called me 'dear' and offered to do things for me that were ludicrous. (Quoted in Sutherland, 1981: 59)

Jones's (1975) study of institutions for people with mental handicaps in contrast reveals them to have a more explicit orientation towards infantilizing practices, a feature also reported by Perring (1989) in her recent study of the rehabilitation of long-stay patients. Jones shows how the nursing staff took on parental roles which 'made possible the occasional indulgence and the exercise of considerable authority' (1975: 22). Patients were allocated to the 'big girls' or 'little girls' wards and nursing staff subjected them to the same rules which they employed at home: 'the doctors say we should treat them as our own kids, so that's what we do' (1975: 109). Perring (1989), in her field study, confirms that the model of the family – parents and children – was an explicit care regime for the elderly mentally handicapped people she encountered.

Dependency as a cultural construct

The illustrations considered so far – and many more will be provided – have shown how particular ideas and images of ageing are mobilized through language and how these images both condense and mask the impact of particular culturally specific forms of oppression and power. Through ascribing a central social

role to independent adulthood, those who are in any way dependent are effectively marginalized. Moreover, even those large
numbers of elderly people who lead fit and active lives may, on
some occasions and at certain times, become involved in the practices and actions which stem from this cognitive system. Thus, the
illusory symmetry of binary oppositions is revealed (Bauman,
1990), for it is only through the domination of the defining
narratives of independent adults in and through social practices
that the dependency of others becomes seen as marginalized.[5]

As we have shown, there is a continuum within social practice,
from small acts of unasked for assistance through to explicit infantilizing actions. Therefore whilst infantilizing practices may, in
some cases, already be widely recognized and deplored, it is
misleading to see them as simply unfortunate aberrations within an
otherwise caring response to those 'less fortunate than ourselves'.
Their extensive semantic range and classificatory power means they
cannot be so easily dismissed. To be fully understood, as we have
argued, infantilization needs to be placed within a continuum
which is underpinned by the wider cognitive system through which
dependency is created and managed within Western society. Rather
than seeking to eradicate what might be seen as the 'pathological'
responses of unsupported informal carers or under-resourced
institutions merely by changing funding priorities or care routines,
practices that reduce dependent people (and others who are old
and/or disabled but not at all dependent) to a child-like status need
to be challenged within their wider conceptual framework. For
unless they are so contextualized change may well be ineffective.
Through exploring in some depth the ways and means through
which metaphors of the child image the process of ageing, we have
already begun, therefore, to lay out a cultural approach to understanding dependency. In line with other approaches more recently
developed in the social sciences, it is one which sees dependency,
whether through old age, physical and/or mental impairment, as
socially constructed (Phillipson, 1982; Lonsdale, 1990; Oliver,
1990).

For example, within the elderly population, many of those above
pensionable age remain fit, vital and healthy, making an active
contribution to society (Thane, 1987). Thus, as Phillipson and
Walker describe, the conceptual linking of dependency with old age
must be seen as a product of 'a particular social division of labour
and a structure of inequality rather than a natural concomitant of
the ageing process' (1986: 11–12). Often, indeed, it may be the
social milieu in which elderly people find themselves which proves
more disabling than the biological fact of growing old; for

example, hypothermia may strike as a result of poverty and poor housing conditions, not simply because of a person's age (Laurance, 1988). In other instances, residential homes for the elderly may effectively encourage social dependency by reducing people's opportunities for independence and self determination (Martin, 1979; Hockey, 1990). Similarly, and providing us with a parallel example, the experience of impairment must be located in its socio-cultural context. Whilst the term 'disability' describes the loss of particular physical or mental abilities, 'handicap' refers to the social experience of living with a disability. Thus it is that impairment itself can be seen as a sufficient, rather than necessary, condition of dependency. Whether a particular impairment proves disabling or handicapping for an individual relates to the social contexts and experiences which he or she encounters (Shearer, 1981). Confinement to a wheelchair for an artist or musician does not, for example, impose upon them the same handicap as it would for an athlete. Nor does it necessarily entail dependency: 'physical disability per se need not impose a state of dependency on someone, but an unaccommodating and hostile environment or prejudicial attitudes will certainly do so' (Lonsdale, 1990: 81). Those who are physically impaired may not be socially dependent; conversely, those who are socially dependent (such as women with pre-school children) may not be physically impaired. In just this way, then, the partnership of dependency and old age is by no means straightforward or indeed inevitable.

The concepts of ageing and disability should therefore be regarded as social constructions, rather than simply as descriptions of biological processes. Although at the level of cultural representation and social practice, the conditions of deep old age and disability are, as we have seen in this chapter, often expressed and imaged through metaphors of dependent childhood, this is done through a process of 'naturalizing' what is a very particularized cultural construct. It derives its persuasive power from the very coherence of the cognitive structures which are its source: a systematic mode of thought informs practices at the institutional and socio-structural level, as well as structuring more intimate social encounters. It is a way of giving meaning to the idea of dependency which is historically and culturally specific and, as we shall continue to explore, is one which denies full personhood to those who are dependent.

A cultural approach to dependency

Clifford Geertz offers an approach to these issues when he writes that

> peoples everywhere have developed symbolic structures in terms of which persons are perceived not baldly as such, as mere unadorned members of the human race, but as representative of certain distinct categories of persons, specific sorts of individuals. (1975: 363)

These symbols systems are not given in the nature of things, but are 'historically constructed, socially maintained and individually applied' (1975: 363–4). Following Geertz, then, we shall show how infantilizing practices can be understood as a metaphoric strategy which maintains conceptual boundaries in the life course, separating off as marginal the social categories 'children' and 'the elderly' through maintaining the dominance of able-bodied adults. Infantilizing practices, then, are not simply an unfortunate and inevitable response to human dependency, but a culturally specific vehicle for comprehending and coping with it. As Coupland (1991) shows, this metaphoric strategy is one in which elderly people themselves may at times participate. Here the anthropological literature on ritual has particular salience in shedding light on the spatial and temporal conditions within which metaphor operates. This will be discussed in detail in Chapter 2. Suffice here to note that it is in society's key, or root, metaphors that many of the tensions and contradictions inherent within a particular culture are overcome. As Turner (1974) argues, these root metaphors work to maintain structural divisions and power, such as that between dominant and marginal social groups (see Chapters 5 and 6).[6] Through unravelling the logic and working of the particular cognitive structure sustaining childhood as a root metaphor it will become possible, therefore, to see how dependency was and is conceptually created and perpetuated as a characteristic feature of ageing in the Western context (Thane, 1987).

If, as Fernandez argues, the 'metaphoric assertions men make about themselves or about others influence their behaviour', then, to understand practices such as infantilization we must consider most carefully how it is that figurative speech becomes quite literally translated into action (1970: 42). That is to say, to understand why infantilizing practices occur we must ask first about the culturally specific nature of the images and ideologies of 'childhood' which they encapsulate in terms of their sources and aptness. Secondly, the ways in which they are expressed in daily life must be explored. Both these tasks have been already started in this chapter but to fully comprehend their resonance involves addressing issues of power. It means demonstrating the ideological role which *particular* cultural images play in securing a *particular* framing of dependency. This is not to say that a 'second childhood' is repressively foisted upon frail and/or impoverished elderly people or that child-like roles are uncaringly allotted to those who are in some way disabled. Rather than a set of prescriptive assumptions about how dependent elderly people should behave, we are dealing with a range of social exclusions, prohibitions or limitations. For example, it is precisely through the socially constructed limitations of 'childhood' – for example, immaturity, vulnerability, asexuality – that a source of cultural images of dependency is made available (see Chapters 2 and 3). But whilst such a 'folk model' of dependency may enable carers to confront the physical and/or mental deterioration of those whom they love and respect, *the same model* may also, as we shall see, socially, economically and politically marginalize those in receipt of care (Chapters 5 and 6).

Questions must be asked, then, about the meaning of dependency, questions which involve a consideration of power, ideology, image and metaphor. These will be explored through the notion of social discourse. As already shown, language plays a central role in the creation and re-creation of social meanings. Indeed, Thompson suggests, to study language is 'to study the ways in which language is used in everyday social life, from the most mundane encounter between friends and family members to the most privileged form of political debate' (1984: 2). The notion of social discourse thus offers a fruitful theoretical perspective from which to approach the cultural repertoire of attitudes, expressions and orientations through which the idea of dependency is managed. Whilst being grounded in a logical system, discourses of dependency remain largely implicit; inaccessible to the conscious mind, they nevertheless constitute a coherent system which is inscribed and negotiated through everyday events, utterances and acts; it endures and is reproduced although having no tangible external shape or form. Following Bourdieu (1977), then, what we seek in the following chapters is the generative principles which inform social practices such as those cited earlier in this chapter and an understanding of their ideological role.

Among social theorists, however, there is a marked lack of consensus as to either the meaning or usefulness of ideology as a theoretical concept (Thompson, 1984; Eagleton, 1991). It has been argued, for example, that all social discourse is intrinsically ideological in that it involves the creation, reproduction and negotiation of social reality, or, more often, social realities. Following this argument, the term ideology is not linked exclusively to the exercise of power but is merely 'a system of symbols or beliefs which pertain, in some way, to social action or political practice' (see Thompson, 1984: 130). As Thompson points out, the difficulty with this view of ideology is that it does not provide a way of distinguishing between a system of symbols or beliefs which is politically neutral and one, such as that which sustains practices of infantilization, which embodies and reproduces asymmetrical relations of power. In agreement with Thompson then, it is argued that 'to study ideology is to study the ways in which creative imaginary activities serve to sustain social relations which are asymmetrical with regard to the organization of power' (1984: 6). In the present context it means studying how it is that the image of the child is used to marginalize people through a particular social construction of dependency.

Thompson has identified three key ways in which ideology operates and these will be explored as our argument proceeds. First, an ideological process may be a legitimating process, one which establishes the authority of particular individuals, classes or social categories and the authenticity of their world view. As we shall see, in Chapter 4 of this volume, adult control of older people may be legitimated morally through reference to an essentially Christian conceptualization of family relations. From this perspective it is the duty of younger people to care for their elders. Sick and or elderly people are believed to 'deserve' reciprocity, that is care in return for earlier caring. Secondly, an ideological process may offer a version of social reality which is in keeping with the interests of powerful individuals or groups. These are highlighted, while conflicting interests are down-played. Constructing images of retirement as a time of freedom and unfettered leisure, for example, obscures the extent to which older people may be vulnerable to poverty and ill health or, as we discuss in Chapter 5, feel distanced from the world of work and central social, political and economic institutions. As a result employers' concern to maintain a 'lean', 'fit' adult workforce are upheld. Thirdly, as shown earlier, an ideological process universalizes or naturalizes that which is arbitrary or contingent, removing the historical specificity of a particular formulation of social reality. Instead, it becomes an inevitable and enduring aspect of human experience. An adult seeking to impose their will upon an older person may assert that 'we all have to get old some day', 'you're not as young as you were' or 'you can't turn the clock back'. Thereby they impute an inevitability to what may be an arbitrary procedure, such as moving an elderly person out of their own home into institutional care.

It is suggested, then, that the metaphoric transformation of older people into children can be seen as an ideological process. It is a process which marginalizes and disempowers and, as this volume demonstrates, conceptually distances adults from the possible or probable onset of painful or debilitating life circumstances, highlighting through comparison or opposition their own independence and attractiveness. In arguing, then, that 'ideology is one crucial way in which the human subject strives to "suture" contradictions which rive it in its very being, constitute to its core', Eagleton emphasizes this very point (1991: 198). As we shall see, the social discourse surrounding old age and dependency reconcile contradictions within prevailing notions of what it means to be human, by transforming those we may become into those whose state and status we have outgrown. Adulthood thus retains its profile as an exclusive embodiment of concepts of independence and autonomy, through disallowing physical or mental impairment to feature among its possible manifestations (Sutherland, 1981). Contradictions are in this way 'sutured'. Paradoxically, as Eagleton goes on to note, contradictions can also be constitutive of the human subject: thus, those whom we seek to distance safely from the social category 'adult' provide an effective oppositional social category, the characteristics of which serve to define and delineate the limits of the dominant category 'adult'. For example, adults are deemed to be sexually attractive/active; children and 'the elderly' are not and, as we shall see later, adults may work hard at denying or controlling any sign of sexuality in later life. Indeed the sexualizing of children through abusive practices is seen as the 'theft' of childhood (Kitzinger, 1990). We shall see too how adults have a power and decision-making responsibility which is denied to children and elderly people. Distancing, transformation and opposition are all strategies which are used to sustain the ideological dominance of adulthood. Those who are not perceived as fully adult occupy an ambiguous position on the margins of the adult world, simultaneously threatening and yet constituting its essential nature.

In the following chapters attention will be centred, increasingly, on the way in which ideology sustains relations of power through a transformative process, or strategy, which represents social reality in such a way as to highlight those aspects which serve the interests of a dominant group – able-bodied adults. In this way ideology mediates between a world that is and a world that ought to be. Economic growth, medical advances and a changing demographic profile have all served to multiply the numbers of elderly people surviving within Western populations. Community care policies have, similarly, served to heighten their social and physical visibility. In order to sustain the viability of the 'world-as-it-ought-to-be' – a world where individualism, autonomy and independence characterize adulthood – ideological strategies are brought into play in such a way as to effect a reconciliation with the 'world-as-it-is'. However, this is not to say that elderly people or children are passive spectators of their own exclusion or that the exercise of power by adults holds uncontested sway. Just as there is a continuum of oppression from a hand proffering assistance to regimes of infantilization, there is a continuum of challenge to it. So, for adults, establishing ideological control over the 'world-as-it-is' may also involve combatting and channelling the 'power of the weak' who threaten, from their marginal social position, to challenge or disrupt the social order. Chapter 6 shows the ways in which the authority of adults can become a site of struggle, played out in daily encounters between carers and cared for. As Hall et al. (1976) note, ideological or hegemonic control is never given or static:

> Hegemony . . . is not universal and 'given' to the continuing rule of a particular class. It has to be won, reproduced, sustained. Hegemony is, as Gramsci said, a 'moving equilibrium' containing relations of forces favourable or unfavourable to this or that tendency. (Hall, et al. 1976, quoted in Hebdige, 1979: 16)

The notion of ideology laid out by Thompson (1984) thus provides a way of thinking about the continuum of events, utterances and practices within which infantilization can be situated. It is one in which 'ideology' refers to sets of beliefs which serve to uphold or legitimate the interests of more powerful groups. It does not, however, imply a fixed or rigid quality to those beliefs. In this, it resonates with Bourdieu's notion of culture, described by Bloch as 'not a hard logical grid nor a complex system of rules but an amalgam of sense and emotions' (1985: 31). Thus, it is the embodied, innovative yet regulated nature of the behaviours described in this volume, the creative yet culturally specific uses of language which, we argue, play an ideological role in sustaining the dominance of one social group – 'adults' – at the expense of marginal groups such as children and elderly people.

Its precise mode of operation needs to be considered, however. As this chapter has shown, within social discourse can be traced a shared, logical cognitive structure which, in some way, associates childhood with old age, yet this is not to say that a conceptual system of this kind exists in any tangible form outside social discourse. Very elderly people are patently not, in any way, children. Nevertheless, there exists the possibility of making metaphoric associations between childhood and other forms of dependency. The means and meanings to do this are mobilized within and through social discourse.

To understand how it is that meanings are authenticated or made to stick we need to explore the role of metaphor within human thought and experience. Metaphor can be most simply described as making one thing, one stage, one condition knowable through reference to another. It can be seen, quite simply, as a creative process whereby that which is familiar provides the metaphoric grounding for knowledge of that which is less familiar: 'the essence of metaphor is understanding and experiencing one kind of thing in terms of another' (Lakoff and Johnson, 1980: 5). Drawing on the work of Ricoeur, Lakoff and Johnson point out that metaphor is not, however, just a poetic flourish with which we embellish our more mundane thoughts and feelings. Without metaphor we neither begin to think about nor experience our mundane thoughts, our humdrum emotions. Only through using that which is tangible – for example, our bodily orientations in space – can we describe sad feelings as 'depression', happy feelings as 'elation'. Only metaphor allows us to construe the inchoate. For example, many societies draw upon their country's indigenous and familiar animals to provide a metaphoric grounding through which more abstract, intellectual or emotional dimensions of life can be construed, communicated and experienced (Tambiah, 1973; Douglas, 1975; Geertz, 1975). Thus, while the individual's private cognitive and affective life is constituted through metaphor, its privacy is also breached through the communicative system which sustains it.

Metaphor, then, permits a creative extension of knowledge, allowing us not only to 'know' things but to know about them in particular ways, to 'impose an understanding on what it is that we feel' about them (Lakoff, 1987). As Fernandez argues, it is 'one of the few devices we have for leaping beyond the essential privacy of the experiential process' (1970: 41). Whilst one individual can never know directly what another feels, they share with them basic experiences, such as the orientation of the body in space. And, it is through metaphoric reference to that which is immediate and shared that that which is private can be communicated. As Sperber has argued, figurative language thus makes a 'prism' of conventional reference' not through 'indicating' things, or by referencing them, but by setting pointers or reference points into a relation with one another, by making them into a relation that is innovative upon the original order of reference. It 'conveys' a renegotiated relation, but not being 'literal' in any sense cannot 'point' to it. Thus we may say that it 'embodies' or 'images' its object, figuring sympathetically by becoming itself that which it expresses. (Sperber, 1986: 6)

Metaphor thus relies upon a community of experience. It is therefore cultural and, being cultural, is culturally specific and, for Sperber, the importance of metaphors lies 'not in how they embellish, but how they constitute culture' (1986: 7).

Whilst metaphors are essentially creative in the way described – giving form to that which is intangible – their cultural grounding means that metaphoric connections are not made afresh with each thought, feeling or communication. Poetry may be acclaimed for its originality, its metaphoric creativity, yet in its choice of image or metaphor a poem must also connote the familiar in ways which are recognizable, in order to make newly accessible the strange or inchoate. Those poems, or indeed, paintings which are subsequently described as 'ahead of their time' may well have drawn on unfamiliar images or metaphors which failed to resonate with the audiences of the day. They may, however, later become the source of images through which experiences are subsequently understood. Brown (1977) cites the remark of Picasso when told that his portrait of Gertrude Stein failed to resemble her. Said Picasso, 'Yes, but it will.' It is in this sense that Ricoeur argues that words are 'metaphor[s] on the road to extinction' (1978: 143). Culture – in the form of language, ritual and imagery – represents society's fund of available metaphors, inscribed within social discourse. Commonplace though they now may be, they are none the less metaphoric in origin.

Through participation in social discourse, then, the individual is exposed to and manipulates the metaphoric construct or models through which a particular framing of reality is constituted. But, as we have seen, while the familiar plays an important role in allowing the unknown to be construed, metaphoric elaboration allows particular cultural ideas to be extensively explored and more cogently expressed. Thus, the metaphoric repertoire of a given society is drawn selectively from the range of the familiar, some items being foregrounded, others discarded. Through such choices, then, particular, culturally specific accounts of that which is unknown or problematic are created. Old age is such an instance and, crucially, it is within this process of selection that power can be exercised. Metonymy also plays a powerful role in processes of cognition and can be distinguished from metaphor as a part-to-whole relation, rather than as one of reference. The wrinkled skin of the elderly person is made to stand for the whole person, the 'wrinkly'. Therefore, whilst metaphor provides us with 'a way of conceiving of one thing in terms of another', to assist understanding, metonymy is referential and 'allows us to use one entity to stand for another' (Lakoff and Johnson, 1980: 36). But, in its part-to-whole function, metonymy permits a specific focus or aspect of the referent to be highlighted. Thus it is that a bent figure with a walking stick is used as the traffic symbol for elderly people crossing, a wheelchair for people with disabilities and a white cane for someone partially sighted. Described by Sutherland (1981) as 'badges of office', these illustrate the power metonymy has to shape our understanding. Like metaphor, metonymy is selective, enabling evaluations and qualitative assessments to be made in relation to which part is taken to represent which whole, a process which Chapter 3 shows is neither arbitrary nor random.

Metaphor and metonym thus provide subtly different kinds of ideological processes for overcoming ruptures within conceptual systems and for sustaining forms of cultural and social differentiation. Lakoff and Johnson argue that 'whether in national politics or in everyday interaction, people in power get to impose their metaphors' (1980: 57). Thus, although specific metaphors/ metonyms may rest partially on their links with the familiar, their resonance derives from the extent to which they are the symbolic capital of dominant social categories or groups. As the material in this volume shows, it is primarily able-bodied adults who impose metaphors of childhood upon those who are in deep old age.

Spring chickens and Christmas turkeys

The following incident, which took place in a residential home for the elderly, two or three weeks after Christmas, reveals how metaphors of childhood can, subtly and unintentionally, inform everyday interactions, through drawing on the cultural repertoire of metaphors of ageing described in this chapter:

Hetty [a female resident] was leaking over the floor and I took her for a change. Maude [another resident] was complaining about her, saying that 'She wants drowning!' Karen [a care assistant] disinfected Hetty's wet cushion as Maude would complain about the smell. After lunch Hetty was shouting again and Karen said [loudly in her ear] 'Shut up. Stop shouting. You've had coffee and been to the toilet. You're upsetting people, shouting. Maude's going to bang you.' Hetty had quietened down, saying 'We'll see about that!' Karen said to Hetty: 'You're no spring chicken. You're more of a Christmas turkey.' (Hockey, unpublished data)

This distressing account of incontinent old age is rich in metaphoric allusions and shows how commonplace they are. Although not specifically using metaphors of childhood, Hetty's behaviour is interpreted by both Maude and Karen as childish. They do this in different ways. For Maude, Hetty's incontinence signals both her physical weakness and social distance from herself. Hetty is more frail than she, and through complaining, Maude not only makes Hetty more marginal, but also justifies her own dominant social position. She suggests that 'she wants drowning', the treatment meted out to the runt in a litter of kittens. Is Hetty the poor, weak baby of the bunch that no one wants? Karen too, treats Hetty as a totally dependent baby–child. She has taken care of her physical needs – feeding and toileting – what more does she want? Why is she still shouting, she asks, as one would of a baby still crying? Hetty's spirited retort is greeted with derision by Karen, who changes her strategy of metaphoric control. The 'spring chicken', soft, fluffy, small and vulnerable, endearing in its antics and symbolic of Easter and resurrection is contrasted with the 'Christmas turkey', large, old trussed and very dead. Through recourse to the cyclical structuring of calendrical time, common as we have seen in metaphors of ageing, Hetty is thus denied the pleasant depiction of old age. She is no 'spring chicken', at the start of the year/life, but instead, the old turkey which signals, through its demise, wintertime and the end of the year/death. When care becomes control the mask of childhood is allowed to slip and Karen, punitively, asserts Hetty's literal rather than figurative position within the life course.

In this encounter, then, can be seen the discursive use to which metaphors of ageing can be put. As Lakoff and Johnson (1980) argue, the way in which meaning is made to stick through metaphors depends upon their location within a shared and logical system. Metaphors do not stand alone, each one making an independent connection between previously unrelated realms of human reality. Rather, they are thought through in terms of root metaphors which carry a series of entailments across a range of contexts and experience. For example, infantilization practices and metaphors of childhood extend beyond the specific arenas of ageing and disability to describe and pattern many other social relations of dependency and power in Western contexts. The use of 'boy' or 'girl' to refer to those in domestic service, irrespective of age, and the diminutive phrases used of wives by their husbands would be such examples (see Arluke and Levin, 1984). This is why we shall speak of discourse for it enables us to appraise the way in which metaphors of childhood operate in social time and space for, in performing their persuasive, authenticating work, metaphors rely upon social context and social interaction. The social identity of those who speak and those who listen, coupled with the physical and social reality within which their interaction takes place, provides the site within which meaning comes into being. Thus the framing of old age and disability through metaphors of childhood can be seen as an interpretation of physical and social reality. Though the internal metaphoric system can be abstracted and elucidated, this in no sense provides a sufficient account of its operations. The chapters which follow describe a living and lived system not some abstract logical structure. As Turner notes, the two thoughts which constitute a metaphor are dynamic, and being 'active together, they "engender" thought in their coactivity' (1974: 29).

Notes

1 The term life course is discussed on pp. 49–51.
2 Featherstone and Hepworth (1986) draw on Elias's historical account (1982) of the growing social regard accorded to bodily control, and its converse, the disgust felt when bodily control is betrayed through age or disability. Whilst acknowledging the historically variable and therefore socially constructed nature of the stigma of ageing, the authors argue that attempts to alleviate the negative signs of ageing, the new interests and commitment to exercise, are unlikely to produce universal change. Rather they can be seen as a bid for power and social status which emanates from particular social groups, such as the *petit bourgeoisie* (see Bourdieu, 1984). Indeed, even the best attempts of those who would challenge the depredations of socially constructed stigma must reckon with the bodily, and particularly the facial, decline which can mar the elderly person's attempts to participate on an equal footing in interactions with younger people (see Chapter 3).
3 The term 'liminal' receives full discussion in Chapters 5 and 6.
4 See the poem 'Ellipse' reproduced in Chapter 3.
5 Bauman (1990) argues that oppositions of this kind contain an illusory symmetry. Although 'friends' and 'enemies' appear to be mutually self-defining, it is the friends who define the enemies, controlling the processes of classification and assignment. Thus, the friends' 'narrative', their commentary on the world, is dominant. However, Bauman also points out the role of the ambiguous stranger, neither friend nor foe, whose presence threatens the binarism constructed between friend and enemy. This volume explores these ideas in arguing that the dependent adult, whether disabled in early or mid life, or constrained by the biological effects of the ageing process, represents such a disordering anomaly (see Chapter 3). These individuals combine the features of adulthood with a failure to live up to its preconditions, hence their relegation to a less than fully adult social status.

However, what we are witnessing increasingly in contemporary society is the demand that adulthood be recognized as a less than rigidly defined or ordered condition, that it shall admit of variation which may involve dependency (see Chapter 6).

6 Turner (1974: 25) exemplifies the concept of the root metaphor through reference to ways in which the notion of 'society' has been conceptualized. He draws on root metaphors as diverse as a 'big animal' and a 'big machine'. Whilst the 'big animal' metaphor can be seen at work in functionalist thought, which highlights equilibrium at the expense of conflict, the 'big machine' metaphor reflects the mind/body split of Cartesian thought and thereby downplays the holistic nature of social life.

2

CONSTRUCTING PERSONHOOD: CHANGING CATEGORIES OF THE CHILD

The approach to the conceptual management and ordering of dependency so far outlined raises questions concerning the distribution and articulation of power within the life course. It has been suggested that passage through the life course – from birth to death – involves the withholding and attribution of personhood at different times and that power is asymmetrically wielded as individuals move between marginal and central social positions, between different conceptions of personhood. Parents, for example, are persons in a way which small children are not; adults are persons in ways in which 'the elderly' no longer are. And, in each relationship, power is unevenly exercised. We are suggesting, then, that dependency is not an intrinsic quality, a property of particular individuals. Neither is it simply an aspect of particular stages in the process of biological maturation or of certain physical and mental abilities. Rather, dependency is primarily a social relationship resting upon the exercise of power (Walker, 1982). As such, it is tied into the specific social, political and economic relationships which pattern the life course of any individual in any particular culture. In this sense dependency is created (Oliver, 1989). The form which dependency assumes in any society is thus expressive of the relationships of power within that society. In this chapter we show that the Western experience of dependency – commonly one of stigmatization and loss of self-esteem – is a function of the historical emergence of particular sets of ideas about individualism and about childhood. This chapter begins, then, to consider how exactly it is that power is gained and lost during the life course by exploring the conceptual links between concepts of dependency and those of personhood in Western cultures. The denial, granting or withdrawal of personhood is, we suggest, inextricably tied to *perceived* dependency and it is 'the child' which provides the dominant symbol of this dependent state within many Western cultures such as those of Britain and the United States. Taking Britain as a case study and focusing upon the ways in which a particular ideology of childhood has developed over time and is currently employed, it becomes possible then to understand the powerful role of infantilizing practices in sustaining an asymmetrical distribution of personhood for people who are dependent. This chapter sets out the historical background.

Personhood and power

Social class and, more recently, ethnicity, sexuality and gender are now recognized as fundamental bases for forms of social differentiation which carry implications of dominance and subordination, or oppression. Biological ageing and impairment have similarly been recognized as preconditions for socially constructed subordination, rather than a period of 'natural' dependency (Phillipson, 1982; Morris, 1991). However, accounts of such processes of social differentiation often tend towards polarizing explanations: individuals occupy either/or social positions with respect to gender, race, age and indeed social class. People are described as female *or* male, black *or* white, old *or* young, working class *or* middle class. The fragmentation of the marxian social classes 'bourgeoisie' and 'proletariat', for example, is often vigorously contested within sociological discussion, despite the difficulties of empirically assigning class membership either to individuals or to social groups. Admission of fragmentation is seen to risk denying the underlying relationships of power, dominance and exploitation (Rinehart, 1972).

In addressing age- and ability-based social inequalities, the proposed cultural approach to dependency challenges such polarized accounts of social identity or social placement. It emphasizes variation and fluidity in the attribution of personhood throughout the life course of any one individual and between individuals, noting the cultural relativity of Western conceptions. Reaching the 'age' of adulthood, for example, may be no guarantee of personhood in Western cultures for it is simultaneously constituted through differences of gender, ethnicity and social class. Similarly, 'the elderly' are often conceptualized as a homogeneous category, as if they were no longer subject to stratifying social relations. As Arber and Ginn (1991) have pointed out, such factors as class and gender may impact considerably on their access to and exercise of power. The personhood of elderly people thus varies extensively. In the category 'the elderly' may be found High Court judges and Members of Parliament alongside the 'little old lady' and 'grand old boy' of the tabloid press. Health and ethnicity, too, are important aspects of social differentiation and comparably powerful markers of distinction in the attribution of personhood and social identity. A parallel case can be argued in reference to disability. We are all differently abled so why is it that some people may find themselves stigmatized as disabled? Indeed, the category 'the disabled' encompasses both those who are denied effective personhood through the controlling regimes of institutional care *and* those who retain power and status despite some form of impairment (Ashley, 1973). An advertisement for the Spastics Society featured in the *Independent* newspaper on 15 November 1991 plays upon this theme. Two naked children stare out of the full page advertisement. The slogan runs: 'One has cerebral palsy. The other has full human rights.' Further on the advertisement states that 'people will notice she's different. They'll start treating her differently. Her rights to education, employment and housing will be out of her control because she can't control her limbs.' Cross-cultural material shows the socially constructed nature of such categories. Indeed, as Reynolds-Whyte notes, in other non-Western cultures a general category of 'disabled people' is absent:

> being blind or mad or lame [are] characteristics of certain individuals; they [are] differences in the human condition, rather than common handicaps entitling a minority group, 'the disabled' to certain rights. (1990: 202)

Monolithic and culturally specific categories – 'the disabled', 'the elderly' and 'children' – work as stereotypes, to gloss over and homogenize the wide diversity of social experience which belongs to those assigned membership of such categories. In our quest for the cognitive structures through which dependency is managed, therefore, an understanding of the social construction of the life course through such categories plays a central role. Indeed, it provides us with a guiding concept. Moving beyond simple notions of material or social inequalities, or the varying life chances of members of different social categories, a more fundamental relationship can be addressed: the power relations operative within the life course between those who are without full personhood and those in possession of it.

This begs the question as to what is implied by the concept of personhood for it is clear that the meaning of what it is to be a 'person' is neither fixed nor somehow intrinsic. It is not part of the natural order of things, but an aspect of particular cultural orders. Ethnographic examples from non-Western cultures provides some useful illustrations and points of comparison when exploring what it means to be a person, that is, what any particular society provides as 'confirmation of that identity as of social significance' (La Fontaine, 1985: 124).

The first example is drawn from the Chewong of the Malay peninsular. In this society infants are denied not only personhood but also human status, a state of affairs which continues for a number of years (Howell, 1987). For the Chewong, human status as persons is only reached after the individual's first child is born. By contrast, in other cultures, children may be accorded an 'adult' role at a much earlier stage in their lives than many Westerners would find appropriate. A working life or betrothal and marriage may take place at an age when Westerners would be concerned still to maintain 'childhood innocence'. Hausa society provides our second comparative example. Here a girl may be married at ten years old but, although 'she may not cook for her husband or have sexual relations with him for some time . . . she enters purdah and loses the freedom associated with childhood' as she takes her place among adult women (Schildkrout, 1978: 130). In Western cultures, the 'age of majority' – nominally 21 but more often now 18 years old – signals an assumption of full adult rights of citizenship, of personhood. However, in Britain, though a 16-year-old might marry and bear a child, she is not yet entitled to exercise other rights of adulthood, such as entering hire purchase agreements or voting, until she becomes 18 years old.

From these examples, it is clear that, although in many cultures the concept of personhood entails some idea of completeness and wholeness, in the sense of achieving full membership of society, the constituents of that 'being whole' are culturally prescribed. Thus, personhood can be defined as that identity which is socially constituted for an individual, not with respect to his or her own sense of uniqueness, but with respect to a particularized set of cultural ideas about what it means to be fully human (Mauss, in Brewster, 1979). For example, for the Tallensi of Ghana, personhood is conferred on individual human beings in recognition of their moral worth, rather than their humanity: 'personhood varies according to social criteria which contain the capacities of the individual within defined roles and categories' (La Fontaine, 1985: 133). If a woman or man does not become a parent and produce offspring for the continuation of society, they never attain the status of persons. In this sense, all Tallensi 'are individuals but not all are recognized as full persons; those that are exercise powers and must accept responsibilities, which are attributed to their office' (1985: 134).

However, the historical emergence of a highly valued individualism in Western cultures (MacFarlane, 1978) has led many to argue that in this context the concept of the person and individual are uniquely fused: the person is both 'a compound of jural rights and moral responsibility' *and* the 'unique and transient human being' (La Fontaine, 1985: 124). This implies a great difficulty in separating out the idea of the person from that of the individual. However, it can also be argued that this characterization of Western personhood ignores the extent to which, even in Western cultures, social role retains vestiges of classificatory power with respect to certain individuals, as La Fontaine notes with respect to gender (1985: 131). Though Enlightenment thought, as manifested in the French Revolution and the Constitution of the United States of America, may have led the members of Western society to adhere to the belief that 'all people are equal', the subtlety of social practice and the complexity of social encounters none the less mean that some adults may effectively not be allowed the status of persons. They are denied it by those who have a degree of power or control over them. Thus, very elderly people may find their freedom to choose for themselves progressively whittled away by the care they receive and, consequently, experience a deepening sense of lost status as persons. Crump, for example, in discussing current debates about nursing elderly people, describes how overprotective regimes of care may well lead to loss of self-esteem:

We thrive on risk and without it life would be dull and repetitive. In discussing self-care, it is suggested that nurses are reluctant to take risks to promote maximum independence as an 'incident' may occur with all the subsequent recriminations and form-filling. Risk is an integral part of promoting independence and maximizing self-care, if there is risk from activity then there is a greater risk from no activity. (1991: 19–20)

Similarly, although the 'age of majority' may legally mark the assumption of personhood, not all individuals make this transition, and not necessarily for always. For example, people with mental handicaps, often described as having the mind of a child in an adult's body, may never *in practice* be allowed to be 'persons'. They may be forbidden to exercise choice and self-determination (Jenkins, 1990). In this way, at the level of social interaction, such as that which exists between carer and cared for, the attribution of personhood to individual people belonging to a category such as 'the elderly' may vary.

The focus on the life course is important in providing a suitable frame within which the relationship between concepts of personhood and those of dependency can be developed. Whilst, as we have seen in Chapter 1, in everyday life a cyclical folk model of a life 'cycle' continues to pattern popular conceptions, 'life course' is the more useful analytical concept. The term 'life cycle' implies a rigidly prescribed movement from one age-based status to the next (Bryman et al., 1987) as, for example, in the medieval conception of the seven ages of man or the wheel of fortune and fate present in Christian religious imagery, one movement leading from dust to dust. Life course, on the other hand, reflects more accurately the linearity of Western perceptions of life which, through the secular medical model, are seen to be both unidirectional and to culminate in an endpoint, death. It also allows for an exploration of the process and experience of becoming old or sick at different points in time. It does not assume a rigid structuring of those experiences and allows us to see how the status of an elderly person is gradually taken on through a progressive withdrawal from certain aspects of social life which varies between individuals.

The concept of the life course is also more appropriate to the patterning of contemporary British and many other Western industrialized cultures where, unlike more traditional societies, there are few rituals to provide formal markers of movement between different stages of life (Van Gennep, 1960 [1908]). Although in the recent past there were subtle indications of chronological age and position in the 'life cycle', even these are rapidly disappearing. In inter-war Britain, for example, age status was easily discernible in dress. Individuals below the age of 14 wore short trousers, if male, and had unstyled hair and no make-up if female. They were 'children'. At 14 they became 'adults'; trousers extended to the ankle, hair was styled and make-up worn. Old age for women was similarly more easily identifiable by dress than bodily state, with older women characteristically wearing the dark clothes of widowhood. This contrasts radically with the 'shell suits' (lightweight brightly coloured tracksuits) currently worn by individuals of all ages and of both genders. Clothes no longer identify an individual's age in Britain but act more often as indicators of class. Shell suits, now past the zenith of their popularity, are in this way seen as indicative of working class membership, whereas the 'green wellies' and Barbour jackets (in the recent past signifiers of membership of the rural upper class), now indicate the aspirations of their middle class urban wearers.

For present purposes, therefore, the concept of life course is the more useful in illuminating such experiences. In rejecting the rigidity of the life cycle model in favour of the more flexible theoretical concept of life course, we are able to show how it is that some, but not all, members of certain social categories come to be dependent upon or are made subordinate to the members of others. It allows us to see the passage from birth to death not as a simple unidirectional movement, but one which has false starts, changes in direction and hidden obstacles. It allows us to explore how power is continually negotiated in processes of domination and submission, as people assert very different social identities during their lives through the attribution or denial of personhood. As Harris has argued, 'biography and history can be seen as mutually constituting and conditioning processes, but are better seen as different moments of a total social process which has collective and individual moments' (1987: 22).

The creation of dependent persons

The social and cultural construction of dependency through the denial of personhood, indicated by the examples cited in Chapter 1, has taken its particular form in Britain, we suggest, in response to the historical emergence of the concept of individualism. This chapter traces the ways in which perceptions of personhood have been shaped and documents their practical effects with respect to the allocations of power in contemporary British society. In doing so it provides a framework within which the particularized understandings of organic aspects of old age, to be discussed in Chapter 3, can be contextualized.

In Britain and many other Western societies both old age and childhood, as currently understood and experienced, are recently emergent social categories (Thane, 1983). They have arisen out of the shift from a rural, agrarian society to an urban industrialized one. Taking Britain as our main example, it is possible to see that urbanization involved initially the marginalization of old age, as very elderly people were often left behind in their villages. But, as the nineteenth century progressed, there was a comparable marginalization of children. By the end of the nineteenth century, both children and elderly people were no longer seen as 'workers'. Other categories, such as women and disabled people, had also begun to find themselves marginalized from the world of work (Oliver, 1989). Accompanying this movement was a comparable reduction in the numbers of those defined as 'persons' as, increasingly, the 'work' society came to provide the measure of personal worth and social status (Kohli, 1988; see also Chapter 5).

Despite the persuasiveness of this materialist account of the historical background to the emergence of contemporary categories of dependency, however, it implies that prior to industrialization age and impairment were no bar to personhood in the West. This was not in fact the case. Again, looking to Britain as an example, accounts of institutional care – the workhouse and Poor Law provision – suggest that the care of dependent people within the home during the nineteenth century had precedents in earlier limited forms of care provided by both the Church and state (Thane, 1983). Similarly, cross-cultural comparison reminds us that frail elderly people were also often ousted within more traditional societies. Sharp makes reference to the 'grim treatment', including the abandonment of 'elderly' persons in times of stress among the Chipewyan, a hunter–gatherer society living in Northern Canada (1981: 102). Competence in adult economic and social activities is the hallmark of personhood among the Chipewyan, and Sharp reports intolerance of those deemed incompetent. Therefore, alongside accounts which prioritize work as central to personhood must be set material which suggests a broader approach to the constitution of dependency and personhood in Western societies.

A key aspect is the negotiated rather than fixed nature of power. Neither feudal nor hierarchical, underpinned by neither royal nor divine charter, British society cleaves to the values of individualism. Both formal policy and individual decision-making are informed by a commitment to the freedom of the individual to pursue his or her own ends, rather than being committed by birth or kinship to the needs and objectives of any one social group or category. Linked to the growth of Protestantism, but with its roots in the vigorous entrepreneurial activity of the thirteenth century (MacFarlane, 1978), individualism in Britain encouraged a market-orientated approach to life and brought with it a particular conception of personhood. These attributes, as we shall see, were epitomized in the self-made man of the nineteenth century. However, independence, in social and economic terms, was acquired by individual men through their life course at the expense of others – the women, children, elderly and disabled people who became dependent. If the concept of personhood came to rest heavily upon membership of the workforce during the nineteenth century, this development should not mask its historical antecedents in the more long-standing association between individualism and autonomy.

Returning to the nineteenth century, the question arises as to how and why these particular sections of the workforce – women, children, elderly and disabled people – came to be seen as expendable? It can be argued that in a rapidly advancing industrial society, such as Britain in the eighteenth and nineteenth centuries, very elderly people did not possess the stamina and strength to participate in the new heavy industries and that their traditional knowledge and skills were of little value in that setting. Roebuck

(1978) charts changing definitions of 'old age' from the eighteenth century onwards, describing the range of ages at which individuals in the 1870s–1890s in Britain might receive pensions. Roebuck notes:

> The ability of an individual to support himself at an advanced age varied according to the individual and his occupation. For example, by the 1890s men over 50 who lost their jobs because of illness often found it difficult to find work when they recovered; miners generally would not work past 60; the best wages in the iron and steel trades were made between 25 and 45, and by 55 a worker's earnings were generally reduced by one third to one half. (1978: 420)

Similarly, disabled people were less able to participate in the new industrial work processes (Oliver, 1990). However, these explanations are only partially satisfactory, for they do not account for the removal of both women and children, from the workforce. Children, for example, alone have the physical capacity to enter the confined spaces of a loom, and women share with them a socialized passivity which equips them to cope with the demands of highly repetitive work.

More insightful is an explanation which focuses on social relations. With industrialization came the rise of an aspiring middle class who, although finding wealth, lacked the status and respectability of those who retained unquestioned traditional power up until the late eighteenth century – the aristocracy or landed gentry. In the lifestyles of this new middle class is revealed their desire for this status, as they gradually appropriated aristocratic symbols: the family mansion, the lady wife and domestic servant. In particular, the middle class home came to signify rank, respectability and refuge in what was becoming an increasingly bleak and inhospitable world of work. As mothers and domestic managers, middle class women's confinement to the domestic world similarly disclosed the successfully protective roles of their wealthy husbands. These 'self-made men' could afford the luxury of a wife at home. Their philanthropic concern for the lifestyles of the poor was in part a function of their own aggrandisement: nonconformist mill owners and their Methodist overlookers had an 'invidious reputation as week-day child-drivers, working their mills till five minutes before midnight on the Saturday and enforcing the attendance of their children at Sunday school on the Sabbath' (Thompson, 1968: 381). In time, it was their wives and daughters who took over the philanthropic role by encouraging working class women and children also to withdraw from the world of work. Towards the end of the nineteenth century, the introduction of compulsory education combined with industrial legislation officially completed the marginalization of children from the workplace and placed upon women the main burden of caring for them at home (Wright, 1987). Having campaigned through the trade unions for better working conditions, those men who were now in receipt of the new 'family' wage were able to provide financial support for households within which immature, sick or frail individuals could be looked after by women who stayed at home. In this way, then, the family forms appropriated from an earlier aristocracy had permeated throughout the entire class structure, providing a model both for the factory worker as well as his employer (Davidoff et al., 1976). In a parallel movement, as Oliver (1990) points out, it was the change in social relations, rather than industrialization per se, which effectively barred disabled people from 'working'. Over time their traditional roles as beggars or 'village idiots' became progressively less acceptable in industrial settings.

In the light of these developments, briefly indicated here, it becomes clear how the burden of pauperism, the threat of the workhouse, the asylum and debtors prison became, for poor, disabled and elderly people of the nineteenth and early twentieth centuries, a source of stigmatizing and individualizing identities (Oliver, 1990). The links between industrialization under capitalism and the emergence of dependent social categories had ensured that labour force participation was by now central to the attribution and withholding of personhood. To be socially respectable – to be a whole person – an adult male required a place within the 'work society' (Kohli, 1988). But each individual, in that they passed through childhood and moved, potentially, towards old age, of necessity would experience periods of exclusion from the workforce. Potentially, then, maturity brought both personhood and then later its denial. And those who cared for the young and the elderly – the female partners of those men entitled to full labour force participation – became similarly dispossessed, both socially and economically. Contemporarily, as we shall see, the 'work society' continues to be a source of and for social identity so that those who, for whatever reasons, are debarred from it may find themselves stigmatized in their dependency. The ways in which this occurs are discussed in more detail in Chapter 5.

The child as a dominant symbol of dependency

Against this broad historical background of the social and cultural construction of dependency can be situated the growing independence of the category 'adult'. Thus it is that to be a 'person' in Britain – and indeed in many other Western cultures –

means being independent, and that, in contrast to the experience of members of other cultures, dependency may therefore bring with it the denial of personhood. Parallels in the experience of dependency were introduced in Chapter 1, when attention was drawn to the use of childhood as a dominant or root metaphor for all that dependency entails. However, why was it that 'dependent childhood' came to symbolize dependency for all? If the power of particular metaphors to shape and express social experience lies in their cultural fitness or appropriateness, derived from shared experience – what Sontag (1990: 6) describes as their 'felt aptness' – what is it about the idea of 'the child' which seemingly allows it to speak so evocatively about other social statuses? And, why is it that through using this particular metaphorical voice, the life experiences of members of dependent social categories are in practice frequently denigrated, marginalized or stigmatized through the creation of asymmetrical relations of power?

Drawing on the work of Black (1962), Turner's theoretical discussion of ritual (1974) allows an exploration of these questions. A root metaphor has been described as the 'systematic repertoire of ideas by means of which a given thinker describes, by *analogical extension*, some domain to which those ideas do not immediately and literally apply' (Black, quoted in Turner, 1974: 26). Turner argues that root metaphors gain their power and dynamism to shape perceptions and everyday experiences through the metaphoric process of bringing two previously unconnected thoughts together in a single word or phrase. It is not simply a process of substitution or comparison. Therefore, Turner suggests, to look for the historical antecedents of root metaphors may be to discover their full panoply of meaning which is currently masked. Over time, 'the more persuasive the root metaphor or archetype, the more chance it has of becoming a self-certifying myth, sealed off from empirical disproof' (1974: 29). It is this which accounts for the embeddedness of metaphors of childhood for dependency in many Western cultures and which explains their resistance to change.

Only by unpacking the past, then, can we discover the signifying potential for metaphoric strategies which is intrinsic to the concept of childhood in the present. The motifs and themes threaded through past and present representations and images of childhood are woven into the particular contemporary Western vision of what 'the child' is and what 'childhood' is all about. Arguably, then, 'childhood' is not simply a descriptively neutral term for the early years of life, but, like the concepts of dependency and personhood already explored, is a way of conceptually ordering and classifying.

Broadly, the form which childhood has taken on in Western cultures is one which stresses the differences between children and adults, rather than their similarities. It is this peculiar historical construction which has progressively increased children's social, political and economic dependency and marginalization. In this constitution of the child as 'other' – a positively approved symbol of difference – lies one reason why 'childhood' seems an apt metaphor for other experiences of dependency.

The idea that childhood is socially constructed (James and Prout, 1990b) was first pointed out by Van Gennep (1960 [1908]). He argued that the so-called puberty rituals of traditional societies were primarily markers of changes in social status during the life course, rather than a recognition of physical maturity. He was quick to emphasize that physical and social puberty only 'rarely converge' in the transition from the status of 'boy' to 'man' or 'girl' to 'woman' (1960 [1908]: 65). However, it is not until the 1960s that we find an acknowledgement that childhood in Western societies might also be seen as this kind of social construction or cultural classification. The French historian Philippe Ariès (1979 [1962]: 115), in making his now famous pronouncement that 'in medieval society the idea of childhood did not exist', unleashed a series of studies both in support of and in opposition to his stance (see de Mause, 1976; Wilson, 1980; Pollock, 1983). Whatever the merits of the ensuing historical debates, their culminative effect has been, in the end, to underline the very point that Ariès was endeavouring to make: that the institution of childhood is socially constructed and that concepts such as 'the child' and 'childhood' are not fixed and immutable. Rather, they have a cultural specificity which varies in relationship to the biological state of immaturity (see Prout and James, 1990). It is, for example, this perception which frames Ennew's more recent statement that 'childhood has a changing historical and ethnographic appearance' when she writes of the sexual exploitation of children cross-culturally (1986: 11).

What expectations and assumptions surround childhood in contemporary Western cultures? What image or images of 'the child' are popularly portrayed? In Firestone's critique of childhood (1971) the images which have gained contemporary currency are for the most part nostalgic or sentimental. For Holt too, in another radical account, the Western 'child' is idealized as a 'mixture of expensive nuisance, fragile treasure, slave and super-pet' (Holt, 1975: 22). The mythical creature he describes is locked into the social institution of childhood, popularly portrayed as 'a kind of walled garden in which children, being small and weak, are protected from the harshness of the world outside until they become strong and clever enough to cope with it' (1975: 22). Ennew provides a more explicit depiction, arguing that the childhood of contemporary Western societies has two main characteristics. The first is 'a rigid hierarchy which permeates the whole of society and creates a distance between adults and children' (1986: 17). This is obvious in the multitude of specialist services and products devised and marketed specifically for children in Western cultures: children's clothes, films, toys, books, food, games, play spaces, schools. Recently, this specialism has extended into other child-centred services, such as special telephones lines for those children suffering abuse, counselling and legal services and the instigation of Ombudsmen to serve children's perceived needs. Whilst adults may not be forbidden access to these goods and services, in the way that children are denied those in the adult world, few avail themselves of the opportunity. Thus, childhood is visualized as a special period in the life course, within which time itself takes on particular qualities (James and Prout, 1990a).

The second feature of modern childhood identified by Ennew is 'the myth of childhood as a golden age' whereby children are 'obliged to be happy' (1986: 18). For Ennew, the theme of innocence is a particularly persistent and powerful representation of the mythology of childhood. A.A. Milne personified innocence in the 1930s, through a curly-haired little boy in wellington boots. Christopher Robin, who whiles away his childhood 'in complete isolation from adults in the Hundred Acre Wood, accompanied by sexless woolly animals', continues to inform our ideas about childhood (1986: 11).[1] It is a childhood conceived in terms of 'a period of lack of responsibility, with rights to protection and training but not to autonomy' (Ennew, 1986: 21).

Another set of images, whilst presenting a stark contrast to those founded on ideals of innocence and happiness, nevertheless stem from the same root and, precisely through their opposition, sustain and nourish them. Drawn largely from the Third World, they are images of starving children, homeless children, victimized children, abused children, abandoned children. These images, in photographs splashed across the newspapers of the First World, are representations of 'incorrect childhood' for which correction must be sought. As Ennew writes, the largely uncritical incorporation of a Western ideal of childhood on to the agenda of international agencies working on children's behalf means that 'an association is constantly made between white children who have a correct childhood and black children who have none' (1986: 22). Thus, the consequences of this globalization of childhood in the everyday lives of Third World children themselves can be particularly damaging for it is, as we shall see, tied into the specificities of the historical and cultural conditions which produced it (Boyden, 1990). Recent controversies about child sexual abuse in Britain have similarly revolved around this image of the innocent and vulnerable child, further sustaining this concept of childhood in society: 'the discourses of childhood innocence, passivity and innate vulnerability' which permeate contemporary visions of what 'the child' is, effectively socialize abused children into 'victimhood' and oppression (Kitzinger, 1990: 158).

The elements comprising the mythology of childhood can be well illustrated by the signifying words and images used to portray children in contemporary popular culture. As exemplified in the advertisements described below which were found in the national press, particular motifs work together to sustain a particular image of childhood. The first is for life insurance:

> 'Bonds, securities, trusts, futures. This is what investment's really about.' These headline words are accompanied by a photograph of a naked woman clutching a naked baby to her in a protective embrace. In the half light of the photograph the woman, who is turned away from us, looks into the distance whilst the baby, head resting on his/her mother's (?) shoulder, dreamily contemplates us, the readers.

A second advertisement is for fuel:

> A woman and girl, perhaps mother and daughter, are walking hand-in-hand across green fields. Their backs are turned away from us, the viewers, as they stride forever onwards: 'We won't ask your children to pay the earth for today's energy.'

A third advertisement is for cars:

> A close-up photograph of a man and child greets us. Only half the man's face is visible as he presses it affectionately against the child's, a child who stares out at us from the page. The caption reads: 'The best thing in your life?'

The fourth image appears in an advertisement for a medical systems company:

> A line drawing depicts a woman cradling a (her?) baby above the caption, 'We bring technology to life'. It is the baby's face which gazes at us, the woman looks down and away.

Clearly these images, 'mythologize' childhood in the manner described by Barthes (1973). Open to interpretation, they re-invent 'the child' in culturally significant ways for the reader, through a complex interplay of dominant motifs of childhood. But they do

so in a way which makes them appear both natural and unproblematic. For example, the viewer assumes that the woman in the
fourth advertisement is the mother of the child she holds. Whilst
we do not know this for certain, we are led to this assumption by
the way in which she holds the child, and by the associations in the
text between 'giving birth' and 'giving life'. Similarly, in the second
advertisement we naturally take the figures to be those of mother
and daughter. However, the mere juxtaposition of an adult and a
child does not necessarily constitute parenthood: we are led to
know it is 'her' child rather than 'a' child by their bonds of affec-
tions, here symbolized in their joined hands. At the level of myth,
then, the clasped hands and cradling arms connote the child in its
dependent relationship: as belonging to someone, as dependent,
rather that as independent, as an individual in his or her own right.
In this way 'the child' is also firmly drawn into the bosom of the
family which is, as shown in Chapter 4, itself a metaphor of
nurturance which plays upon the notion of vulnerability. Thus the
child's dependency is doubly secured.

Secondly, the child, who is speaking to us (for it is the child's
face which engages us in three of the advertisements), is a young
baby. Being small, helpless and infinitely dependent, the baby is a
most voluble image through which to promote the particular
childhood mythology of innocence and vulnerability. Although the
child-as-baby has no language, it addresses us. It is special and
different, and literally embodies the words it cannot speak.
Thirdly, the naturalness of children, as well as their supposed
natural innocence, is symbolized by their nakedness. Unlike the
naked bodies of women, it is through the presumed sexual
innocence of children that a naive honesty can be affirmed. Being
sexually innocent, their nakedness is both unprovocative and
unproblematic. Wide-eyed and truthful, the baby's gaze confronts
the viewer, challenging us to negate its innocence. Fourthly, the
specialness or otherness of the child also lies in its construction as
a thread of continuity between the past and the future, the 'moon-
shot' model of the child (James and Prout, 1990a). Inscribed in
both the text of the adverts – 'investments', 'securities', 'life',
'tomorrow's advances' – and in the visual image of protection and
dependency, is the idea that the child should be cradled and
cuddled, shielded and protected, in preparation for what is to
come. And it is the natural world which best prepares the child for
this future; portrayed as enfolded and cocooned in the green fields
of a future Jerusalem, rather than the satanic mills of the past, the
temporality of childhood mediates between the past and the future.

These advertisements have indicated the consistency through

which a particular mythology of childhood is evoked and drawn upon in everyday life. They are not, however, the inevitable byproduct of biological infancy. Instead, they represent a cultural construction of that infancy which has only gradually emerged in Western societies. The processes which both produced and sustained a growing social separation between the worlds of adults and children in the West and which denied children their personhood, at the same time made 'natural' this partitioning of a period in the life course as a time of dependency predicated upon the special nature of children.

The history of childhood in the West is therefore, more accurately, the history of a particular and changing vision of what it means to be a child. However, although broadly historical in tone, we shall not present an exhaustive history of childhood. This has been variously written and its details hotly debated elsewhere (see Pinchbeck and Hewitt, 1969, 1973; Demos, 1971; de Mause, 1976; Ariès, 1979 [1962]; Wilson, 1980; Walvin, 1982; Pollock, 1983). Instead, some predominant themes and motifs will be outlined – thus making it 'intelligible by reconstituting its conditions of existence and its conditions of emergence' (Cousins and Hussain, 1984: 3) for it is in the particularity of these themes and motifs that the metaphoric potential of 'childhood' lies. We shall therefore look to these histories to discover some of the more significant shifts and changes in the social, political, moral and economic climate at particular points in time which created the conceptual space for the gradual emergence of a modern Western 'childhood'. From these various accounts of contemporary Western childhood four characteristics can be distilled:

1 the child is spatially and temporally set apart as different, as 'other';
2 the child is said to have a special nature, and to be associated with nature;
3 the child is innocent and therefore
4 vulnerably dependent.

Whilst not always explicit, these characteristics nevertheless subtly structure the ways in which children are thought about in Western cultures. They are therefore integral to the persuasive power which childhood has as a root metaphor for other experiences of dependency such as that of deep old age (Turner, 1974). In these expressed attitudes and ideas about 'the child' and 'childhood' lie the hidden meanings which the root metaphor of childhood contemporarily entails. Our 'history' focuses, then, on the 'categories of language and thought' through which children were and are perceived, rather than following a sequence of historical events (Samuel, 1981: xliii). Once again, Britain serves as the case study.

A child can be classified as 'other'

The importance of the temporality of childhood is only just beginning to be recognized as being of heuristic value in social analyses of childhood and of children's lives (see James and Prout, 1990a). This comparatively late development is surprising given that time is a key feature of contemporary representations of childhood. It is, for example, through reference to 'age' – time passing – that childhood as a separate domain of human experience, a distinct period in human life, is made explicable. Children are, through age, given justification of and for their separateness and exclusion from mainstream social life and central social institutions. They are confined to age-based and child-centred social arenas – schools, playgroups, nurseries, youth clubs etc. – where contact outside their peer group may be limited to the family (see Holt, 1975). It is only through increase in numerical age – time passing – that access to the adult world is permitted. Thus little children receive birthday cards which proudly proclaim their age; each year passed is a step towards full personhood at 18 and/or 21 years old. Quite literally, the 'coming of age', calculated as a numerical quantity, signals the end of childhood.

But such numerical accuracy is neither an inevitable nor necessary aspect of 'age'. To meet the demands of a fragmented and technological society, such as Britain, it is used to locate, most precisely, a person's position in relation to access to work or schooling, wage packets or pensions, bingo halls and betting shops. In other cultures such exact measurement and calculation of time passing may be neither relevant nor even known and, in many traditional societies, age is much more a social than a numerical concept. Its cognitive value lies in attributing position within a group with reference to the quality of its social function and relationships, an age set or grade, rather than registering the quantity of time which has passed (Baxter and Almagor, 1978; La Fontaine, 1978; Spencer, 1990). In Western cultures during the Middle Ages, 'age' had this kind of classificatory function.

Our first theme, which centres on the child as different, as other, can be illustrated then by tracing how age and physical maturity came to predominate as a differentiating feature of childhood. In medieval society there were seven 'ages' in a person's life linking, through the great chain of being, the 'destiny of man to that of the planets' (Ariès, 1979 [1962]: 19). A coherent conceptual universe with an essentially fatalistic perspective, it 'fostered the idea of a life cut into clearly defined sections corresponding to certain modes of activity, physical types, social functions and styles of dress' (1979 [1962]: 22). Although these ages of life roughly corresponded to the process of biological maturation, their significance lay in specifying *social* functions. Each 'age' was perceived to be characterized by particular social rather than physical attributes, and it was these which defined the nature of personhood.

The historical emergence of individualism, which as we have shown, became central to Western concepts of personhood, can be linked in to the increasing temporal specificity which 'age' gradually acquired in Western cultures. This can clearly be seen in the changes in British education. During the fifteenth century, schools were not seen as predominantly for children, nor was education confined to schools. Education for the poor often took the form of apprenticeship to a trade or guild, whilst schools, primarily for the rich, catered for older as well as younger people (Wardle, 1974). However, during the sixteenth and seventeenth centuries, which as Wardle (1974) notes witnessed the burgeoning of a variety of educational schemes, such as charity schools and industrial schools, education took on a narrower remit. Children had become the target for educationalists, both reflecting and refracting a growing awareness of childhood as a distinctive and special stage in an individual's life, rather than simply one part of a cycle. By the late nineteenth century compulsory schooling was introduced for children, with specific age limits set to mark out the intended population.

In a similar manner, the Factory Acts of the nineteenth century used age to segregate out specific categories of children who were to be excluded from work, or limited the number of working hours for particular 'ages' of children (Pinchbeck and Hewitt, 1973). The end of schooling and the start of work thus became the age at which British childhood ended and adult life began. Describing how, in 1883, his grandfather left school, aged 11, Williamson notes that:

> there is no record of his early start in pit work creating in him any feelings of dread or despair. In fact, such evidence as there is suggests he was keen and utterly unperturbed, despite the fact that he faced a ten-hour shift underground. Indeed, it was likely that he felt quite elated by the idea, for starting work was the essential step to becoming a man and would confer on him a new position of authority in the family and give him a lot of freedom from home. (1982: 30)

In this way, age reckoning – the calculating of a numerical

quantity – became a marker of an individual's social status. It was the accumulation of age which literally marked out the men from the boys. For working class girls, the transition into service provided a similar function when they reached the 'age' when compulsory schooling ended, as Flora Thompson (1979) has so vividly described.

A child has a different nature

A second theme which predominates in contemporary images of Western childhood centres on the child's nature as being different from that of adults. The gradual separation of children from the adult world into age-based institutions – the making of children as other – was, as noted, in part a function of the changing constructions of time in Western cultures. However, their separation, and later marginalization, was also fostered by growing philosophical speculation upon the nature of this category of 'child'. The child rendered as 'other' was the precondition for attempts to understand its nature. Ennew remarks that contemporary Western conceptions of 'the child' are, to some extent, paradoxical, seeming to have a 'built-in ambiguity with constant interplay between good and evil' (1986: 11). There is nothing new about this ambiguity. Like the arc of a pendulum, conceptions of 'the child' have swung first in one direction and then the other, as debate followed debate about its fundamental nature. Herein lies the beginnings of the child as a root metaphor for 'otherness'.

By the end of the sixteenth century a radical reappraisal of the old medieval order had taken place. No longer was humanity seen to be at the mercy of the natural and supernatural world. Instead salvation rested upon the individual's own faith and contrition in the sight of God and, according to Calvin, the predestined elect would be revealed through their display of the virtues of thrift and abstinence. As Thomas argues this was 'a conscientious attempt to impose order on the apparent randomness of the human fortunes by proving that, in the long run, virtue was rewarded and vice did not go unpunished' (1973: 125–6). It was these arguments which framed the Puritan doctrine of Original Sin and out of which emerged a particular view of the child. Liberated from fate, through the conception of human beings as self-controlled and self-determined, the Puritans faced a particular problem: in their apparent helplessness, newborn children lacked the very qualities which defined humanity and thus the child was, to the Puritan mind, innately sinful. But, through strict discipline of the body and rigorous training of the mind, its will could be broken, its sin removed. In this way children could be trained out of the natural state of sin into a state of grace:

> So long as no one cared about them very much, they could be left to run wild, or in the hands of nurses, servants and tutors. But the Reformation – and in Catholic Europe the Counter Reformation – drive for moral regeneration brought with it an increasing concern to suppress the sinfulness of children. A pedagogic movement, which had begun a century earlier with the Italian renaissance and a glorification of the purity and innocence of the child was twisted in its late sixteenth- and early seventeenth-century northern religious transplantation into a deadly fear of the liability of children to corruption and sin, particularly those cardinal sins of pride and disobedience. (Stone, 1979: 124)

The Puritan period in the seventeenth century therefore saw not only the increasing separation of children from the adult world through schooling, but also the growth of a doctrine concerning the particularity of the child's nature. Children – the literal manifestation of the sins of the flesh – represented uncontrolled and irrational beings. They displayed qualities which were in direct antithesis to Puritan morality. For them, rational thought and hence salvation was only possible through control of the physical body, humanity's animal nature, and children were in this sense more animal than human. The doctrine of Original Sin therefore provided both an explanation for their disordered state, and a pretext for its remedy.

Explicit parallels were drawn by the Puritans between the nature of children and that of animals. This view created further conceptual distance between children and adults: their special nature, being more natural, compounded their separation from the adult social world. Although there is disagreement about the extent and severity of Puritan parents' disciplinary regimes, the supposed sinful 'animality' of children precipitated the need for training (see de Mause, 1976; also Pollock's (1983) critique). As Stone depicts it,

> the early training of children was directly equated with the bating of hawks and the breaking-in of young horses or hunting dogs. These were all animals which were highly valued and cherished in the society of that period and it was only natural that exactly the same principle should be applied to the education of children. (1979: 116)

Children were made, for example, to kneel before their parents to receive their blessing. This was a sign that their stubborn will was under control, that their animal nature was becoming socialized. They were continually exhorted to lead pure lives, for example through being introduced to the exemplary and godly children in Janeway's book *A Token for Children* (1671). These children, too good to live, achieved deliverance rather than damnation when they died. The first child-training manuals appeared at this time and recommended methods of child-rearing to encourage righteous behaviour. The Puritans, who saw in their children a medium for promoting their faith, argued for the necessity of their moral control. The animality of children meant that innocence and godliness could only be obtained through social control of that special and different nature.

By the eighteenth century the situation was reversed. As Thomas (1973) notes, whilst significant emphasis was still given to the particular and special qualities of children's nature, it gradually became more favourably looked upon. Cases were cited of children who, through their innocence and chastity of body and mind, could divine the face of a thief in a crystal ball. Examples of child prophets were held up as symbols of the innocence of children, and, on account of their tender age, as evidence for the neutrality rather than the essential sinfulness of human nature. Four tracts related in verse and prose the achievements of one Charles Bennet, aged three, of Manchester. Hailed as a prophet, divinely inspired he foretold of the King's death.

> His parents were but mean People, getting their Livings by their daily labours and Imployments. This is no fallacy nor premeditated Instruction taught by device nor Art of men, for was it so, the Child could not be perfect in every cross question, the which amongst the learnedest of men requires some deliberation, then what we can imagine less than that those parts and early Docilities proceeded by Divine Inspiration: and who can tell what Mysteries Omnipotence may veile that tender form, the which in time may shine more perfect to the World, till when let us admire and with the Prophet say, It is the Lords doing and is Marvellous in our eyes, etc. (Axon, 1902: 50)

It is in the writings of John Locke that this changing perception can be best seen. For Locke, all knowledge was to be gained from experience of the world: it was experience which, with age, produced reason amongst human beings. In contrast to the Puritan view, Locke argued that the mind of the newborn child was a *tabula rasa*, a blank sheet upon which sensations were imprinted. These experiences were gradually accumulated and ordered in the mind of each individual, so that reason was achieved as maturity was reached. The social and moral education of the child was therefore crucial to the realization of humanity's potential. For Locke, human nature was not innately sinful; rather each child was born with a capacity to learn, to receive and order experiences. The ways in which learning took place were therefore of paramount importance.

It is in his essay *Some Thoughts Concerning Education* (1693) that Locke proposes his philosophy of education, one which 'encapsulates what was clearly a new and growing attitude towards child-rearing and education' (Plumb, 1975: 67). Locke stressed the importance of a lib.ral attitude towards children in his educational writings which stood in stark contrast to the previous emphasis placed on corporal punishment and authoritarianism in child-training methods. The child, he reasoned, should be encouraged, rather than forced, to learn. Such ideas paved the way for the increasing institutionalization of childhood in the eighteenth century and stimulated the opening up of markets specifically for children. They were becoming identified as a separate and distinct consumer group. By the eighteenth century, then, the containment of the child within a distinct and special category was established not only in terms of the child's life and activities, but also in terms of ideas about its special nature. This concern became, in the nineteenth and twentieth centuries, the focus for the new science of psychology through the study of child development.

The child as innocent

As noted, increasing industrialization in the nineteenth century had led to the effective marginalization of children, along with women and elderly people, from the world of work. This process undermined their personhood as individualism, increasingly symbolized through wage work, became the mark of significant social status. Children's growing distance from the adult social world was compounded by more radical ideas about the particular qualities of the child's nature which rendered the child vulnerable to the pressures and corruption of industrialization. The third theme of innocence can be located here but its roots lie in the eighteenth century.

Discounting, like Locke, earlier Puritanical suggestions of the inborn sinfulness of the child Jean-Jacques Rousseau argued for its original innocence through his 'cult of sensibility' (Coveney, 1957: 6). For him, the mind/body of the child was naturally pure, rather than the blank sheet which Locke had argued for. Countering Locke's educational philosophy of the seventeenth century which, although not seeing the child as sinful, had stressed social training. Rousseau suggested that it was through contact with the 'natural' rather than the social world that this primaeval nature could best be protected. For him it was Society which was to blame for any departure of the child from its natural state of innocence: 'God makes all things good, man meddles with them and they become evil' (1969 [1762]: 5). Social experience for Locke was a positive force; for Rousseau it was fraught with danger. As he saw it, from the moment of birth the child's original virtuous nature was subject to, and threatened by, the corrupting influence of society. Thus in *Emile*, published in 1762, Rousseau proposed a system of education which would allow the child to develop naturally, according to its own nature rather than society's whims.

The importance of Rousseau's philosophical contribution lies not in its practical application – *Emile* had little direct influence upon later educational developments, unlike Locke's thoughts on education – but in its ideological import. Rousseau stressed that the child could retain its innate innocence if allowed to grow up in harmony with the laws of nature, rather than those of men. The child would be Nature's pupil. According to Rousseau the child matures 'not by a gradual unbroken process of accretion' (Locke's philosophy) but 'by a periodic movement through certain distinct stages' (Wardle, 1974: 33). The child passed from a stage of sensual experience through a period of intellectual and analytical thinking, before reaching a time when it could appreciate moral and aesthetic issues. So that the child might mature in this natural and orderly manner, Rousseau was opposed to formal schooling. Books were banned at an age when a child was experiencing sensual pleasures; only later would they be allowed.

> Nature would have them children before they are men. If we try and invert this order we shall produce a forced fruit immature and flavourless, fruit which will be rotten before it is ripe; we shall have young doctors and old children. Childhood has its own ways of seeing, thinking and feeling; nothing is more foolish than to try and substitute our ways. (1969 [1762]: 54)

The corrupting influence of society was the only source of evil in children so that through allowing the child to learn naturally, according to its own stage of development, maximum protection from social pressures would be achieved: the child should do 'only what Nature asks of him; then he will never do wrong' (1969 [1762]: 57). This idea of stages of development, located in Rousseau's depiction of the child's innocence, was incorporated into the growing perspective of the child as a symbol of Otherness. During the nineteenth and early twentieth centuries, for example, it was fundamental to the developing science of child psychology and can clearly be seen in the writings of Freud and Piaget. Contemporarily, it remains one of the mainstays of developmental psychology.

Rousseau's image of the child was a true product of its age. During the late eighteenth century the New World discoveries had begun to broaden the social vision of certain Western intellectuals who saw in the 'noble savage' an alternative and better mode of thought and lifestyle. The cult of primitivism (Boas, 1966) embraced the simple life. Untrammelled by the complexities of industrial society, the 'noble savage' was portrayed as living life instinctively in harmony with nature. The appeal of this vision was widespread, for it seemed to offer a solution to the problems of an industrial society, popularly seen to be caused by a ruthless individualism and the predominance of rational thought over natural human instincts. Rousseau's fictitious child was akin to this 'natural' human being, another symbol of an innocent and uncorrupted life. Thus it was that in his innocence Emile came to embody a vision for 'childhood' itself. As Hendrick argues, 'the factory child seemed to symbolize profound and often little understood changes in British society, changes which appeared to threaten an imagined natural order' (1990: 40).

The child is vulnerably dependent

The contemporary representation of the child as different from adults in its youthful and innocent immaturity was, therefore, already established by the end of the eighteenth century. Indeed, it was this special vulnerable and dependent nature which prompted social reforms on the child's behalf. In Wordsworth's 'Ode on Intimations of Immortality' from *Recollections of Early Childhood* (1802–6) the child is portrayed as different from adults, an integral part of nature. But, unlike Rousseau's vision, the child is not Nature's pupil, but rather possessed of a particular nature. As Coveney argues, this poem is a *locus classicus* indeed for nineteenth-century literature on childhood (1957: 39). The Ode portrays the increasing pressures upon the child, 'shades of the prison door' which 'begin to close/ upon the growing boy'. Social reformers, such as Robert Owen, echoed these concerns in their consideration of the social consequences of industrialization in terms of the cognitive and moral development of the individual. Owen understood human character to be moulded in childhood, its shape determined entirely by the social environment. Echoing Locke, such a view also referred back to Rousseau: blame for social ills cannot be attached to individuals since it is society, rather than nature, which is at fault. Therefore, to eradicate social evils, society has a responsibility to provide a decent environment within which individuals can lead good and honest lives. These themes of social reform, characteristic of the late nineteenth century, were echoed in the more theoretical works of Engels and in the call for radical social change initiated by Marx. By the end of the nineteenth century, this concern focused upon the care and protection of children, embracing as it did so the particular cultural motifs of childhood which, as shown, can be historically contextualized. As a 'root metaphor' for dependency, then, childhood speaks volubly about particular qualities of living and particular views of humanity (Turner, 1974). It is not a neutral term, devoid of value judgements and attitudes. Within its simplicity are entwined a set of cultural beliefs about children who, as humanity in the making, are not yet conceived to be persons. Their distinctive qualities separate them off from the social world of independent adults. Herein lies the semantic power of the metaphoric extension of concepts of childhood to other categories of people, a cultural strategy which this book sets out to question.

Fostering the dependence of the child

The mythologizing of childhood, here historically schematized through a set of recurring motifs, embraces the set of ideals – separation, naturalness, innocence and vulnerability – which characterize contemporary beliefs about the dependency of the child. However, given that the child must eventually leave childhood, must become independent, wise and social, this culturally specific understanding of 'the child' and childhood is riven with contradictions. There is then, for Western cultures, a continual problem of effecting a reconciliation between them.

For example, the mythology of Western childhood innocence cannot embrace children's sexuality, either contemporarily or in the past. As Foucault (1979) notes, its repression dates back at least to the eighteenth century and, as knowledge of children's sexual life was made public through the theories of Sigmund Freud, this repression intensified (Ennew, 1986). Sexuality and innocence make strange bedfellows. In other cultures, where innocence is not a precondition of childhood, children's sexuality does not present the same logistical problem (see Berndt and Berndt, 1964; Shostak, 1976; Collier and Rosaldo, 1981).

However, the central contradiction with which the Western ideology of childhood is riven centres on dependency itself, on that very quality which, as we have seen, defines the child as different, natural, innocent and vulnerable. During the life course of individuals in Western cultures, dependency must somehow be shrugged off in favour of an individualistic, knowledgeable, independence which is the mark of adulthood. There is, as Benedict (1955) noted some years ago, a discontinuity, rather than continuity between child and adult social experiences in Western societies. This contrasts with the process of socialization in many non-Western cultures. For example although the teasing games played by Canadian Inuit adults with their children – threatening the death of a child's mother or the self – may, in the light of Western visions of childhood, seem harsh, they are instructive for Inuit adult life:

> [Inuit children] can't sit back comfortably, passively absorb the fruits of adult wisdom and experience, and conclude that the wisdom embodies final and permanent answers. Instead of learning to depend passively on 'the authorities' and 'experts', they learn to rely on their own sense in interpreting their own experience, to be watchful, doubtful, alert to hidden meanings and intentions and to keep testing others, as the adults have tested them. (Briggs, 1990: 38)

Such abilities have many uses, both in the social and the physical environment of the Inuit. Children quickly learn to be observant and watchful of the world around them. As adults, this enables them to notice the dangerous first trickle of wet snow from an iceberg, or the sour smell on a person's breath which denotes illness. The Inuit understanding of 'the child' respects 'the ability of three-year-olds to understand and to use in their own lives, emotionally complicated and difficult lessons' (Briggs, 1990: 38). By contrast, conceptualized as a dependent Other, Western children's emotional and intellectual lives are largely under an adult's rather than their own control.

As the following chapters demonstrate, the contradictions with which Western childhood is beset become magnified for those whose lives are touched by the metaphoric extension of the concept of childhood through infantilizing practices. How is it, then, that the model of childhood dependency which had emerged by the eighteenth century succeeded in masking these contradictions? Again we return to a consideration of questions of power. During the nineteenth century the reforming activities of a variety of philanthropic and child-saving movements aimed to provide for all children the 'happy' childhood which existed for the few (Hendrick, 1990). However, it was the middle and upper classes, so placed as socially, politically and economically to afford 'childhood' for their own children, who were its main instigators. Yet, as Musgrove points out, 'protective measures are a two edged device; while they may signify concern for the welfare of the young they also define them as a separate, non-adult population, inhabiting a less than adult world' (1964: 58).

The concept of childhood dependency, which like all other dependencies rests on an asymmetrical power relationship (Walker,

1982),[2] developed as a feature of the emerging nuclear family and was justified through recourse to a cultural mythology which was developing simultaneously in relation to the child. Thus it was that the extended family, where the social unit reigned supreme over its individual members of which children were simply a part, gave way to the nuclear family of which children were a distinct and separate group. This change had already begun by the middle of the seventeenth century and children's social dependency was fast becoming a key feature both of the family and of childhood itself. For the Puritan regime of discipline and control, education and training, subordination was an essential prerequisite: children were subject to parental control within the emerging nuclear family and, later, through schooling to that of their teachers, standing *in loco parentis*. Education was a method of equipping 'the child with accomplishments that would secure for it gainful employment' and a way of teaching the idea of 'sobriety, obedience, industry, thrift, benevolence and compassion – that educationalists regarded as the virtues of a successful man' (Plumb, 1975: 69). Before this stage was reached the child remained dependent upon its parents.

For children of the wealthy, this dependence was encouraged by their active participation in the rapidly developing markets for children. Educational reforms stimulated a growth in the production of books for children, books which would be used by parents to encourage children to read. In 1745 the Newbury publishing house first began producing books specifically for children and by the mid-eighteenth century the toy industry was rapidly developing. As Plumb comments, although this time of commercial expansion positioned children as a new group of consumers, it was not children, but their parents, who were buying these goods or paying the educational fees:

The image of the child which the schools, as well as children's literature projected, was the image of an ideal parent's child – industrious, obedient, constantly respectful and indeed a pet, never too spoilt, but occasionally indulged as a reward for virtue. (1975: 80)

For the wealthy, 'children had become counters in their parents' social aspirations' (Plumb, 1975: 80).

The child labour reforms of the late nineteenth century contributed to the growing dependency of all children through denying them a source of income. Combined with the introduction of compulsory schooling in 1870, economic dependency came to represent and form a boundary to the idea of childhood itself. Further protective measures soon followed and, through these, the dependency of the child upon the nuclear family and its exclusion and marginalization from adult centres of power and control was finally effected. For example, the Infant Life Protection Act was passed in 1872 and in 1889 this was supplemented by the Prevention of Cruelty to Children Act which allowed the courts to deprive irresponsible parents of their children. The 1891 Custody of Children Act made it impossible for parents who had abandoned their children to reclaim them and in 1895 the National Society for the Prevention of Cruelty to Children received its Royal Charter. Underscoring this mass of legislation for the protection of children, which was introduced during the nineteenth century, is an image of children as belonging to a distinct social group, set apart as a special category with specific and special needs. As Pinchbeck and Hewitt note, 'in effect nineteenth century legislation gradually imposed on the working class family a pattern of child dependence which the middle and upper classes had developed several generations before' (1973: 651).

In this way, therefore, social, political and economic dependency has become 'naturalized' as the key feature of a Western child's experience of the world, through the historical development of a particular ideology of childhood. The physical dependency of infancy, common to all cultures, now stretches into a social dependency in the late childhood and adolescence of the members of Western cultures, bringing with it the denial of their personhood. Thus it is that, when used of those who are not children, metaphors of childhood are potent in their stigmatization of individual selves. Drawing on his personal experiences of disability in American culture, where 'independence, self-reliance and personal autonomy are central values', Murphy reflects on this process:

> lack of autonomy and unreciprocated dependence on others brings debasement of status in American culture – and in many other cultures . . . Overdependency and non-reciprocity are considered childish traits, and adults who have them – even if it's not their fault – suffer a reduction in status. This is one reason why the severely disabled and the very old are often treated as children. (1987: 155)

Notes

1 Its continuing power as a cultural image is evident in the recent call for the introduction of Christopher Robin and the *Winnie the Pooh* books into the National Curriculum for English school children, to replace more 'progressive' children's books. It may be that these 'progressive' books are seen to threaten the sentimental, regressive vision of Western childhood.
2 See below pp. 104–12 for a discussion of dependency and power.

3

YOUNG AT HEART

The metaphor 'young at heart' is but one of a number which, we are suggesting, establish conceptual links between categories of persons at different points in the life course in Western cultures. Such usage draws explicit parallels between those at each extreme: old heads are said to be on young shoulders, very elderly people may be described as entering a second childhood or as going 'gaga'. It operates to produce two effects. First, it appears to suggest similarities between the life experiences of very elderly people and children. Secondly, it makes elderly people into metaphoric children. That is to say, a one-way process of metaphoric transformation links the two social categories.

In continuing to challenge the use of such metaphors and to explore their role in defining boundaries to and negating aspects of personhood in Western society this chapter focuses upon the social construction of the body. This extends our argument beyond a purely theoretical discourse for, as we shall see, the body provides one critical pathway along which the figurative association of dependent elderly people with 'the child' is made literal through infantilizing practices in society. This is no isolated or aberrant social phenomenon but a widespread process which can also impact upon the life experiences of other people, besides the very elderly and infirm; for example, people who are dependent and receive constant care such as those who are chronically sick and some disabled people (see Jones, 1975; Thomas, 1982; Perring, 1989).

This focus upon the body will reveal, then, some additional and more subtle aspects of this process of re-assigning personhood. Through selected historical case studies, we show in detail how and why 'the child' has come, quite literally, to embody the dominant model of dependency in contemporary Western cultures, one which now encompasses and structures the lives of those who are physically dependent, yet who are not children. Thus, through continuing to make explicit the complexities of the metaphoric system which the image of 'the child' implicitly entails, we are able not only to reveal its ideological role in recreating relations of power, but also to indicate the implications of these infantilizing practices for the health and welfare of individuals and of society as a whole.

Ellipse

The doorbell rings
And flowers are delivered.
Visitors arrive; creep in to see.
Even a casual passer-by will know
If this is a coming, or a going.

In the bedroom, centre of attention,
Someone small and wrinkled lies awake,
Too young to smile or speak, or even watch.
All she can do is take
Her mother's milk; cry, excrete, and sleep.
In return she gives them joy and hope,
Delight in her new life, her innocence.

Bustling woman, seldom sitting down,
Deceives herself that all she does is give
To children, parents, others who, to live
Must feed and ask, depend on her, and take.
Sometimes so much to do she doesn't know
If she is coming or going.

In the bedroom, centre of attention,
Someone old and wrinkled lies awake,
Able to smile, but lacking strength to speak.
Nappies again, and needing help to drink;
All she can do is take.
In return her eyes give out her love.
She watches with concern as other grieve
To lose her gifts, not knowing she will leave
A store of wisdom and experience.

The ellipse of life has perfect symmetry,
Wide in the middle, ends
Both gently narrowing.
There's mystery in
This similarity
of coming and
going.

Averil Stedeford

From Averil Stedeford, *Facing Death* (Heinemann Medical Books, 1984)

The body as a signifier

A wealth of anthropological material reveals the body being used in many societies to make statements about changes in social status. These range from permanently marking the body to simply decorating it in particular ways. For example, in non-Western cultures genital mutilation (male and female) is commonly performed at initiation ceremonies, thereby registering a change in social status from boy to man, or girl to woman. Heads may also be shaved to register this passage through the life course. Among the Nuer of Sudan, on the other hand, it is scarification of the body which by tradition symbolically marks the permanence of the movement out of childhood into adulthood. Different forms of body decoration – such as body painting with henna or ochre – register other culturally significant changes in social status. Among Hindu women, for example, a red circle is painted on the forehead to indicate their marriage and, traditionally, Chinese girls' feet were tightly bound, their restricted growth symbolizing high social status. From ear lobe stretching, inserting lip plates and filing teeth to more common practices such as ear and nose piercing, the physical body is literally changed or altered in some way to signify socially significant points in the life course (Polhemus, 1978).

In Western societies there is a continuum of forms of bodily alteration. Whilst not necessarily signifying status change in terms of the life course, invasive plastic surgery procedures such as breast enlargement or nose reshaping and non-invasive practices such as dieting and hair styling nevertheless reveal the powerful role which the body can play in registering more subtle aspects of status. For example, within middle class British families the piercing of girls' ears before puberty is often avoided in that the act signifies a shift into 'premature' sexual maturity, a development seen as common or vulgar because it is often associated by the middle classes with working class culture. In other cases bodily alterations may be performed to conform to ideals of feminine beauty or, as we shall see later, to mask the signs of ageing through strategies as diverse as hormone replacement therapy, facelifts and the wearing of wigs. Indeed, according to Helman, the contemporary spare part surgery now common in industrialized societies 'may symbolize a type of partial immortality', as the mass-produced parts – from artificial bones and joints to pacemakers – 'age much slower than the body itself' (1988: 15). In non-Western societies particularly, bodily alteration serves to move the individual forward in time to their future location in social space. By contrast, many Westerners make such interventions in order to reverse the direction of the life course, their wealth being literally expended to 'buy' time.

In addition to taking on this literal signifying role, the body can also assume a figurative one in the process of social signification; that is to say, the body becomes a vehicle of meaning-making or meaning-creating, rather than a repository of meanings (Crick, 1976). Douglas, for example, has shown the ways in which, in many cultures, the body's boundaries and their symbolic breach provide the medium through which ideas of social purity and pollution are expressed, with the caste system in Hindu India providing the most evocative illustrations:

> The whole system represents a body in which by the division of labour the head does the thinking and praying and the most despised parts carry away waste matter. Each sub-caste community in a local region is conscious of its relative standing in the scale of purity. Seen from ego's position the system of caste purity is structured upwards. Those above him are more pure. All the positions below him, be they ever so intricately distinguished in relation to one another, are to him polluting. Thus for any ego within the system the threatening non-structure against which barriers must be erected lies below. The sad wit of pollution as it comments on bodily functions symbolizes descent in the caste structure by contact with faeces, blood and corpses. (1966: 123)

Similarly, as argued in Chapter 1, it is the experience of the body in space which provides, for British and American people, a grounding for the metaphors they use to express their moods and feelings in everyday language: hence, 'elation' (up) is contrasted with 'depression' (down), being 'on a high' compared with experiencing 'a low' (Lakoff and Johnson, 1980).

Whether literally or figuratively, then, the physical body bears a particular and peculiar relationship to the social body and it is in the work of Marcel Mauss that this idea was first articulated. He argued that even the apparently natural movements of the body such as walking and running are culturally engendered and should be regarded as 'techniques' that are 'assembled for the individual not by himself alone but by all his education, by the whole society to which he belongs' (in Brewster (ed.), 1979: 105). Elaborating on this theme, Bourdieu has more recently argued that the signifying role which the body has – as illustrated in the examples above – reveals the workings of the cultural 'habitus' – the 'commonsense world endowed with the objectivity secured by consensus on meaning' (1977 [1972]: 80). It is this which provides a socially specific meaning for the body and it is the 'habitus' which, within Western cultures, constitutes for the body and the person 'an implicit pedagogy, capable of instilling a whole cosmology, an ethic, a metaphysic, a political philosophy, through injunctions as insignificant as "stand up straight" or "don't hold your knife in your left hand"' (1977 [1972]: 94).

Thus it is that, despite the dominance of 'scientific' or rational approaches to the body in Western society, the body has not, as might have been expected, been divested of its role as a source of social imagery and understanding. Paradoxically, as Sontag (1983, 1990) has argued, it may have strengthened or furthered it. Subtle and implicit images of the internal changes within the cancerous body and, more recently, the HIV-positive body have become powerful reference points for social signification in other domains. Therefore, although there is a variety of sources that, as we shall see, contributed to the potency of the metaphoric strategy embedded in practices such as infantilization, the primacy of the physical body in late capitalist societies for definitions of personhood makes it a first and key site for exploration (Featherstone, 1982).

Many accounts point to this relationship. Elder writes of old age:

> The wrinkled skin, the sagging chin, the sunken eyes, the thinning hair, the liver-coloured blotches on the backs of hands, do not exactly inspire confidence and self-respect in our society. After all, the structure and functions of the body provide the basis for our personal identity. (1977: 28)

A woman with a disability writes:

> Some people say that 'you can't tell a book by its cover'; this is a very nice ideal but in reality the cover - the person's physical appearance - is always judged before their personality. (Campling, 1981: 5)

The personal testimonies by MacDonald and Rich (1984) and Elder (1977) confirm the close relationship between perceptions of the body and of personhood, vividly depicted in Vesperi's account of old age in Florida. She describes how elderly people are judged by their adult children, and their peers, as to whether or not they are growing old gracefully. For one woman, 'wearing a "youthful wig" could only be justified when bolstered by frequent expressions of approval from others' (1985: 65). Gradually, however, she began to discard 'her pre-established adult identity', no longer thinking it 'appropriate to attract attention to her physical appearance' or 'to accept compliments about her musical ability' (1985: 70).

Other ethnographic accounts similarly reveal the importance of the body as a locus of metaphoric strategies amongst dependent elderly people, where the needs of the physical body are used by carers to define the social body - the person - as being child-like. Hockey (1990), for example, describes how the frailest residents of

Highfield House – those whose bodies and or minds had become impaired in some way – were socially distinguished from fitter residents through different kinds of naming practices:

> Those who become incontinent, unable to walk without support, or perceptibly 'confused in their minds' will find themselves moved downstairs to what staff refer to as the 'frail' corridor . . . in the dining room 'frail' residents are moved forwards close to the hatchway into the kitchen. Referred to as 'the little people' – who receive smaller meals – it is this group who will be addressed by Christian names only and will tend to be given nicknames. (1990: 100)

The bodily condition provided the literal grounding for their social identity, through registering their loss of physical abilities in terms of a loss of their adult social status as Mr or Mrs (see also Martin, 1979; Hazan, 1980).

Jones's study of mentally handicapped adults provides a parallel process of assigning category membership through recourse to the body's condition. She describes how nursing staff took on parental roles with their adult patients in response to a particular perception of bodily dependence as child-like; they were unable to feed or dress themselves. It also shows these adults' emotional needs being construed as like those of children:

> Usually for tantrums of a verbal or physical kind nothing more is needed than a telling off and perhaps sending upstairs till the next meal to produce repentance and floods of tears. (1975: 25)

In both these examples, however, this social construction of physical dependency as being child-like is particularistic. It represents a *partial* and a *selective* reading of the bodies of *both* adults and children. They are, after all, very visibly different kinds of bodies in terms of both competences and appearances. Our questioning, from this point on, centres then on two key issues: firstly, why is it that the child's *body* provides much of the literal grounding for the metaphoric use of childhood in shaping the experience of dependency and secondly, what are the implications of this metaphoric use of childhood within the context of dependency? This latter question is particularly crucial for, as already indicated, there is a powerful conceptual relationship between the physical body and social identity. Not only is this common to the everyday experiences of those whose bodies differ in some ways from an implicit 'normality', as shown in Goffman's work (1968) on stigma and identity, but this relationship is registered in the very language we use and the stereotypes which we employ to think about the social world.

For example, it was argued earlier that in Western cultures, such as those of Britain and the United States, elderly people are often marginalized through negative stereotypes. Many of these portray the experience of ageing as the experience of bodily decay or mental deterioration. Old age, according to such a perspective, means being 'constantly plagued with "unsightly age spots", constipation, denture problems, baldness, arthritis, chronic backaches, gray hair and facial wrinkles' and elderly people themselves are often characterized as 'lacking commonsense, acting silly or being eccentric' (Powell and Williamson, 1985: 39). Whilst, as we shall see in Chapter 6, there are notable exceptions to these kinds of stereotypes, and views of the ageing body may be changing (Woodward, 1988),[1] the power of traditional stereotypes of old age remains firmly grounded in negative perceptions of the body. Thus, as Kitching, Low and Evers critically point out, an old person may be described by nursing staff solely in terms of a diagnosis such as 'dement' or 'depressive', as if this were the most critical aspect of their personhood (1990: 9).

Once again, a parallel can be drawn with the experiences of some disabled people who find themselves dependent upon the care of others. Whilst there are some indications that the image of disabled people in the media is changing, many depictions remain within the tradition of marginalization through 'monster and criminal characterizations' (Shakespeare's Richard III, the Hunchback of Notre Dame, the Phantom of the Opera, Doctor Strangelove and Captain Hook), or individualization through 'dramas of adjustment' which stress the 'emotional choices, courage and character of the individual' (Longmore, 1985: 33; see also Morris, 1991). For those who become their subjects the effect may be devastating:

> On leaving hospital and finding the mantle of 'disabled' placed firmly upon my unwilling shoulders I entered a world which was alien, absurd and ultimately defeating. My weak grasp on my identity was no match for the massed forces of society who firmly believed themselves to be 'normal' and myself just as firmly as 'abnormal'. I found myself inhabiting a stereotype. I became my illness, I was of interest only because of it. (Campling, 1981: 48)

Outward appearances of personhood

From these examples it is already becoming clear that perceptions of the body play an important ideological role in the allocation of category-specific social identities and that the process of transformation effected by metaphors of childhood is based upon both a highly selective reading of the body and a particular understanding of dependency. To develop our explanation of why the child's

body in particular should provide so apt a metaphor for the dependent body, and why this process of metaphoric transformation is
both powerful and destructive, we can begin by situating our
arguments in terms of some more generalized perceptions of the
body in Western cultures.

Featherstone (1982) writes that the body has taken on great
social significance in late capitalist society, and that this has
involved a process of bodily reassessment: 'within consumer
culture, the inner and outer body became conjoined: the prime
purpose of the maintenance of the inner body becomes the
enhancement of the appearance of the outer body' (1982: 18). For
Featherstone, this shift in emphasis has had particular social consequences: 'with appearance being taken as a reflex of the self the
penalties of bodily neglect are a lowering of one's acceptability as
a person' (1982: 26). Those whose bodies do not visually conform
to current ideals may therefore find their social status correspond-
ingly reduced. Statistical information from the various 'body'
industries reveals the primacy of the body's surface in the allocation of identity: in 1986, for example, British women spent £113.2
million on skin-care preparations, £143.6 million on fragrances and
£124.4 million on make-up (*Independent*, 22 October 1988).

Nevertheless, the ageing process or chronic illness all leave their
mark upon the physical body and in Western cultures, where
ageing is devalued rather than esteemed, its bodily manifestations
are, likewise, unwanted. Indeed, they may be deemed ugly and
unsightly. This may explain why, in the light of a contemporary
emphasis on the body's appearance, advertisers in Western cultures
rarely depict people in the 50-plus age group (Grant, 1991). This
is in marked contrast to the Chinese traditional veneration of old
age:

> In direct contradiction to the American custom advertisers in Hong
> Kong who wish to promote such luxury products as expensive brandy
> or watches often depict the birthday party of an elder as the appropriate
> occasion for such a gift. Ancient laws allocated special meat rations to
> those who had attained advanced ages. These allotments were similar to
> the status markers denoting the nobility. (Sankar, 1984: 271)

In the contemporary consumer cultures of many Western societies
there is, then, a 'self preservationist conception of the body',
expressed in trends towards health, fitness and beauty
(Featherstone, 1982: 18). This means that those whose bodies are
old, fat or disfigured are provided with little affirmation of the self
as desirable. Writing from the personal experience of becoming
disabled, Brooks comments that 'the continuing struggle to remain
alive', which is daily played out through the experience and

appearance of the physical body, results in a 'tattered identity and dislocated sense of self' (1990: 96).

Affirmation that it is young bodies which are the most beautiful bodies abound in contemporary popular culture. Here we consider two contemporary advertisements. The first promotes a face cream as being able to 'help keep you looking young'. A naked woman clutches a young child, beside the warning 'Your skin is only ever four weeks old.'

> About once a month you get a new skin. Unbelievable but true. During this time, the top layer of your skin is shed to reveal a fresh new one. Unfortunately, however, it doesn't provide an antidote to wrinkles. The problems start as the years go by. When your skin was young, it could fend for itself. Keeping in moisture to protect it against all manner of evils. The weather, central heating, to name but a few. With age, the skin's inner layer loses its elasticity. It's no longer as efficient at retaining this crucial moisture. If you're not careful, this is when lines start to creep up on you. Now, don't despair there is something you can do . . . (Ponds Moisturiser advertisement, *Good Housekeeping*, August 1990)

Physical ageing is here described in entirely negative terms: wrinkles need an antidote, lines creep up; the body is under attack from 'all manner of evils'. Old skin needs protection and care. The textual imagery of the advertisement cleverly combines and confuses the vulnerability of infancy with that of the ageing body. The image of the child enfolded in its mother's arms affirms the reader's pre-existing belief in the infant's need for maternal protection, a form of care which will ensure its eventual maturation into a beautiful, sexual adolescent. As a result, the proposed care of the 'ageing' woman's skin, being intertwined, through the image, with the maternal care of the child, is naturalized and legitimated. An elision is created between the controllable, transitory vulnerability of the child and the ultimately uncontrollable decay of the woman's good looks.

A second advert for shampoo and conditioner similarly warns against the ageing process: 'conditioning formula actually reduces the breaking and thinning of hair that naturally occurs with age. It enriches the hair to bring back body and shine. So it will look and feel more alive' (Empathy advertisement, *Family Circle*, 1988).

In both these adverts, it is the achieved rather than ascribed qualities of dominant adulthood in late capitalist Western society which are highlighted. Having overcome the social and physical limitations of dependent childhood, the adult is portrayed as threatened with the subsequent loss of dominant status and power through the predations of the ageing process. As noted earlier, '[hegemony] . . . is not universal and given to the continuing rule of a particular class. It has to be won, reproduced, sustained' (Hall et al., 1976, quoted in Hebdige, 1979).

From the 1960s onwards the West has seen a growth in access to products orientated towards an attractive appearance, now no longer the exclusive province of members of wealthy social classes but more readily available in off-the-peg chain store purchases. As a result there has been a stigmatizing of unshapely, wrinkled appearance – whether in terms of the body itself or its outer clothing. This process – a familiar aspect of women's experience as Sontag (1978) notes – has gradually been expanded in the reconstruction of men's bodies. Men from their late teens onwards are increasingly aware of the role of a fit, well-groomed body in bolstering the adult individual's social power and status. Although spending less than women on their bodies, British men spent around £42.4 million on toiletries in 1986, registering a 15 per cent increase on hair preparations between 1982–6, and a 65.8 per cent increase on deodorants and anti-perspirants (*Independent*, 22 October 1988).

In late capitalist societies the clothed body is another important way in which personhood is marked out, and again children, elderly and disabled people may find their status prescribed by attitudes towards the suitability of particular types of clothes. Children's clothes have moved away from the pastel, 'baby'-blue for boys, pink for girls and white for newborn babies, characteristic of the immediate post-war years, towards more vibrant primary colours. That adult leisure clothing now mimics these, registers the youthful appeal of children's bodies in averting the onset of ageing (see Chapter 2). But extension of this kind, or colour of clothing, into old age is seen as somehow amusing or eccentric. Jenny Joseph's poem of defiant old age encapsulates this. She uses many images of clothes to suggest how an elderly person might break away from social convention in old age. 'I shall wear purple with a red hat which doesn't go and doesn't suit me', she writes, 'and summer gloves and satin sandals', 'slippers in the rain and terrible shirts'.[2] Outside the poem, despite some change, there remains a prosaic uniformity of colour – browns and beiges, darker colours – manifested in the fawn mack and zip-up jacket frequently worn by old men and the cream or pastel coloured clothing of older women. The phrase 'mutton dressed up as lamb', draws on the imagery of the natural world to denigrate those women who resist a strongly gendered requirement that they should dress according to their age.

For elderly people within institutional settings the ways in which clothes are often allocated reinforces their marginality as Ford makes clear in her critique of such regimes. Arguing that 'among the most basic of requirements for most people is the right to be able to dress according to their own taste and to wear their own clothes', Ford shows how the very fabric of many institutions infringes this entitlement:

> The storage aspect of individualized clothing is, in many ways, the key factor on which the whole exercise depends. Without adequate storage facilities, access is in the control of other people. Security is a rather hit and miss affair, choice is reduced because the availability of items cannot be fully appreciated and privacy is reduced as items of personal clothing kept in communal storage areas tend to resemble a . . . jumble sale. (1991: 16)

Defining bodies

The links between the body and concepts of personhood, which we are beginning to draw out, have been underlined by Turner in his insistence that social analysis should take account of the 'corporality of human life' (1984). Such an approach requires recognition of the body on two levels: first, an acknowledgement that people have bodies which change and become subject to the effects of accident, disease and time passing, and secondly, that the body itself is 'also an effect of cultural historical activity, a site for the construction of meanings' (1984: 49). In this section we ask what meanings are attached to 'the child's' body in Western cultures and how it is that the child's body has come to provide the metaphoric grounding through which other people's bodies may be known?

To answer these questions we argue that children within Western cultures are defined primarily by their bodies. This is not a retreat into crude socio-biology. Indeed it is deeply opposed to any such idea through the suggestion that the predominant Western conceptualization of 'the child's' *physical* body sustains and is itself partly defined by the *social* institution of childhood. In Chapter 2 it was noted that childhood is contemporarily represented in the life course as a time of innocence, a perception which derived from particular past socio-economic changes. This conception of the special nature of 'childhood', moreover, was both reflected in and refracted through particular perceptions of the child as vulnerable, sexually innocent and dependent in body and mind (see Ennew, 1986). Contemporarily, then, it is in terms of this mutually informing and sustaining mode of thought that a perceived lack of responsibility and autonomy denies the child an effective personhood, according to Western individualist concepts of the person. Those therefore who, through physical dependency or mental impairment, are said to have child-like bodies may be similarly threatened with a loss of personhood and an accompanying social, economic and political dependency. Herein lies the grounding of the destructive reshaping of personhood which practices such as infantilization promote.

It is not immediately apparent just how the child's physical body came to play so important a role in defining the social institution of 'childhood'. However, the historical development of the idea of childhood provides some clues. As noted, from the medieval period onwards, there was the growing recognition of childhood as a distinct period of the life course within Western cultures. This led to the gradual marginalization of children from mainstream social life into specific child-centred institutions and activities, a change which both reflected and reinforced a conceptual shift in thinking about children. First, as we have seen, this was predicated upon a view of the child's nature as being essentially different from that of an adult's. For example, the Puritan emphasis on Original Sin urged a necessary control and training of the child's body to promote its innocence, which the Romantic backlash translated into the desire to protect and nurture. This shift in perception was part of what Foucault (1977) describes as the growing discipline of the body through surveillance. In this way the social institution of childhood came to throw its mantle around children's conceptually frail and vulnerable bodies, and created distinctions between the kinds of things which adults could do and those seen as peculiar to children.

We shall take but one of many historical examples to illustrate the manifestation of these ideas in practice. During the early nineteenth century, the smallness of children's bodies enabled the offspring of the poor to gain employment as chimney sweeps or as workers in the cotton mills and mines (Thompson, 1968). In a similar way the size of children's bodies is exploited in other cultures as young children tie the knots of oriental carpets or roll cigarettes with their small and nimble fingers (see Fyfe, 1989). Significantly, it was a growing sensibility about those same small and vulnerable bodies which later motivated a rallying cry for the removal of children from the sphere of wage work altogether. Whilst this call was, in effect, one for a more generalized humanitarian reform of working conditions, it found its symbolic focus and force in the body of the child (Thompson, 1968).

By the late nineteenth and twentieth centuries concepts of 'childhood' were becoming more rigidly tied into ideas about the child's body through the new theories and accounts of child development (Hendrick, 1990). Freud and Piaget, for example, both demonstrated that children's mind were in essence 'different'. These theories were largely predicated upon the physical body, upon the child's physical weakness and dependency and, despite or indeed because of Freud, upon its constructed sexual innocence. In this way depictions of 'the child' as 'embodied childhood' became increasingly commonplace and provided further reinforcement for discriminatory social attitudes and practices towards children (Bradley, 1986). As Armstrong (1983) describes, in the new medical gaze of the early twentieth century, children's bodies were used literally to classify 'types' of children:

> Nervous children, delicate children, neuropathic children, maladjusted children, difficult children, oversensitive children and unstable children were all essentially inventions of a new way of seeing childhood. (1983: 15)

The process continues to unfold. In the 1990s, 'the abused child' and 'the hyperactive child' can be added to the list. In this way, individual children can acquire a kind of personhood – that is, they can acquire a socially significant identity – but only through the pathologizing of their bodies.

Armstrong notes that such classificatory practices construed the child as only 'precariously normal', necessitating 'constant vigilance' by adults of the child's body (1983: 27). Although he suggests that in the post-war period this paved the way for a change in attitude which located deviance as external – in society – rather than internal – in the child's body – surveillance is, we suggest, still practised by adult carers.

For example, although emphasizing diversity in biological development, child welfare professionals at the same time see the Western child's progress from infancy to maturity as marked out in fixed stages of bodily achievement and control, ticked off on growth and development charts. The new mother must watch anxiously for the physical signs which are the prerequisites for learning more social skills: sucking, rolling over, sitting up, crawling, chewing, hand to eye coordination, walking, talking, running, jumping, bowel and bladder control, hopping, climbing, skipping. Each stage reached and gladly encouraged represents movement along the path to being grown up; failure to reach a stage at an appropriate moment is closely monitored, supervised and kept under surveillance by health visitors, doctors and therapists. In Booth's study, for example, the mothers' accounts of their babies' mental handicap were offered in terms of observation of the body:

> The bulk of clues which first prompted the parents' concern about their child referred to aspects of their child's physical condition or

appearance – 'It was the smallness of his head that bothered me'; to the rate of physical or social development – 'He was a bit backward in coming forward'; or to the prominence of certain behavioural quirks and mannerisms – 'His reactions were slow. He didn't ever seem to smile on cue.' (1978: 209)

As Wright (1987) points out, this construction of 'normality' through emphasis upon the health and development of the child's body both reflected and justified nineteenth century social interventionist practices and state control through gradually defining infant care as a largely medical problem.

Through these examples, then, it is possible to see how the child's body gradually became a primary ideological marker of the child's social status. This not only relates to the pathologies Armstrong (1983) identifies, but also to the stages of physical and psychological development in 'normal' bodies. Differences in children's bodies are seen as direct and intrinsic functions of their different ages which, as we shall see later, creates the 'problems' of both precocity and backwardness. It is the constantly changing and rapidly maturing nature of children's bodies which generates new definitions of the child as it moves towards full personhood. The phrase, 's/he's quite a little person', or 's/he's a person in her/his own right', used of an unusually sentient and independent two- or three-year-old child, reveals that children, in the Western context, are not normally deemed capable of being 'persons' in the ways that adults are.

The increasing proliferation of terms for distinguishing different types of child reveals the importance of the body in the process of acquiring personhood, registering the cultural value attached to the upward and onward movement towards adulthood. Contemporarily, childhood may be seen as beginning before birth, as testified in arguments about abortion, a debate which recent developments in the care of premature babies have further complicated. Now that the survival of infants born at 26 weeks is becoming a possibility, it is argued that this forms the first category of 'child'. Low infant mortality rates, combined with the increased attention to and knowledge of the physical and mental development of the child, have made the categories 'newborn', 'toddler' and 'pre-school' clear stages in childhood. However, these categories are increasingly subject to further fragmentation. Penelope Leach, the author of a child-care manual (1977), identifies seven stages of childhood under the age of five years old: 'the premature baby' (36 weeks); the birth (40 weeks); the newborn and unsettled baby (0–2 weeks); the settled baby (1–6 months); the older baby (6 months to 1 year); the toddler (1–2½ years); the pre-school child (2½–5 years). Each stage is predicated upon changes in the child's physical ability and development of its mind. Thus being able to grasp toys signifies the settled baby, whilst crawling is a sign of being an older baby. The stage of childhood, from five to 12 years old, is that of the 'school child'.

At the other end of the spectrum, where a proliferation of bodily changes constitutes a slow and insidious decline towards death, there has been little proliferation of linguistic categories. Thus the social category 'the elderly' or 'old age pensioners', encompasses a huge age range, from 60 to 100+. Spanning 40 years, 'old age' represents more than double the time span allotted to 'childhood' and 'adolescence' combined. This suggests that whilst the movement towards personhood by the child is celebrated and anticipated, ageing is seen as an unwelcome movement out of personhood, as something to be hidden or disguised. It suggests that changes in the aged body are best not remarked upon. MacDonald and Rich make this point in discussing their own experiences of ageing:

> the fact is we spend our lives conveying to others how we feel in our bodies . . . suddenly in my sixties, when my body was doing all kinds of things, sending me all kinds of messages, I am not supposed to talk about it. (1984: 109)

In the light of increasing numbers of fit elderly people and perhaps in response to the preservation of their bodies, there has been a call for a distinction to be made between 'types' of elderly people and in these the primacy of the body for definitions of personhood is emphasized. This contrasts with the moral distinctions made in previous generations between the deserving and undeserving elderly. Thus, new corporal categories – the 'young old' and the 'old old' – are contemporarily used to distinguish between those who are over and under 75; to make distinctions and create a controlling distance between those who are hale and hearty and those who are sick and decrepit.

The body is therefore an important vehicle through which personhood is constituted and, for children, it is the immaturity of their bodies – perceived in terms of particular physical needs – which both legitimates their dependency and sanctions their social vulnerability (Woodhead, 1990). The physical immaturity of their bodies denies children their social status as persons so that only through the maturing of that same body will dependency be relinquished and personhood, as an adult in society, be acquired. Western childhood is thus largely 'anticipatory' and 'transitional', a body becoming more than being (James and Prout, 1990a;

Qvortrup, 1990). Among children, adults are referred to as the 'grown ups', those whose social status emanates from a prolonged period of bodily growth in a positively perceived upwards direction. The question asked of children by adults, 'What do you want to be when you are grown up?', fosters the perception that as children their social status is marginal, and that their personhood is not yet confirmed.

A childish body

Contemporarily, the symbolic marking out of an ideology of childhood through the medium of the physical body occurs in two ways. The first stresses, through contrast with the mature version it will become, the child's body as deficient, as lacking skills and abilities, whilst the second, sentimentalizes the specific abilities and qualities which the child is seen to possess. In this section we examine the first of these, through an appraisal of some definitions of the child.

Tucker's book *What is a Child?* (1977) provides a useful starting place. Whilst acknowledging cultural variability in concepts of childhood, he none the less argues for a universal definition of 'the child', one which emphasizes the primacy of the physical body. However, the physical body in his account is largely to be conceived in terms of the *absence* of adult skills. Variously the child's body is described as follows: a child has 'intermittent concentration and intellectual limitations' (p. 28); a child is 'prone to misconceptions' (p. 29); 'innate fear and credulity' (p. 29); a child has an 'immature physique' (p. 42); it is characterized by 'nonfertility' (p. 45); a child is 'small in a world where those in authority over him will be tall' (p. 46); children show a 'lack of differentiation between the self and the outside world' (p. 77).

Although we in no way wish to deny the biological base of childhood, what is significant, at the *ideological* level, is that such accounts of the child carry exclusively negative connotations. They *cannot* be written positively. They stress the child's disabilities, rather than its different abilities. This suggests that in Western societies it is the adult body and intellect which provide the dominant yardstick by which other bodies and minds are to be judged or to which children should aspire. James's (1993) work, for example, shows how children regard upward growth of the body as an important marker of their social status and that those children who are smaller than their peers risk having their identities called into question (Ablon, 1990). Looked at from children's perspectives, it would be possible to argue that 'growing up', in fact, involves the *loss* of certain abilities – running, jumping, falling, whirling and squeezing into small and secret spaces. However, the ideological power which the concept of upward growth holds precludes this possibility. Thus it is that whilst adults remain physically capable of some, if not all, of these activities, they have access to them only when formalized as sports, and confined to the times and spaces reserved for adult leisure: race tracks, long jump pitches, sky diving and potholing. Adults who indulge in such activities outside these specified contexts may be condemned as acting 'childishly' or, even, as irrationally. As the radical writer Holt observed:

> we tend to think that children are most cute when they are openly displaying their ignorance and incompetence. We value their dependency and helplessness. They are help objects as well as love objects. Children acting really competently and intelligently do not usually strike us as cute. They are as likely to puzzle and threaten us. (Holt, 1975: 91)

Contemporary attitudes towards 'gifted' children illustrate this point (Freeman, 1979). Careful account and indeed explanation of their talents must be provided, for through their exceptional abilities, they are seen as having overreached their status as children. They are 'out of time' with the pace of a child's 'normal' development through childhood (see James and Prout, 1990a). Under the headline, 'Boy cleverest since Middle Ages', the following account appeared:

> A boy of 11 studying for a mathematics degree at Surrey University is believed to be the youngest undergraduate to take a place on a degree course since the Middle Ages. (*Guardian*, 19 November 1990)

A key concern for his father was the maintenance of a normal childhood for his son. Is it for this reason, then, that the boy is described in the newspaper report as attending 'tutorials wearing a Dennis the Menace T-shirt'? Did this somehow safeguard his childishness and signify that, despite his considerable academic achievements, he remained a child? A parallel example to the 'gifted child' is the 'whizz kid' of the adult world. Out of step with his or her contemporaries, the 'whizz kid' literally outpaces them on the route to success in the workplace. But, both the whizz kid's success (competence), and any subsequent failure (incompetence), is accounted for through this very disjunction in time. The anomaly of his or her position is rendered safe and less threatening through analogy with childhood.

In other cultures exceptional talent proves less problematic. Strong links are not sought between biological childhood (physical immaturity) and a child's ability. As Richards and Light (1986) point out, the idea that 'social context is, at a variety of levels, intrinsic to the development process itself' is a perspective still not widely embraced within Western developmental psychology (1986: 1). Much work within traditional academic discourse continues to portray 'social arrangements as if they were fixed laws of nature' (1986: 3). And yet early anthropological studies had already called into question a strict biological determinism. Benedict described, for example, how the Cheyenne trained their children in adult practices such as hunting from an early age: 'the gravity of a Cheyenne Indian family ceremoniously making a feast out of the little boy's first snowbird is at the furthest remove from our behaviour' (1955: 24). The latter she describes as follows: 'the child is praised because the parents feel well disposed regardless of whether the task is well done by adult standards, and the child acquires no sensible standard by which to measure its achievement' (1955: 24). Western socialization practices, such as those of the United States and Britain, reflect the separateness of the social categories 'child' and 'adult', emphasizing discontinuity rather than continuity between them. This is expressed in the view that the child has the potential to acquire and develop lacking *future* skills, rather than as having a particular level of *present* skill (see James and Prout, 1990a), a subtle but ideologically powerful difference. Observations from an East African village are revealing:

> A child of three to four years of age is helping his mother to sort out the dry from the wet coffee beans which have been laid out in the sun. In carrying out this task he is demonstrating and perfecting those skills of visual discrimination, concept formation and fine manual control which his western counterparts acquire through play with picture dominoes, manipulative toys and the like. His work is not a reflection of the patronizing 'let the kid have a go' attitude of the 'good' white middle class parent. He is, within the limits of his developmental capacity, making a genuine contribution to the economy of his family in the context of a society which expects and respects this. (Farrant, 1979: 127)

The special categories of equipment – 'toys' – provided by Western parents for their children – construction toys for the nascent engineer and fashion dolls for the woman-to-be – are the child's exclusive property. They mark out their separateness as a social category, and are the literal representations of the roles available for them to play in the future.

In Western cultures, then, an emphasis upon inability and incompetency underscores children's historically constituted dependency and 'need' for protection (Hendrick, 1990). Other cultural models of the child's body are, by contrast, more positive in their appreciation of the *different* abilities which children have. For example, in her description of child-rearing among the Papagoin of Arizona, Benedict observed that no adult rushed to help a three-year-old girl to shut a heavy door: 'it was assumed that the task would not be asked of her unless she could perform it, and having been asked, the responsibility was hers alone just as if she were a grown woman' (1955: 23).

Similarly, recalling childhood in Bali in the 1930s, Mead suggested that 'there is little acceptance of any task as being difficult or inappropriate for a child' (Mead, 1955: 40). More recently Schildkrout (1978) has shown how in urban Kano children of seven or eight are expected to look after younger children and perform many other tasks in Hausa society. Indeed, the institution of purdah means that adult women, in particular, are dependent upon their children's work:

> Were this not the case, women, except in wealthier families, where paid labour can replace the services of children, could not remain in purdah and carry out their domestic responsibilities, not to mention their economic activities. (1978: 126)

A Western appraisal of children's physical competence as being a deviation from adult 'norms' is mirrored in the ideological framing of their emotional and intellectual development. Childhood is prized as a necessary period of cocooning and enveloping, with happiness being its key (Ennew, 1986: 18). This blissful state is understood to be best achieved through 'ignorance', rather than knowledge, a perception of children's 'needs' again thrown into relief through cross-cultural comparison. Hendry's account (1986) of Japanese child-rearing highlights a subtle difference in attitude underlying Western and Japanese practices. British and American children have their fears calmed by parents' reassurance that dangers do not exist; for Japanese children, on the other hand, dangers are acknowledged but security provided through reassurance of parental protection:

> In general, the encouragement of fear, and eventually courage, seems to be quite an important part of child training. The word for 'danger' (*abunai*) is used a great deal by adults with small children, as I learned first of all by having to translate it endlessly before my own children could understand any Japanese. I noticed then that in English we would be much more likely to use the positive phrase 'be careful' than the negative one 'that's dangerous'. In the country, some old people went further, especially at night, and pointed down dark alleyways suggesting that there might be a ghost or a big dog lurking there, so that the child should remain close to the safety of the adult's side. (1986: 113)

These warnings to the child are given as advice for the child to follow and learn. They present a radical contrast to an image commonly used in English in recent times to intimidate or punish children – 'the bogeyman will get you'.

These alternative models of child-rearing reveal that an insistence on the primacy of children's physical inabilities and emotional immaturity is particular to a Western construction of the biological differences between older and younger bodies. They are not, however, constitutive of that difference for, in contemporary Britain, there are many children who, in their everyday experiences, contradict the dominant model of incompetence and vulnerability. Children who run households, care for disabled parents, engage in prostitution, contribute to family income and take charge of younger siblings reveal the extent to which these images of dependency are ideological rather than actual.

A recent report estimates that there may be as many as 10,000 young carers below the age of 16 but, as no one of this age can claim an invalid care allowance, exact figures are unknown (Fallon, 1990):

> One case concerned an 11-year-old who won the Most Caring Child in Britain award for taking care of her disabled mother. It seemed incongruous that a child with such responsibilities should be presented with a huge Care-Bear. Her concern was to get back home as soon as possible to look after her mother. . . . For a young carer it is not uncommon for the day to start at 5.30 am with preparation of breakfast and attendance to the personal needs of the parent. The child may call home at midday to toilet the parent and prepare lunch. In the evening shopping, cooking and cleaning may take priority over homework. Often a child puts the parent to bed and sleeps in the same room in order to turn him or her during the night. The involvement in personal care such as changing of sanitary towels and catheter management has also been reported. (Fallon, 1990)

According to Fallon, young people found one of the more frustrating aspects of caring to be professionals' belief that they were too young to be involved in negotiations and decision-making.

The body and the person: the accomplishment of metaphor

The perception of the child as an incomplete adult, incompetent and immature, is based therefore upon a particular reading of children's bodies and minds which both justifies and initiates their protection and exclusion. It is a highly selective reading which, through denying them competences also denies them personhood. Children's different qualities – such as being 'healthy, vital, vivacious, enthusiastic, resourceful, intelligent, intense, passionate, hopeful, trustful and forgiving' – that is, children's most positive and autonomous qualities, are interpreted as but a sign of their immaturity (Holt, 1975: 85). Holt argues that these 'childish' or 'naive' qualities are expected to be eroded through the passage of time. Retained into adult life, such abilities may lead to vulnerability and be interpreted as signs of immaturity and weakness. In old age, they become signs of senility:

> It is with affection and nostalgia that adults regard the innate creativity of unsocialized children. But usually they are blind to the creativity of desocialized elders at the other end of the life cycle, people whose reemerging originality – stemming from social detachment, long experience, the urgency of a foreshortened future – may be as delightful, surprising, and fruitful as anything to be found among the very young. . . . Intolerance for 'bad behaviour' among the elderly is part of our blindness to their gifts. (Myerhoff, 1984: 311)

This difference in expectations between children's and adults' bodily behaviour had already found eloquent expression in the late nineteenth century through Lewis Carroll's famous depiction of the relationship between youth and old age. 'You are old Father William, the young man said' and then went on to list the old man's eccentric behaviours, eccentric, that is, because of Father William's age. Father William reveals competencies which old people should not have. His robust appetite for food – goose, bones, beak and all – and his gymnastic skills – back-somersaults, head stands and balancing eels on his nose – are called into question by his son who asks: 'Do you think at your age it is right?' Drawing attention to the old man's age, loss of hair colour, his uncommon fatness, weak jaws, unsteady eyes, it is the physical body which provides the son with the source of Father William's social identity. It legitimates his request that Father William act in an age-appropriate manner. Father William, however, is effectively resisting re-classification as a member of the social category 'old' through choosing to act 'childishly'. He strategically reinterprets the young man's 'adult' authority as 'giving himself airs' and then threatens him more directly: 'Be off, or I'll kick you down stairs' (Carroll, 1960: 70 [1865]).

These illustrations show, then, how a selective and culturally specific reading of the body and mind of the child forms both the basis for the Western conception of childhood as a period of social dependency and provides the grounding for the parallels perceived between their bodies and those of very elderly or disabled people.

It also, therefore, forms the basis for the denial of their personhoods.

In British culture, the complexity of this interplay between the literally and figuratively old and young finds widespread and general expression in everyday language. For example, the adjective 'wrinkly' is often used as if it were a noun to refer to elderly people, as in the following headline to a newspaper story about a bank-raider in his late sixties: 'Wrinkly in an old-up' (*Sun*, 4 July 1990). Here a metonymical (part-to-whole) relationship is established between the old surface of the body and the social identity of the person: through a highly selective reading of the body – its wrinkled skin – a single part of the person is substituted for the whole. But this relationship is neither fixed nor consistent, for elsewhere wrinkled skin may not be understood to denote old age. Babies' skin, for example, is also wrinkled but, in this instance, we choose to focus on its smoothness, rather than its rippled texture; in this way babies' skin is positioned as pleasurable, admirable and desirable. 'As smooth as a baby's bottom' we say in admiration, forgetting what, in everyday life, the smooth-skinned baby's bottom is often covered in.

As earlier examples revealed, at the level of social practice a similar creative metonymic relationship is established through the process of infantilization. It would seem that one or two physical features – such as incontinence, lack of rational speech, or faltering step – are taken as defining criteria for the whole body. Thus, for example, the elderly person who has poor bladder control becomes seen as incontinent, just as the elderly person with Alzheimer's disease is referred to as 'dementing'. One aspect of their body's behaviour is used to refer to the whole person. In turn, this metonymic relationship is used both to justify, and is itself justified by, the metaphorical assertions of their child-like qualities made explicit through infantilizing practices. Thus, in Hazan's study (1980), elderly people applying to an old people's home are assessed as suitable in terms of the capabilities of their physical bodies, rather than their personal qualities or social needs:

> The factors considered relevant are: Physical: mobility, dressing, feeding, continence, sleep; Mental: orientation, communication, co-operation, restlessness and mood. (1980: 31)

The whole person becomes known through the functioning and competences of the body's parts. This denies elderly people their personhood through effectively 'obliterating their life history and social identity, and reducing them to their physical and mental disabilities' (1980: 30).

Fieldwork within Highfield House, a residential home for elderly people (Hockey, 1990), shows that, once admitted, the bodily 'inabilities' of elderly people increasingly come to provide the primary focus of the regime of care provided. Through a bodily based social construction elderly people are made, as children are, to conform to rigid bodily routines: sleeping, washing and eating are all timetabled, snacking, staying up late, or prolonged lie-ins are all inadmissible. Distinctions are made between 'fit' and 'frail' residents:

> One by one, failing residents are moved downstairs to bedrooms on the 'frail' corridor, within a few yards of the two sick bays where dying people are cared for. . . . Such residents find their armchair in one of the lounges supplanted by a seat in the open alcove at the beginning of the 'frail' corridor. Increasing immobility and the need for regular 'toileting' rapidly curtails their movement outside those areas of the home associated with illness and death. It is in this way that care staff are able to create a somewhat precarious distance or spatial boundary between 'fit' and 'frail' residents. (1990: 117)

Indeed, it is through reference to residents' bodily condition – 'frail' – that the social space within which they age – the frail corridor – comes to be identified.

In a parallel example, Thomas argues that often 'among the most potent sources of social identity given to a disabled person is his or her impairment' (1982: 174). People with disabilities may find their social identities continually reflected in their physical bodies. Through such attitudes 'social oppression . . . is rationalized by appeals to biology' (1982: 179). Jones's work provides an example: 'the severely subnormal were often called "the babies"; the "boy's ward" might contain 50-year-old patients; a ward for women patients would be divided into "big girls" and "little girls"' (1975: 33). The justification for such attitudes was phrased in terms of physical needs and dependency: a nurse is quoted as saying, 'we have to do everything for them – feed them, dress them, take them to the toilet .. but more than that, we have to think for them' (1975: 106). The patients' different abilities were not used as classificatory criteria.

The metaphoric and metonymic power of language by which conceptual links between physical dependency, bodily inability and social status are established in Western cultures is illustrated by Kate Cooney. In a newspaper article, significantly entitled 'The *girl* can't help it' [our emphasis], Cooney evocatively recounts her experience of having had rheumatoid arthritis since the age of 18. Now, at 31, it is the lack of autonomy which she sees as crucial to the eroding of her identity as an independent adult woman:

It's not easy being 'cared for'. It's not just the messy bits. It's no longer being able to nick a chocolate biscuit out of the fridge, or experiment with make-up, or grab just the right scarf to set off your jumper as you rush out the door. Always, always, you have to ask. These things may seem insignificant nit-pickings compared with the more obviously dramatic changes wrought by disability, but taken together they are as momentous as the arrival of the wheelchair or the loss of your job. As they are given up, a little bit of what outwardly makes you an individual is eroded. (*Guardian*, 2 January 1991)

Barnes's account of accompanying some young adults with physical handicaps on a shopping trip similarly reveals how, in everyday encounters, through selective assessment of the physical body, qualitative judgements about identity come to be made. This may mean disabled people being given the status of metaphoric children:

> At the shopping mall the lift operator commented to me on the lack of facilities at the precinct, and almost as an afterthought asked my wheelchair-bound companions, Bruce and James, in a maternalistic tone, which I considered would be inappropriate for an eight-year-old, if they were having a 'nice time'. When he had moved away I asked them both if such situations bothered them. Bruce shrugged his shoulders and said nothing, James replied, 'it doesn't bother me, you get used to it' and Bruce agreed. (1990: 165)

Whilst acknowledging that such perceptions may call forth 'the kind of tenderness and protectiveness usually reserved for children', it is none the less humiliating for adults to be classed as children (Jones, 1975: 23).

Perceptions of physical dependency or loss of competency as 'childish', whether in old age or through disease or illness, are however culturally specific. They represent a particularized reading of how the body should be and should perform, and, as Oliver has argued with respect to disability, 'the kind of society that one lives in will have a crucial effect on the way the experience of disability is structured' (1990: 11). The same can be said of ageing.

MacCormack (1985), for example, offers an alternative conception of the ageing process from among the Sherbro people of Sierra Leone. If the speech of elderly people becomes incoherent or incomprehensible, this is perceived as a positive sign that the old person is in close communication with the ancestors, with the ultimate source of social blessings and misfortune. Within this context old people are cared for reverently as they grow into sacredness. While a daughter may have to give the kind of physical care to her helpless mother which she as a helpless infant received, that care *endorses*, rather than diminishes, the status of the elderly woman. Similarly, amongst the Venda-speaking people of southern Africa 'old age' is a pleasure and its first hints – the birth of a grandchild or greying hair – are welcomed as signs of a person's approaching contact with the 'real' world of the spirits (Blacking, 1990). Even in cultures where old age is seen to be akin to childhood, this does not necessarily entail a reduction of social status:

> Within the Chinese medical system old age is thought to create a special susceptibility to disease. In this respect it is structurally similar to infancy and childhood. Both phases of the life cycle are characterized by having insufficient yang and by a soul that is not firmly attached to the body. (Sankar, 1984: 250)

However, as Sankar goes on to say, this is not thought of as belittling, for the system of gerontocracy which was established under Confucian tradition remains as a conceptual frame:

> The affection and respect accorded the elderly still remain, especially in rural areas. There the parents still maintain considerable control over the social and economic lives of their adult children. With social space allotted to them, the importance of the sick role to legitimize dependence is in effect negligible for the elderly. In fact, the opposite attitude very much obtains. Elderly people whose children are successful enough to care for them take great pride in the fact that they are able to rely on their children. (1984: 273)

In relation to disability, a contributor to the volume edited by Campling (1981) describes her experience of moving between cultures:

> During a trip to Kenya I was pleasantly surprised and relieved by the black Kenyan's attitudes. . . . They looked upon my disability realistically, no psychological hang-ups. This seems part of a fatalistic philosophy absent in the West, plus a natural acceptance of daily hardships. 'Okay, so you wear baby-type knickers but everyone has their problems', said a black male friend, who found me mentally and physically attractive. (1981: 18)

Such attitudes were, in her experience, rarely to be found within Western societies.

These feelings of humiliation and degradation which infantilizing practices of any kind may engender in elderly people and in others who are dependent in Western cultures deepen and intensify in encounters involving bodily intimacy. Indeed, it is here that the most explicit parallels may be drawn with children. Like that of children, the sexuality of elderly people is commonly deemed inadmissible and, in this denial, their status as adult people is reduced. Might it be that the centrality of sexual relationships to concepts and definitions of independent adulthood is threatened by its association with those people who are dependent?

Newspaper reports bear adequate testimony to these perceptions, as headline captions seek to distance and neutralize the idea of sexually active elderly people:

> Able Mabel, 84, elopes to wed. (*Sun*, 12 July 1990)

> A cartoon in the *Daily Mirror* (20 July 1990) depicts an old couple at Sunset Old Folks' Home. The man, sporting a buttonhole and carrying a wine glass, is being berated by a woman: 'Go away! It's unlucky to see the bride without her teeth in.'

Through captions and cartoons such as these, we are introduced to the comedy of marriage during toothless old age. The images invite us to laugh, not at the people concerned, but at the very idea that sexuality and age could go together. And through our laughter the danger is averted.

A second way of culturally distancing the sexuality of elderly people, if not by laughter, is through its representation within the discourse of romantic love, for although elderly people are not expected to have intimate sexual relations, they are, as children are, required to show loving kindness and affection. Described as a controversial campaign, a 1991 advertisement for Fuji film broke new ground through its depiction of 'geriatric eroticism':

> A man and a woman in a launderette, kissing passionately. He is in his 70s, she is in her 80s. They aren't even married to one another. (Grant, 1991)

The campaign was developed in response to research which showed that the 50-plus age group were rarely represented in advertising. One of the designers, however, refutes the charge of breaking the 'final taboo' – that older people have sex – by describing it instead as a picture 'that is about love'. Similarly, through populist images we are encouraged to admire the enduring love and romance of long-lived couples: the remarkable marriage of Harry and Sarah is detailed under the headline 'True love. Married for 80 years they are still sweethearts' (*Bella*, 11 November 1989). Under the caption 'Will you still love me tomorrow?' and alongside a photograph of a man, aged 84, presenting a woman, aged 102, with a bunch of flowers, Garvey describes the couple's relationship as one of sexual fulfilment. This, as she notes, is not unusual but what is significant is that the couple are 'exceptional in admitting to it' (*Guardian*, 5 June 1991). A consultant geriatrician is reported as saying that

> many old people feel that sex is something they should have grown out of; they feel guilty it's still going on and although they may have

physical problems such as lack of lubrication or arthritic limbs, many elderly people are reluctant to ask for help and advice for fear of ridicule or, worse, disgust. They don't want to be dubbed a Dirty Old Man or Not Quite a Lady. (Garvey, 1991)

For elderly people in residential homes their sexuality may be particularly problematic. There is often very little privacy and 'the ability to be a complete and sexual being is denied by the staff who label it as "dirty" or "not nice"' (Hutchings, 1988: 29). There may be no facilities for married couples, not even a double bed.

In the residential home studied by Hockey care staff scoffed at sexual desire in old age through the derisory remark: 'surely they've had enough by their age'. Male residents who had a reputation for making sexually explicit remarks or gestures towards female care staff were managed through metaphoric elaborations which reversed the direction of power. Hockey notes:

Albert, confused and unsteady on his feet was, when physically supported by female staff, wont to touch them in a sexual fashion. Whilst being dressed by them one day the following exchange took place which, through humour, distanced and controlled Albert's perceived disordered sexuality:
'Well, I never thought I'd come to this?'
'What, having two women dress you? Some people pay a lot of money for this sort of service you know.' (Hockey, unpublished data)

But outside institutional walls, life may be not much better: 'children can react with particular horror to the idea that their own parents are taking up with] someone else. Worse, if the parent is living with them, children' may have the power to enforce their prejudices' (Hutchings, 1988: 29). Dawson's study of clubs for elderly people in the North-East of England showed that many elderly people themselves viewed new pairings with seeming distaste. Couples who got married in old age were seen as misguided. However, this disapproval was not so much a comment on their sexuality but upon 'their futile denial of the inevitability of physical decline in old age' for 'marriage involves a series of commitments which may not be satisfactorily executed in old age' (Dawson, 1991: 2).

In Western cultures, the media can be seen as an important source of images of sexuality in old age. The notion that ageing and romance are at odds with one another makes certain pairings newsworthy, others amusing. For example, A.J.P. Taylor's love letters to his 'soulmate', Eva, written from his early fifties onwards are presented by the *Observer* newspaper (23 June 1991) under the headline 'Love in the Twilight', whilst a headline in the *Sun* (15 March 1990) reads 'My secret toyboy by Barbara Cartland, 88'.

BBC television's *Last of the Summer Wine* offers for amusement the examples of (1) a dishevelled old man who lusts after an elderly woman, presented as a 'battleaxe', who constantly rejects him and (2) an adulterous older couple, he a 'henpecked' husband, she dressed in the sexually alluring clothes of a teenager. Humour is found in the eagerness with which the two men and the second woman attempt to engage in sexual activity while constantly being foiled by rejection or discovery. The same theme of the humour of love during later life is echoed in another British comedy programme, *Open All Hours*, in which an old-fashioned shopkeeper lusts vainly but persistently after the robust figure of the district nurse.

Cross-cultural material reveals again the relativity of such cultural values and perceptions. Amongst the Vanatinai of Papua New Guinea, for example, elderly people are expected to be sexually active well into their old age (Lepowsky, 1985). Similarly, the Kaliai, also of Papua New Guinea, have no expectation that during old age women will end their sexual activity. Whilst social disapproval may greet indiscreet actions, no more scandal would be attached to it than amongst younger people. For the Kaliai, 'because there is no marked boundary between "elder" and "decrepit" person, the way in which a person is classified depends largely on the way he presents himself' (Counts and Counts, 1985: 141). Sexual activity is therefore encouraged for older people, as an effective way to maintain a sense of self and personhood. Those who become dependent solely because of their age are regarded intolerantly, for the majority of elderly people work hard to maintain and demonstrate their status as an active elder.

The distancing of elderly people's sexuality in Western cultures parallels the attitudes that shape perceptions of disabled people's sexuality: in that physical dependency denies them the status of fully independent adults, then an independent adult activity, such as sex, seems also to be withheld from them. Physically handicapped adults may find attitudes to their sexuality highly ambivalent. There is, for example, little information about sex provided for people with disabilities. As Lonsdale observes: 'assumptions are made that they do not have sexual feelings, that they will never get married or have a relationship that includes sex and, by implication, that they will not have children' (1990: 7). Tony Arber, writing from his own experience, tells how his local authority made him a downstairs bedroom but the room was too small for a double bed. He wryly comments that 'perhaps they felt disabled men don't sleep with their wives' (1991: 23). Reporting on work carried out by SPOD – a British charity formed ten years ago to make public the sexuality of disabled people – Cheaney (1990) writes that often carers will not acknowledge the sexuality of disabled people:

> many of them simply don't want the people they are looking after to have sexual relationships. In a lot of homes if a disabled person dares to suggest such an idea, they are simply told there are no double beds. . . . Many social workers and parents deny that disabled people have sexual feelings and see no reason to promote such an idea.

This metaphoric neutering can take place through carers' and professionals' approach to the naked bodies of those in their care. For example, the lack of privacy experienced by many elderly and disabled people in their daily lives may extend even to the very surface of the body which carers and other professionals poke, explore and touch, without seeking permission, just as they feel free to do with the bodies of children. Lonsdale describes the constant exposure of disabled women's bodies to professional eyes, which may be done with little regard to the person's sense of decency and sexual self. In a society where sexuality is made evident through clothes that revealingly conceal – skin-tight jeans, Lycra swimwear and transparent blouses – such naked exposure is an indication of sexual immaturity. Like children, disabled women may find themselves positioned as sexually innocent in their nakedness. But, unlike children, the bodies of elderly or disabled people can at the same time be conceived of as in some way 'disfigured' or 'abnormal'. Such baring of the flesh may therefore only occur in institutional and not public settings. Naked revelation of difference in public, as those with facial disfigurements often find, may lead to ostracism (Welford, 1990).

Younger adults who have a mental handicap and elderly people whose faculties are diminishing are similarly metaphorically 'neutered'. For example, Jones's study shows that whilst affection and cuddling were encouraged as acceptable modes of interpersonal relationships among mentally handicapped people, more sexually aware responses were regarded as problematic: 'many staff feel that affectionate behaviour by patients is morally correct – it reinforces the child-like image and their own status as surrogate parents' (1975: 110). Visible signs of a patient's own adult sexuality, such as masturbation, were, on the other hand, regarded with disgust or anger by the staff for such actions did not fit within the 'family' model of the care regime provided (see Chapter 4).

In the often implicit, metaphoric extension of childish bodies to those of dependent adults, through caring practices, the question of sexual intimacy raises particular conceptual problems concerning social status. Jenkins (1990), for example, has argued that the sterilization of a mentally handicapped woman without her consent, or the immediate removal of children born to mentally handicapped parents, would be unthinkable actions in the case of non-handicapped people. His analysis of court reports suggests that, despite being seen as chronologically or even biologically adult, the people concerned were deemed to be non-adult in a social sense.

This chapter has traced the growing ideological role of the body as a marker of social identity, showing how the perceived limitations of the bodies of members of dependent social categories preclude the granting of full personhood. Furthermore, material drawn from personal and ethnographic accounts of dependency reveals the prevalence of the image of the child, and the models of parental care, in the management of this experience. In that the bodily limitations ascribed to childhood are seen as acceptable, indeed desirable attributes, they provide the literal grounding for the metaphors through which otherwise very threatening bodily conditions – such as chronic illness or deep old age – are framed. Crucially, we need to understand the importance of these metaphors for adults themselves, and indeed to see their use as emanating from the adult world. The threat of old age and illness with respect to personhood is extremely powerful, as is evidenced by the vigilance of members of the dominant category 'adult' to resist any diminution of their capacity for self-reliance and physical attractiveness. Even the slightest bodily lack or disfigurement may mark the onset of the eventual undermining of their personhood in old age.

The marginalization, and often indeed the infantilization, of members of dependent social categories evoke varying responses. In childhood, dependency is seen as not only entirely natural, but also desirable. Child prodigies threaten the adult world. But the powerlessness of children is itself beginning to be called into question in the light of evidence of child abuse of all kinds. The corporal punishment of school children, until recently seen as central to learning discipline, has been redefined, in some quarters, as physical violence. Accounts presented in this chapter have also indicated the sense of humiliation experienced by sentient dependent adults whose personal circumstances and social identities are shaped in terms of the model of childhood. Those unable to articulate their views may, it can safely be assumed, experience a similar erosion of self-esteem and self-will as a result of their exposure to this framing. At present, however, childhood continues to be seen as an acceptable form of dependency and, as such, persists as a model for other experiences of dependency. As we have shown, the imposition of such conditions upon younger dependent adults, those whose ages, but not bodies, otherwise confer full personhood, erodes the personal attributes which might otherwise sustain their autonomy and self-esteem. This chapter questions the connections between a particular framing of the body and social identity, asking about the structuring of power relations across the life course and about the use of the metaphor of the child to amend the powerlessness of individuals whose bodily conditions threaten to render them socially marginal.

Notes

1 Woodward opens her discussion of twentieth-century representations of ageing in Western fiction and psychoanalysis (1991) with an account of the exhibition of an unadorned photograph of an elderly man, naked but for his slippers. She argues that the anger expressed by viewers towards the photographer, for 'exploiting' the man, was in reality an anger associated with the unequivocal representation of the fate of the viewer's own body.

2 The full version of this poem appears in Chapter 6.

4

DEPENDENCY, FAMILY AND COMMUNITY

An awareness of the culturally and socially specific nature of 'childhood' provides initial insights into why children should provide the literal grounding for the metaphors through which the experience of members of very different social categories is shaped. This chapter develops the arguments so far raised by considering the notion that children, in their relationships with their parents, provide, through the idea of the 'family', an acceptable model of the relationship between 'dependent' and 'independent' individuals. It argues that, as a result of a process of metaphoric transformation, familial relations provide a model for relationships of dependency of all kinds. Another layer is therefore added to earlier discussion of the way in which the social construction of the child's body, as an image of limited but developing human ability, is used metaphorically to deflect awareness of the reality of ageing, deterioration and death. The question remains, however, as to why the model of child/parent relationships has a part to play in making human dependency cognitively manageable.

If this question is to be addressed effectively, the implications of both dependency and independence in Western cultures need to be considered. Both are integral to the conception of personhood in the West, as argued in Chapter 2. In suggesting that the family provides a model for the structuring of power relations within society as a whole, this chapter raises central questions about the social organization of power. In the examples to follow, it becomes apparent that the metaphoric use of the position of the child within the family provides the means through which the reality of human need, whether biologically given or socially constructed, is reconciled with the central cultural value attributed to independence within Western cultures.

Dependency and independence

'Dependency' is a possibility at any point in the human life course, for any individual. Furthermore, dependency carries no single meaning; it encompasses a range of different contexts, embracing a wide continuum of social experience. Despite this, in the context of a Western industrial society such as Britain, 'dependency' is often used to refer to a narrow, rather than broad range of social contexts and to identify particular categories of people.

For example, its locus as a source of fear – through the loss of biological function or social competencies – is frequently dramatized in advertising campaigns seeking funds to improve provision for specific categories of disabled people. For example, multiple sclerosis was highlighted through a campaign which offered variations on a theme of 'On Monday she danced. On Wednesday she went lame.' Recent critiques of such campaigns point out their negative positioning of disabled people, whilst at the same time acknowledging the dilemma that it is precisely through the depiction of physical dependence that public response to such campaigns is encouraged (*Guardian*, 10 December 1990).

Dependency can be permanent or temporary, fleeting or extended, partial or overwhelming, but, again, the apparently self-evident meaning of the term 'dependency' conceals a number of assumptions.

First, as a description of the circumstances of individuals perceived to be poor, handicapped, needy, deteriorating or immature, it carries the suggestion that there will be others upon whom the individual will be able to depend, that their social relationships will include a cooperative, indeed altruistic dimension. In identifying dependency in this way, as a relational term, questions are immediately raised about the nature and quality of that relationship. Walker (1982: 127) argues, for example, that conceived in these terms dependency is primarily a social relationship which rests upon the exercise of power.

Secondly, the term 'dependency' often carries powerful negative associations in Britain and America, even though in reality it can be a fleeting and partial experience. For example, 'I'm depending on her to give me a lift' suggests a very minor experience of need. My car is being serviced; she is saving me the inconvenience of the bus and the expense of a taxi. Thus, through becoming 'dependent' in this way I am beholden to her. My dependence presages exchange, later reciprocity, an act of friendship to be repaid. At the other extreme, when dependence is an overwhelming and permanent state, the term is assumed to carry weighty implications, a state of far reaching lack, an enduring position of powerlessness.

Why should human need be described in terms of dependency, and, through the use of this term, be associated with powerlessness? Some clues have already been given, and here we consider in some detail the historical background to ideas of dependency and powerlessness. Discussing the nature of person-hood in Chapter 2, for example, it was argued that economic dependency was the result of the exclusion from the workforce of certain categories of people during the development of industrialization under capitalism. For example, Thane (1983) locates 'the problem of the elderly' as a late nineteenth century phenomenon, occurring within a capitalist system under interna-tional trade pressure. Gradually marginalized as paid workers, elderly people became unable to operate autonomously within a free-market economy, and so found their personhood as individual members of British society invalidated.

Chapter 2 also drew attention to the development of a culturally specific form of personhood, the product of a tradition of English individualism. Thus, Dalley (1988: 28) describes individualism as a cluster of notions which give precedence to the individual as an independent centre of consciousness, one which by right is private and protected from intrusion. It is a possessive individualism,

> the conception of the individual as essentially the proprietor of his (sic) own person and capacities, owing nothing to society for them . . . The human essence is freedom from dependence on the will of others, and freedom is the function of possession. (Macpherson, 1962, cited in Dalley, 1988: 28)

For Dalley it is possessive individualism which links gender-based inequality and the family. The freedom and the privacy understood to be the right of the individual is, she argues, the prerogative of the male household head alone.

Whilst the development of industrialization under capitalism may indeed have exacerbated the marginalizing of members of certain social categories, their previous position within a society long committed to the pursuit of individual freedom is unlikely to have been either central or dominant. For example, Quadagno (1982) notes a tradition of exchanging retirement contracts between British farmers and their children from the Middle Ages to the nineteenth century. In these families, 'care' was an item of carefully negotiated exchange, and not a spontaneous response by adult children to the needs of their elderly parents. MacFarlane (1978) similarly questions the historical account of the relatively recent, mid-sixteenth century emergence of a capitalist economy out of a preceding peasant society. Drawing on a careful reinter-pretation of sources such as parish registers, he argues that 'since at least the thirteenth century England has been a country where the individual has been more important than the group and the hierarchy of ranks has not been closed' (1978: 197). Rather than a peasant economy where production was deeply embedded within the life of the extended family, MacFarlane points to the presence of nuclear families in England from the thirteenth century onwards. Within those families were to be found the 'rampant individualists, highly mobile both geographically and socially, economically "rational", market-orientated and acquisitive, ego-centred in kinship and social life' (MacFarlane, 1978: 163).

Thus, those nineteenth century men whose campaigning trade union activities fell into line with middle class philanthropic movements to ensure the exclusion of members of certain social categories from the workforce (see Chapter 2), held to a long-established, rather than newly emergent set of beliefs concerning the rights of the individual to improve their social lot. Late eighteenth century Enlightenment thought, which called for equal rights for all men, turns out therefore to be grounded in an already established belief in individualism.

However, the powerful diffusion of egalitarian beliefs during the eighteenth century in Britain rapidly raised questions about the implications of individualism, questions which continue to be addressed in contemporary society. For example, feminist thinkers such as Wollstonecraft 1962 [1792] pointed out that the demand for equal rights for all men rested upon the willingness of women to forswear any possibility of individual freedom. Individualism, and its eventual expression in a capitalist economy, contains an endemic contradiction. Equality of opportunity to pursue one's own ends inevitably creates an unequal society, for not all members of that society share the same capacity to generate wealth. The independently effective, individual entrepreneur is but one member of a mixed and constantly changing cast. His role, like all others, is also vulnerable to accident or increasing age. Thus individualism is irreconcilable with human dependency, for if the pursuit of individual freedom is the hallmark of personhood then all those unable, through dependency, to hold to this aim are cast in less than fully social roles.

The individualism which developed within the nuclear, market-orientated families of thirteenth century Britain, is, however, an organizing principle specific to Western society. It contrasts radically with concepts of dependency in other cultures. Anthropological accounts of non-Western societies provide, for example, plentiful evidence of social strategies orientated towards the creation, rather than avoidance of personal indebtedness, towards dependency as a positive ideal. In such societies, dependency may be created through brideservice (Collier and

Rosaldo, 1981), bridewealth or bloodwealth payments (Evans-Pritchard, 1951). Brideservice, bridewealth and bloodwealth payments can be seen as social practices which involve the exchange of goods, livestock or labour between people either along kinship links created through marriage, or as a means of settling feuds between kin. *Potlatch*, as described by Boas (1965 [1911]), is the staging of a feast and the display and destruction of property amongst native Americans for the benefit of a rival group. This group is, through its participation, obligated to repay. Similarly, *moka* and *kula* are forms of ritual exchange practised between trading partners in Mount Hagen, New Guinea (Strathern, 1971) and the Trobriand Islands (Malinowski, 1922), respectively. These too establish relations of dependency. In each example, then, carefully patterned, reciprocal networks of indebtedness are created and maintained as a form of social organization described by Mauss (1966 [1925]) as a 'gift relationship'. Following from the patterning of these reciprocal exchange networks, a society's economic, political, religious and kinship systems are organized.

In each of these examples, dependency or indebtedness is seen as a transitory experience in which power is lost and gained and then lost again. It is not an all-encompassing social identity, a permanent state of powerlessness. Looked at more broadly, the exchange of goods or services is an activity which extends over time, binding succeeding generations of individuals and kin groups in networks of exchange. For example, the Nuer bridegroom depends upon his kin to supply him with bridewealth in the form of cattle. This is necessary to acknowledge his debt to his in-laws in providing him with a wife. In entering into marriage the young man therefore simultaneously enters into a sustained relationship with his own kin group, gradually returning the bridewealth debt through his work as a herder of their remaining cattle (Evans-Pritchard, 1951).

Power none the less remains very much at issue within social relationships such as those which link Nuer kin groups, just as it does within the Western contexts described by Walker (1982). However, these traditional systems of social organization can be distinguished from the dependency relationships which characterize Western individualism in the sense that their members undertake periods of indebtedness as a means of generating or activating networks of relationships through which power and status may eventually be summoned, as and when it is needed. This option is rarely available to dependent categories of people in Western society, though in Chapter 6 the exercise of power on their part is discussed.

Economic strategies such as these contrast markedly with the

Western view of property as something which can be bought and sold with impunity, one role of money being to sever any enduring relations of indebtedness or dependency (Hirschon, 1984). Once sold, it is detached from the seller; there is no formal social character to this exchange of goods and money, or indeed labour and money. Extended indebtedness, rather than creating links between individuals which may be used many times over in the organization of a whole variety of political, economic or religious activities, instead places a constraint on the freedom of the individual to pursue his/her own ends.

The Western cultural framing of indebtedness is particularly evident in the case of dependent individuals and their carers. In her discussion of the continuing absence of adequate provision for carers offered in the Griffiths Report on Community Care (*Community Care: Agenda for Action*, 1988), Glendinning notes the 'steady stream of research since the early seventies [which] has documented the financial disadvantages commonly experienced by those who are living with and providing domestic and personal care for a sick, disabled or frail elderly relative or friend' (1988: 26). The sense of frustration experienced by many female carers, who may emerge from an extended period of domestic labour on behalf of their children only to re-enter this domain as guardians of their elderly parents, illuminates the dissonant position of extended relations of dependency within Western society. One woman writes:

> 'And so there's nothing seriously wrong Mother after all – and I'm so very glad!' Is the spinster friend who said this a saint or a hypocrite? The old lady is a chronic invalid whose diet has to be watched constantly – and a tyrant to boot. My friend, who does secretarial work at home to make ends meet, often has to work through the night as Mother is so demanding. (Quoted in Tinker, 1990)

Thus women's domestic labour is often used to underwrite the freedom of men to pursue their own ends. Whilst men may make use of their incomes to discharge their obligations to dependent kin without risk of censure, women are more likely to maintain caring relationships over time, caring for, in order that they may be seen to care about. None the less, many men do take on a carer's role, a trend which Tinker speculates on in her survey of the literature on caring, pointing out that 'more than one writer has asked whether the father who changes the nappy will later take on the changing of the incontinence pad' (1990). However, whilst many men do willingly undertake the care of an elderly relative, such as a spouse (Pollitt et al., 1989), for others financing care still remains an acceptable way of demonstrating their care (Dalley, 1988; Tinker, 1990). In asserting the value of personal freedom,

individualism in Western societies erodes the multiplicity of obligations through which family members might otherwise be tied to,
and be potentially supportive of one another. As a result, many
isolated female carers, for example, find themselves constrained as
individuals, creating an indebtedness which engenders no
reciprocity. A woman writes of her involvement in community
care. 'Jack' is an 87-year-old man, confused and incontinent, who,
because he is not sick, has no state assistance with his care. After
months of voluntarily helping Jack, cooking, cleaning, putting him
to bed and coping with his incontinence, she expresses both her
anger on his behalf and the frustration she herself feels:

> I do not want to do his washing any more. I do not want to take my
> children to his house when I change his bed, though I know he likes to
> hear my two-year-old son say 'Hello Jack'. It makes him smile. I am
> not sure what it will mean to Jack if we cease to help him. But this is
> the end of the road for me at least . . . he deserves a decent end to his
> life. (McCormack, 1991)

Those who are dependent on care and also isolated from any
effective kinship network provide no access to channels of wealth
or other resources through which, over time, the favours might
gradually be returned. The risks to existing family stability arising
out of the need to care for a dependent member are noted by
Allan, who argues that 'caring for an elderly person, especially in
the same household, can often generate a good deal of friction and
emotional tension in relationships with other family members,
particularly spouses' (1985: 130).[1]

As a result of these circumstances, the members of Western
society stand or fall as individuals. Independence and dependency,
which, in biological and social terms, represent points on a fluc-
tuating continuum that encompasses every person, are socially
constructed as polar opposites. As we have shown, infantilizing
practices both sustain and are sustained by binary thinking and
cognitive practice of this kind. The cultural value attached to the
pursuit of individual freedom therefore problematizes the binding
human needs experienced by very young, chronically ill, handicapped or very elderly people. Within a society of individuals, they
lack access to the resources available in societies where social
interaction is more densely patterned. However extended the family
might be, its size promises little in the absence of an underlying
organizing principle of social reciprocity. In their need, dependent
people are therefore seen to constrain others in their own pursuit
of individual freedom. As a result only those who are without
need, or without obligation to those with need, are able to achieve
full independence and therefore personhood.

Anthropological studies in non-Western contexts highlight the cultural specificity of this relationship. For example, the male members of a hunter–gatherer society such as the Llongots of the Philippines experience adult social status hand in hand with indebtedness. In becoming full social actors on marriage, men become indebted to their fathers-in-law, a debt which binds them in relations of brideservice over an extended period. Through time, the full implications of their indebtedness unfolds, their own daughters attracting a new generation of young men who will labour on their behalf, so providing them with eventual wealth and status (Collier and Rosaldo, 1981).

However, despite both a lack of reciprocity and the constraints which caring places upon them, many members of contemporary Western society, both female and male, do enter into extended periods of labour on behalf of dependent family members, labour which binds them in an enduring sense of obligation up until the death of the dependent person (Pollitt et al., 1989). Tinker (1990) shows that while one million more women than men are caring for a dependent relative or friend, 2.5 million men have none the less taken on this role. Fifteen per cent of women and 12 per cent of men are carers. Rather than an eventual return of the resources which they have made available to the dependent person, a more likely outcome is, as suggested above, a constraint on their participation in the labour force which renders them impoverished and socially isolated. Phillipson and Walker (1986) document the financial, social and emotional costs of caring, highlighting, in particular, disruptions to women's employment opportunities and future pension entitlements. 'Tension, mental stress, physical ill-health and acute tiredness are commonly reported symptoms amongst carers, especially those caring for the mentally frail' (1986: 69).

If independence and dependency are conceptually polarized within Western societies, rather than seen as interconnected human conditions, their occurrence carries implications for ideas of power and status. Not only those who fall by the wayside through accident or illness during adulthood, but also those passing through the stages of childhood and old age, will, in their different dependencies, be denied full personhood and, as a consequence, full access to power. As embodiments of the fragility of biological life, they threaten the adult world, both ideologically and materially, for the notion of individual freedom rests upon the spurious assumption that the individual will be as able and as fit as the next person. Additionally, it takes no account of the central role which an individual may be called upon to play in providing for someone else's freedom, when the caring role involves yielding up most of their own.

Contradictions such as these are endemic within societies such as Britain and the United States, composed of transitory and vulnerable human beings and organized and thought about according to the principle of individualism. Faith in the possibility of individual freedom is always vulnerable to the harsh realities of human dependency, and to the tension between continuity and change. However, anthropological field material again reveals the cultural specificity of this response. It indicates the range of cultural and social strategies through which a sense of permanence and stability is lent to the existing social order, notwithstanding the fleeting lives of society's individual members. Bloch and Parry (1982), for example, describe the deliberate confusion of cyclic and unrepeatable time in non-Western societies where the social order is conceived of as eternal. 'Death', for the ordinary member of Hindu society, takes place not when the heart stops beating or brain function can no longer be recorded, but, instead, mid-way through cremation when the skull is cracked open to release the spirit. The temporal unpredictability of biological death is thus effaced through a social and ritual practice which allows for the culturally controlled release of life. Geertz (1977) has also addressed the tension between transient mortality and an enduring social order. He gives examples of societies where separations of some kind are introduced within the concept of the self, with the result that at death some aspects of the self endures. For example, Balinese life incorporates an enduring system of fixed roles and statuses played out to infinity by a changing sequence of mortal human beings (1977: 485–7).

The parenting of elders

In arguing that within contemporary Western society the child provides the literal grounding for one of the root metaphors through which the anomalous occurrence of human dependency is made manageable, conceptually, emotionally and practically, this volume reveals the metaphor's ideological role. It offers the means of suturing one of Western society's endemic contradictions. While numerous examples of infantilizing practices have been examined, particularly from the perspective of those insiders whose 'dependency' is being managed for them in this way, dependency is, as already shown, primarily a social relationship which rests upon the exercise of power (Walker, 1982: 127). Here we shall consider examples which reveal the shared model through which carer and cared-for are linked: the metaphoric use of the child/parent relationship as one strategy through which the care of elderly people is managed. Thus, Hazan, for example, in discussing a day centre for elderly Jewish people in London, says that: 'some of the patterns adopted by members of staff and outsiders to relate to participants [elderly people] were guided by the paradigm of the relationship with children' (1980: 31). Martin too describes the way care staff in a London residential home similarly drew on mother/baby models of interaction in their work with elderly people:

> Food is dolloped on to the plates and served at great speed by the Care Assistants with unwashed hands. The 'babies' (i.e. the confused) are exhorted to eat: 'Let's play aeroplanes . . . watch' – an over-laden spoon weaves in the air and is thrust into a rejecting mouth. (1979: 17)

In their role as caring 'mummies' and 'daddies', care staff exercise control over their metaphoric children, thereby overcoming an otherwise troubling encounter with the limits of independent adulthood (see also Jones, 1975; Perring, 1989). In this way, the contradictions arising out of the intimate care of individuals who are simultaneously 'adult' and 'dependent' may be made less anomalous. Such contradictions are exemplified in the continuous involvement of care staff in unusually close contact with those to whom they give care, other adults. It is a contact which takes place largely outside a more carefully controlled medical framework, a contact which occurs because an individual is unable to perform certain required bodily tasks for him or herself. Not only do carers make physical and verbal interventions when feeding, dressing and toileting dependent people, dependent people themselves will also tend to make more bodily contact than is customary between adults if, for example, they are deaf, in pain, confused or immobile. If, as noted in Chapter 3, the body and bodily behaviours play a central role within the classificatory processes through which self-identity comes into being, then this bodily contact, unusual in Western societies, is not only ambiguous but also threatening to the identity of those involved. Thus, while the range of social relationships between carer and cared for are varied – for example, dependent people may be strangers to their carers, may become the familiar focus of daily paid labour, or may be the parents, in-laws, or even remoter kin of the carer – each relationship will none the less involve close physical contact, regardless of the social distance between the individuals. Moreover, the intimacy of contact required during much care work of any kind is unprecedented in adult relationships. Lovers may sometimes feed one another, but how many regularly wipe each others' bottoms? Whereas a hospital setting will bring fleeting periods of close contact between patient and nurse, those whose dependency requires an ever-present carer are involved in a closer and more enduring relationship. Furthermore, intimate contact is taking place within a less rigidly structured professional setting than that which pertains within the hospital, a context where these effects are further distanced via medical models (Turner, 1987). Thus, in an individualistic society where personal autonomy is highly valued, the one-way intimacy of the relationship between carer and cared for can produce a loss of social power as well as personal control on the part of the dependent person. An unequal relationship has been created between two individuals, both of whom are adult. The ambiguity of this asymmetrical balance of power is further reinforced by its association with the spectre of inevitable human vulnerability, indeed mortality.

One example of a particularly problematic area within this changed and changing 'adult' relationship is sexuality. If sexual relationships are one of the few sites within which the boundaries of the self are broken or dissolved, albeit in a carefully limited fashion, then dependency may evoke sexual vulnerability. The parent–child relationship, with its legitimate imbalance of power and its apparently 'safer' model of intimate contact, partially resolves this. By 'parenting' a dependent adult, the balance of power ultimately lies within the hands of the parent, not with the adult 'child'. Without the 'safety' of the parent–child model, both an elderly person and their carer can find it difficult to sidestep the danger of being drawn into some form of sexual interaction. Ethnographic material from a residential home for elderly people shows care staff who fear they may be exposed to unwelcome sexual behaviour by male residents adopting a parental, stern mother to small son, stance in response:

> When George, being bathed by Jan, touched his penis in what she perceived to be a sexual fashion, she reproached him, saying, 'Howay [get away with you], stop playing with that!' (Hockey, unpublished data)

Constructing families

Within a society organized through the principle of individualism, constructions of childhood as a metaphor for dependency cannot be made sense of in isolation, for the notion of 'the child' is encapsulated by, indeed resides within, contemporary images of the family. Thus, not only the powerless, but also the powerful, are positioned through reference to family-orientated social discourse, through the rootedness of the parent–child metaphor. As this section demonstrates, the various members of the family, and the relations of power through which they are linked, provide a fund of metaphoric forms through which the relationship between those who are dependent and those who are independent can take legitimate shape. Thus the image of the child's kin relationship with its parents builds upon its age-category status of dependency, one which carries prevailing associations with marginality. It is an image which therefore embodies a more complete, double dependency.

Intimately bound up with the creation of child as Other, as shown in Chapter 2, are relations of power which link the social categories of 'child' and 'adult'. The social construction of the child as Other rests upon the availability of a context, or site, within which that Otherness can be realized. Whether the child is conceived of as an embodiment of Original Sin, a *tabula rasa*, or a creature of primaeval innocence and wisdom, its successful passage into adulthood has become increasingly the outcome of protracted parental surveillance. Thus the initial need to subordinate the child's 'animal' nature to the demands of society underwent the series of changes already described, changes which resulted in the subordination of the child to the state and to the family. This process culminated in the theories of child development. In Freud's work, for example, the Western family is lent a universal status, with mythic family forms from other, ancient cultures providing images through which the psyches of Freud's middle class Viennese patients might be understood.

During the nineteenth century, in particular, the parental role, and consequently the child's role, became elaborated, at a time when the mother, in terms of middle class ideology, was for the first time expected to engage solely in reproductive, rather than productive labour. Ehrenreich and English (1979) describe the requirement, during the nineteenth and early twentieth centuries, that the mother should assimilate a growing body of 'expert' knowledge. Withdrawn from the labour force, women's domestic roles became in this way increasingly professionalized and the possibility of children being reared by nurses or in institutions came to be frowned upon (Donzelot, 1980). Whilst this particular domestic role may have been a reality only for middle class women, commitment to its values resulted in the persistent attempts both by those women themselves, and by philanthropists in general, to promote similar child-rearing practices among working class women who combined reproductive labour with factory work (Steadman, 1990). The family therefore emerges as a site within which relations of power and inequality are reproduced, if not necessarily on a material level, then perhaps more significantly on an ideological level (Bernardes, 1985). Thus not only children, but a particular conception of the child was fostered within the emerging family form of this period.

This interdependence between concepts of the child and of the family can also be seen contemporarily. Coote (1990), for example, argues that the rupture of traditional family models is currently understood by the political Right as a source of 'under-achievement in children, juvenile delinquency, crime and general social disintegration'. If the resonance of the child as a metaphor for the experience of dependency is to be understood, the legitimation of a particular set of power relations through a culturally specific notion of 'family' must be explored.

Sociologists have examined the role of the family in reproducing the social order, both from a marxist feminist and a functionalist perspective (Murdock, 1949; Parsons, 1964; Young and Willmott, 1973; Oakley, 1974; Segal, 1983; Bernardes, 1985). From within an extensively theorized field, key areas of social life such as health, social placement and the hierarchical, gendered division of labour have been shown to be created from within the family. Issues of power and authority, whether in relation to gender or generational forms of differentiation, have been understood through appraisals of familialist ideology. Here discussion will focus on the way in which the positioning of the child within the family serves to position the child within the wider society: images of the son or daughter in relation to its parents, we suggest, orientate all children and all adults in their relationships with one another. For example, incest prohibitions within families provide an organizing principle which is expressed in constraints on intergenerational sexual relationships external to the family. Familial or age-related terms of reference – sugar daddies, toyboys, bimbos and nymphets – evoke child–parent couplings, ambiguous pairings which transgress the intergenerational sexual boundary and, in order to become acceptable, must somehow be accounted for. Murcott's discussion of the social construction of teenage pregnancy illustrates the ambiguous nature of this occurrence (1980). The condemnatory, 'but he's old enough/young enough to be her father/son!' can be softened only through the mustering of extenuating circumstances. Often these justifications highlight a mismatch between adulthood understood in terms of units of time, and adulthood understood in terms of appearance and abilities. This in turn is an ambiguous circumstance, the two being expected to develop or advance in synchrony. If 'he's a surprisingly thoughtful 19-year-old', or if 'you'd never think to look at him that he's over 60', then 'she' may proceed with her affair. Condemnation may none the less be transformed into warning words, such as 'but what about when she's 60 and he's 40/80!' If he is younger he will eventually find her sexually unappealing (see Chapter 3); if he is older he will die well before she does. The likelihood of death or desertion occurring in *any* relationship is overlooked.

The parallel between the intra-familial construction of femininity, masculinity and heterosexuality, and the intergenerational rules in relation to which all sexual partnerships are conducted, highlights the role of the family not only as the social context within which children are raised, but also as a site which is seen to be associated with particular sets of social values. This process operates in two different ways.

First, in a material sense, the family continues to be seen as a haven within a hostile environment, the locus of personal, informal social relations, and a refuge from the formal, hierarchical relations of power which characterize the public world. This view was promoted by functionalist sociologists, such as Murdock (1949) and Parsons (1964). However, as Barrett and McIntosh argue (1982), those on the Left as well as on the Right continue to promote its role as a repository of human values in an otherwise anarchic, uncaring world. Even the challenge to the family offered by the 1970s Women's Movement came to be questioned during the 1980s by feminist authors such as Friedan (1981), Elshtain (1981) and Greer (1984). All three argue that in writing off the family, feminists are writing off the private context within which the dehumanizing patriarchal structures of the public world should be slowly dismantled, a task in which women and men could cooperate informally (Stacey, 1987).

Alongside these perceptions of the material role of the family can be placed its second, and metaphorical role in providing a source, or literal grounding for key metaphors through which power is organized and legitimated within a Western society such as Britain. Not only power, but also the notions of equality and closeness are brought into being through the use of family terms. For example, relations of inequality are reproduced through metaphors of parenthood, as in the case of the dominance of the 'mother' country over her colonies; the ascendancy of God the 'father' over his 'children'; and the apocalyptic threat of the 'mother of all battles' offered by General Saddam prior to the Gulf War. As these examples reveal, parental power in relation to dependent people of all ages is, however, double-edged, encapsulating the twin possibilities of both care and control. By contrast, relations of equality can be created among groups and individuals otherwise structurally set apart from each other, through the metaphoric use of collateral kinship terminology, such as 'sister', 'brother' or 'cousin', rather than that of descent, 'mother', 'father', 'son', 'daughter'. Although divided from one another by social class, age and race, women may none the less use a familial metaphor, 'sisterhood', in order to transcend the family-based boundaries, the ties and loyalties which confine them in their everyday domestic lives. Similarly, women devoting themselves to a religious rather than domestic life join together in 'sisterhood', their shared inequality in relation to God, the 'father', being organized through the metaphor of marriage, each one becoming a 'bride' of Christ (Williams, 1975).

If, as we have been arguing, the child provides a root metaphor through which dependency may be managed, then insight must be developed here concerning the ways in which the family reproduces itself, for this is the material and ideological context within which both children and the concept of the child are fostered. The question remains, then, as to how the family retains its centrality within Western society, regardless of the political perspective which is adopted.

The 'family and other animals'

To address this question, two processes can be considered: 'naturalization' and what can be termed 'super-naturalization'. An examination of the fine grain of family life reveals both these processes at work. Thus, for example, the notion of the incest taboo, by definition an intra-familial issue, none the less resonates within all sexual relationships, as we have seen, stigmatizing alliances between an individual and someone 'old enough to be their father/mother'. The discourse of incest, when examined, can be seen not only to authenticate particular sets of power relations, but also to naturalize them.

Thus, parent–child incest is found to be disturbing in terms of a set of beliefs and assumptions grounded in the 'laws of nature', and indeed in natural 'lore' which proscribes inbreeding among animals. Birds leave their nests and tom cats stay out rather than in all night. Familiarity breeds contempt, and not new life. The perception of incest as a form of child abuse reveals it as a power-based rather than a sex-based issue. However, while incestuous relations are defined as 'pathological', in that they involve an abuse of power, the unequal relations of power expressed in 'healthy' child–parent relations are seen as entirely 'natural', a view which is echoed in traditional beliefs about the 'natural' inequality which underpins adult-to-adult heterosexual relations. Kitzinger develops the link between child sexual abuse and adult power, arguing that:

> Child abuse is not an anomaly but part of the structural oppression of children. Assault and exploitation are risks inherent to childhood as it is currently lived. It is not just the abuse of power over children that is the problem, but the existence and maintenance of that power itself. (1990: 178)

None the less child sexual abuse continues to be seen as an anomaly within an otherwise legitimately unequal social relationship. Gender-based inequality too is naturalized with equal vigour, as Coward (1984) has shown. Wildlife programmes on the television readily demonstrate the dominance of the male of the species over his female mate.

'Childhood' describes a period of the life course when the naturalization of family relations occurs with particular intensity. Children learn, therefore, not only about being 'children' but also about the nature of the family. For example, the material practices which go to make up child-rearing are often, in themselves, heavily loaded symbolic forms. In middle class families, the nightly bedtime story is an important vehicle. Daddy Bear, Mummy Bear and Baby Bear provide a model of the child's immediate family, the human child Goldilocks offering the young listener a point of entry not only into the home of the Bear Family, but also into the text itself. Not once but three times the parallels between Goldilocks, Baby Bear and the listening child are drawn. The listener discovers that Baby Bear's chair, Baby Bear's porridge and Baby Bear's bed are more fitting for the child/Goldilocks through a series of systematic comparisons with those bigger, harder, softer, or hotter beds, chairs, and breakfasts belonging to Daddy Bear and Mummy Bear. In all cases, that which belongs to Baby Bear is somehow lesser than that which belongs to its parents, and is suited only for the use of another 'child'. Trying on adulthood for size, Goldilocks in fact has her childish identity confirmed, finding herself unable to transcend the boundary between childhood and adulthood. It is all beyond her.

At adult-imposed bedtime, the parental narrator readily simulates the deep, gruff voice of Daddy Bear, thereby putting the child in its place, both literally and metaphorically. Confined to its bed, the child understands that its powerlessness in relation to its parent is, after all, only natural. As in another bedtime tale, Peter Pan, the child is encouraged to remain a child (Rose, 1984).

The naturalization of the family through the performance of bedtime story-telling is a far from isolated childhood experience. Animal families proliferate in babies' board and rag books, in three-dimensional cuddly toys that cradle their young, and in sets of farm animals. They provide another vehicle through which the child may be positioned, or put in its place, an urgent task in the light of historical uncertainty as to the exact nature of the child. Fernandez takes up this point, noting that:

> At the earliest moment our infants receive metaphoric attributions: they become sweet peas, tigers, little bears, kittens, little fish . . . how inclined we are to comb the world for cunning animals to surround our children with. Is it that without them we feel helpless to give definition to the infantile inchoate? (1970: 46)

The Rousseaunian identification of child with animal is currently structured, for British and American children, in terms of a set of parallels between the advancing years of the child's life and the shift from domestic to exotic animals. Whilst fluffy baby chicks and ducklings attend the newborn, it is fantasy cartoon figures such as Tom and Jerry, Thundercats and Teenage Mutant Hero Turtles which engage the older child, preparing them for the presently unreal but none the less imagined 'flight from the nest' during their adolescent years.

It is, however, not only through family-based child-rearing practices that the family is naturalized as a unit which is characterized by positively perceived relations of inequality. As noted, the media has an important ideological role to play within the experience of all children and all adults, both inside and outside the context of the family. For example, wildlife programmes not only frame animal behaviour in a way that reflects contemporary heterosexual notions of appropriate human sexual activity (Coward, 1984), they also portray those behaviours as aspects of 'natural' family activity and sentiment. For example, the 'grief' experienced by the female chimpanzee for her lost offspring is heralded not only as a sign of the universality of maternal bonding, but also of the possibility of a shared, cross-species emotional life. Thus anthropomorphic representations of wild animals provide the literal grounding of sets of culturally specific metaphors through which power relations between human animals are legitimated.

Alongside the naturalization of the family through references to the animal 'kingdom', must be placed the 'super' naturalization of the family through sets of parallel images drawn from both religious and aristocratic sources. Representations of the 'Holy' Family and the 'Royal' Family provide a complex, often interlocking commentary on contemporary notions of family. For example, the Holy Family, as depicted at the time of the birth of Jesus Christ is a site within which natural creatures, supernatural beings, 'common man' and 'sovereign man' are brought together. The nativity tableau has as its centrepiece the infant/king, his mother and father encircling him, a second subordinate circle being made up of domesticated animals, local shepherds and exotic kings. In an uncaring world, the baby Jesus none the less finds a haven of love and security within the family circle. In the natural world of the stable, God chooses to manifest himself as the youngest member of an earthly family. Not only the animals and their guardians, but also royalty from far-off lands play a supporting role, surrounding the Holy Family in positions of respectful worship. In contemporary British society, the Holy Family finds form not only in images but also in performance. Significantly, it is children rather than adults who consistently re-create the birth of baby Jesus within the context of school nativity plays. Images of the Holy Family are reproduced too in the Christmas cards through which the links between separated family members are traced. Indeed, in its internal organization of space the nativity tableau bears a strong resemblance to the family photograph. At weddings and christenings in particular, the centrepiece of family photographs is either the parents of a child-to-be or the white-swathed child and its parents and godparents. Indeed the impending arrival of the child may often be the trigger for a wedding. Around the new 'family' the strength of kinship links is manifested as successive circles of parents, grandparents, aunts and uncles, nephews and nieces and friends group in an ever-widening, protective formation. The family, as a key site within which social notions of childhood are reproduced, is thus legitimated in naturalistic, religious and ceremonial representations, all of which are occasioned by, and give primacy to the addition of a child to the family.

Geographical and social mobility in contemporary British and American society may lead many individuals to live in isolation from their family, friendship gaining ascendancy over kinship within everyday life. The family none the less remains central to the formation of social identity. For example, powerful feelings are aroused in connection with the significance of family names. Whilst women may resist the loss of their own family name at marriage, the strength of a desire to incorporate the children of that marriage into the new family name is evidenced in the ingenuity which parents bring to bear in producing a 'family' name of some kind for their offspring. Double-barrelled names may incorporate the surnames of both parents; an entirely new 'family' name may be coined; or the surname of one parent may be listed as one of the child's forenames.

Yet the nuclear family, made up of two parents and their mutual offspring, can be seen as little more than a myth or fantasy in terms of its prevalence within contemporary Western societies. One-parent, gay or lesbian and combined families through marriage provide a range of alternative family forms. Traditional familialist ideology none the less endures and is often expressed in dramatized form at times of calendrical or religious significance. Anthropological studies have consistently documented the ritual expression of fundamental cultural and social values during periods of change, whether of social status, territory or calendrical time (Van Gennep, 1960 [1908]; Hertz, 1960 [1907]; Turner, 1974). Thus, within a contemporary geographically mobile society, the ending of the year still remains an occasion marked by ritual which highlights the family as the desired, natural context for social life. Similarly weddings and funerals both involve rituals of reassembling the family which, outside the 'ritual', may be separated or fragmented. If the passage from coupledom to matrimony, from life to death, or from one year to the next takes place outside the context of the family, there are implications both in terms of the social identity of the (non)participants and indeed in terms of whether that passage has been successfully brought into being. Thus, spending Christmas alone is perceived as either a catastrophe of 'modern society' or an indication of individual perversity; and the hasty or unceremonious marriage by 'special licence' is traditionally seen as a 'shotgun' wedding. Being without a family at Christmas time becomes all the more poignant by virtue of the multiplicity of forms through which familial ideology finds expression. Thus, under the headline, 'Tinsel-time on wards!', the *Middlesborough Evening Gazette* (21 December 1989) showed a nativity-like hospital tableau, made up of *children*, rather than adults, surrounding an elderly dependent woman in a wheelchair – rather than the Baby Jesus. The children had distributed baskets of food and gifts to patients on the hospital's geriatric ward. Drawing on a familial ideology of dependency and care, as well as the supposed affinity between elderly people and the young (see Chapter 1), the children's teacher commented as follows:

> We wanted to highlight to the children the important social need of helping the elderly. When people are old they are so often forgotten and I thought we should take the chance to help them over Christmas.

The family regrouped at the fireside, encircled by Christmas cards bearing representations of the Holy Family, also provides a frame or context within which, in Britain, televised representations of the Royal Family are viewed. Christmas time is underscored as family time when the mother of the nation, the Queen, from her position within the Royal Family, delivers her personal message to the families of the Commonwealth, that 'family' of nations which traditionally orientates itself towards the 'mother' country, Britain (Bennett, 1981). During this key calendrical and religious ritual, a powerful image of 'family' is inserted within the experience of ordinary family life, an image which is fostered throughout the year. Royal activities, and the opinions of Prince Charles and the Princess of Wales, Prince Andrew and the Duchess of York, Princess Margaret, the Queen Mother and Prince Philip and the Queen herself are monitored and measured against notions of appropriate family behaviour and simultaneously, therefore, reinforce a familialist ideology through confirming or denying its truth. Certain themes emerge consistently. For example, the sanctity of both marital bonds and maternal bonds is stressed; royal divorces and extended, childless world tours provide occasions for the censure of individual behaviour in relation to dominant models. The announcement of the separation of Prince Andrew and the Duchess of York rapidly gave rise to heated debate concerning the Duchess's right to (Royal) 'family' membership. Tabloid newspapers reported her 'humiliation' after being requested to enter the palace only by the 'tradesman's entrance'. Billig, in an analysis of families' talk about the Royal Family, cites a fireman in his forties:

'To me . . . they are the sort of figurehead of the family life.' Family life, he went on, should be 'rock solid'. It was the 'foundation' of all morality: 'I don't think anything can function without it.' (1992: 91)

Despite the failure of its individual members continuously to adhere to 'rock solid' notions of family life, Christmas sees the union of the Royal Family, gathered together at Sandringham, flanked by loyal corgis. Those family members who conform most closely to traditional notions of the family appear centre stage. The Queen and the Queen Mother, consistently devoted parental figures, are particularly in evidence. Viewers and Royals alike subordinate their individual choices and lifestyles to the unity of the family at Christmas time (Bennett, 1981).

What must be stressed in relation to the ritual expression of the unity and endurance of family harmony, is the role of the child itself in providing a pivot or focus for the occasion. If Christmas palls, exhausts or disappoints, the child is the reference point in accounts for this deviant state of affairs. 'Really, we only bother for the sake of the children'; 'it's worth all the effort to see the looks on the children's faces'; 'the magic's gone out of it now the children have grown up'. Indeed the onset of Christmas is often first signalled by the intensifying of children's toy advertising on television. As long as belief in Father Christmas endures, the child continues to play its role in re-creating the magic of Christmas (Finnegan, 1981).

Christmas therefore emerges as a ritual site within which representations of idealized child–parent relationships accrue. Family life as lived and family life as imagined are fused at the decorated fireside, the log fire itself reminiscent of 'tradition', 'the past' and old-fashioned family values of hearth and home (Bennett, 1981).

Implications of familialist ideology

Although, as has been shown, pervasive links exist between family life as lived and family life as imagined, this is not to say that we can expect to find a strong degree of congruence between the two. For example, in 1990, one-quarter of households in Britain were one-person households and 15 per cent of children were living in a lone parent family. In 1989, European divorce rates were as high as 13.6 per thousand marriages (Denmark), with the British rate 12.6 per thousand (*Social Trends*, 1992). What can be argued, however, is that the consistent connoting of family forms and values, whether in story book, nativity play, or royal wedding, provides a set of images in relation to which individual lives are lived. Those individual lives may be pursued largely outside the confines of the family, indeed individuals may remain outside the family, right from birth up to death. None the less, the naturalized, indeed, 'super'-naturalized family continues to play an ideological role within the lives of society's individual members, whether in terms of their experience of intergenerational relations of power, or in terms of their experience of dependency of any kind. For Bernardes, family ideology – comprising individualism, materialism, differentiation and idealistic mystification – 'interlocks with gender ideology and wage labour ideology to form the major part of contemporary dominant ideology' (1985: 291).

During the past 20 years, however, awareness has been growing that family relationships can be violent and oppressive. Child abuse, incest, domestic violence, marital rape and women's disproportionate vulnerability to mental illness have all been recognized as aspects of family life, rarely talked about on a personal level and masked through ideological processes which naturalize the family in Britain and other Western cultures. For example, domestic violence has been addressed in the work of Pizzey (1974), Hanmer and Maynard (1987) and Dobash and Dobash (1992). Child abuse of all kinds has also become a focus of attention for academic as well as legal and social work. Eastman (1984) and Steinmetz (1988) have highlighted the prevalence of elder abuse. Taken together, work of this kind underlines the nature of power relationships within the family, a profile which stands in marked contrast with its representation in a whole variety of harmonious 'naturalized' imagery. Rather than making a distinction between 'normal' and 'pathological' families, current debate points more towards the commonality of power relations across all families, that power being made use of in a variety of ways. Care, control and abuse all represent the exercise of power, and reflect the presence of structured inequalities within the family along gender and generational lines. Cross-cultural and historical comparison reveals the variability of conceptions of legitimate care and control and 'illegitimate' abuse. Chapter 2, for example, describes approaches to child-rearing in the past which, in the twentieth century, would be seen as abuse. 'Smacking', only recently questioned in Britain as an acceptable child 'care' practice, is seen as intolerable in Scandinavia. Thus, while the child's relationship with its parents may be seen to provide an acceptable ideological model of dependency, that relationship, in practice, is one which can be both painful and dehumanizing as well as caring and protective.

It is, therefore, through the naturalization, and super-naturalization of family ideology that the subordination of the child takes on its positively perceived dimensions. Barrett and McIntosh (1982) make the significant point that the popularity of the family, as both an institution and an idea, does not imply that its members, and supporters, are 'passive consumers'. They argue that:

> Familism is not a ruling-class or patriarchal ideology repressively foisted on an unwilling population. Or, if we do consider familism as an ideology, we need a theory of ideology that casts people as participants rather than as passive consumers. (1982: 21)

They quote the Frankfurt School proposition that 'Like every proper ideology, the family too was more than a mere lie' (Frankfurt Institute for Social Research, 1973, cited in Barrett and McIntosh, 1982: 21). To explain this paradox, Barrett and McIntosh argue that within the notion of the family is embodied an expectation of acceptance given as a right. Membership is not achieved but ascribed, and the obligation to offer unconditional acceptance and practical aid is powerful among family members. Thus it is that, in Western societies such as Britain, mothers of murdering sons are, fictively at least, believed to stand by them, come what may; that wives repeatedly abused are expected to, and often do, retain their loyalty to their husbands.

In addition to the expectation of unconditional acceptance is the notion of family ties as enduring. Being ascribed rather than achieved, they persist throughout the life course and cannot be severed. In British culture, as well as elsewhere, the stressing of family likenesses from the moment of birth onwards reflects the notion of blood ties which cannot be ruptured. Even the integration of pets within the family is framed within a discourse of physical similarity, as evidenced in the often repeated joke about pets and their owners resembling one another.

Given these assumed cultural dimensions of family life, dimensions which cannot be expected in other social relationships such as friendship or neighbourliness, the participation of individuals within the family can be seen to constitute what Barrett and McIntosh (1982: 21) describe as a 'rational choice'. Outside the family unconditional acceptance and practical aid become problematic. Allan, discussing social constraints on the care of elderly people in the community, argues that 'the essence of good neighbouring lies in maintaining the tension between co-operation and privacy, helpfulness and non-interference, between friendliness and distance' (1985: 136).

Conscious of the paucity of alternative social forms of care for dependent elderly people, general practitioner Dr Keith Thomas, medical adviser to the charity Help the Aged, is reported to have initiated an 'Adopt a Gran!' scheme, bringing together 'single parents, people who had moved away from, or lost parents and . . . elderly women who had never had children' (*Daily Mail*, 9 April 1990). In this way remedies are provided for both the social problems of loneliness, as well as the conceptual anomalies of fragmented family units and childless women. In this, as in other examples, the centrality of the family is drawn upon to make manageable the notion of human need, thereby allowing dependency to be incorporated within a capitalist system grounded in the principle of individualism. This therefore is the ideological source of infantilization practices.

The caring family

Dependency, as noted earlier, implies the likelihood of the offer of care. So broad a term as 'care', however, requires more careful delineation. Given the model of the relationship between the child and its parents incorporated in family ideology, care, at the outset, must be seen as something which customarily involves or generates an asymmetrical relationship. However, the family model leads us to understand care also in terms of a combination of affect and obligation. The 'cost' of family care, whether financial, practical or emotional, is something which, lying outside the public world of market forces, is not, or should not be, amenable to calculation. Not only can we expect to be cared for, as a right, but the nature of that care will not be quantified, nor will it involve any acts of reciprocity.

Moreover, in that the model of family relations renders the asymmetry of the caring relationship legitimate, it also carries the implication that care which does not involve a combination of affect and obligation is inauthentic. It suggests that it is only within the family that authentic care can truly be received. This fusing of affect and obligation within the concept of 'care' is, as feminist critics have argued, a gendered strategy. For example, Dalley (1988) notes that, in Western cultures, just as the woman whose career allows her to pay for institutional care of an elderly relative is seen as uncaring, in that she is forsaking her 'natural' role as the one legitimate source of genuine care, so the woman who pays for her new baby to be reared by a childminder in order that she can pursue her career uninterrupted can also be seen to be withholding her capacity to lavish 'mother love' upon the new infant. Despite evidence from a variety of Western and non-Western sources, the notion of the mother as the primary source of authentic care retains a tenacious hold within political debate.

For example, Coote, Harman and Hewitt (1990) outline the responses to the changing family forms of Britain in the 1980s from the Left of the political spectrum. They argue that the Right is championing a 'traditional' family model of breadwinning father and caring mother, a model which is the 'mainstay of decent, civilized living: if it goes into decline there will be a general slide towards moral degeneracy and social disorder' (*Guardian*, 26 September 1990). The 'mother' or carer is thus central to familial ideology.

We can compare perceptions of this kind with Moyo's account (1973) of child-rearing practices in Matabeleland (part of what is now known as Zimbabwe). In this setting children are often cared

for by their aunt, or other female relative, rather than their
mother. Whilst their biological mother is engaged in agricultural
labour her eldest sister rears both her children and those of any
other sisters. Known as the 'big mother', the eldest sister offers
equal care to her own children and those of all her younger sisters.
Whilst 'mother love' is understood within Western society to be
closely tied to the biological link between mother and child,
Matabele thought perceives this kind of emotional tie as
selfishness. Women who feel a special affinity with their own
children will make poor 'big mothers', being unable to offer equal
care to all those in their charge.

A further example of non-biologically linked mothering is
evident in Schottman's account of fieldwork among the Baatombu
of northern Benin. Schottman makes reference to the mother-in-
law as the child's primary caretaker, alongside 'a good number of
willing backs to tie the baby on to' (1988: 10).

In contrast to the powerful image of authentic care and mothering as something to be found primarily within the family, the
demographic profile of the British population offers the
contrasting picture of many elderly people living alone. In 1990/91
people over pensionable age living alone made up 15 per cent of
all households (*Social Trends*, 1992). Even for those who do live
within, and *receive* care within the family, their care is often at the
cost of the family's well-being (Allan, 1985). Yet despite the
evident mismatch between 'care' as imagined and 'care' as lived,
the social expectation of 'family' care endures.

Whilst lack of clear-sighted planning and adequate funding may,
in part, account for the continued absence of ready alternatives to
current approaches to the care of dependent people, when explored
in depth, however, entrenched familial models of dependency can
be seen to provide major conceptual obstacles to the generation of
satisfactory alternatives. Dalley's historical and cross-cultural
appraisal of ways of caring for dependent people leads her to question the centrality of possessive individualism within Western
society (1988). She traces an alternative strand of collectivist
thought and action, evident in forms as diverse as the trade union
movement and the Women's Aid Federation. This strand, she
argues, is present as a counterpoint to individualism. It does not,
however, of itself, offer any radical challenge to patriarchy. Thus,
if the familial model of dependency is to give way to more collectively grounded models or metaphors, those models must challenge
not only the role of the family within an individualist approach to
social life, but also subordination of women to the autonomy of
men. Care of dependent people in the community, whether young,

old or disabled, creates, in carers, another category of dependents – that is, those who are unable to provide their own income. Among the carers of elderly and disabled elderly people, women outnumber men by one million. The requirement that women provide an unpaid, informal care service for dependent family members has been the focus of critiques from the late 1970s onwards (see Nissel and Bonnerjea, 1982; Finch and Groves, 1983; Ungerson, 1987; Dalley, 1988; Lewis and Meredith, 1988; Qureshi and Walker, 1989). Thus, it is through the labour of one category of dependants that another is being cared for.

This chapter has shown that not only do family ties provide the first call when dependency arises, but familial ideology provides an organizing principle which legitimates the practices which constitutes 'care'. Thus the family provides a root metaphor through which individualism can be reconciled with the reality of human deterioration and dependency. The hegemony of individualism, preserved through family-based metaphors, is evident in 'normalizing' policies which are seen as a desirable alternative to special care for dependent people. They rest upon the assumption that it is the dominant culture, as embodied by the family, which must be extended, thereby incorporating the 'abnormal' who otherwise lie, firmly excluded, at its periphery. As shown in the following chapters, increasing politicization among dependent people has led to the alternative demand that notions of normality be amended in such a way that dependency be included as one of its aspects.

Notes

1 Chapter 3 offers discussion of Fallon's account of children who care for sick or disabled parents (1990).

5

THE MAKING AND SUSTAINING OF MARGINALITY

Understanding childhood and ageing as social constructs, as cultural representations of the passage of time, has been a first step in challenging the metaphoric re-positioning of the members of particular social categories in contemporary Western societies. These representations, as shown, inform both the content and style of everyday interactions and yet it is not only at this level of intimate contact or interpersonal relationships that this ideology is brought into play. The conceptual marginalizing of certain categories of adult as 'child-like' is both sustained by and sustaining of wider processes of social, economic and political discrimination at the socio-structural level. Thus, 'being elderly', or indeed 'being disabled' are social roles which are learned. Rather than 'natural' or 'inevitable' aspects of personhood, they are taken on, voluntarily or involuntarily, by those who are old or impaired (Lonsdale, 1990). It is these practices which are examined in this chapter.

Whilst there is some evidence that the distressing consequences of infantilizing practices are now recognized by those involved directly in caring, the extent of this shift in perceptions and attitudes is less certain (Arluke and Levin, 1984; Dolinsky, 1984; Knowles, 1987). Moreover, though the language and imagery through which old age is understood and experienced may be changing (Woodward, 1988), it cannot be assumed that a more profound conceptual shift has occurred at the socio-structural level. It may, as yet, signal only a growing awareness. Thus, although Abramovitz (1991) highlights one specific group within society, social workers, and argues that in their practitioner role the language they use can have rapid implications for their actions and deeds, we shall consider here how certain structural features of contemporary Western industrial societies continue to present obstacles, rather than opportunities, for change. Examples are particularly evident in the spheres of work and leisure and it is these areas which are addressed in this chapter. It will be argued that the embeddedness of cultural attitudes within structural forms accounts for both their resistance to change and their persistence in shaping social encounters. Taking Britain as a case study, and once again drawing on a wide variety of ethnographic and personal accounts, this chapter shows how specific structural features of a contemporary Western industrial society shore up and are themselves shored up by the practices which constitute the interpersonal relationships between carer and cared for previously described.

However, the ways in which members of different social categories experience dependency, and the constraints which it imposes, vary considerably in socio-structural terms. Any account of the relationship between agency and structure must therefore proceed cautiously. Three important factors need to be considered.

First, within the broad conceptual category 'dependent people', children can be singled out. For them the consequences and implications of dependency are radically different from those faced by elderly or disabled people.[1] While children outgrow their dependency, elderly people may increasingly succumb to its advances and the associated stigma. When compared with the construction of adulthood as independent – standing on one's own two feet, cut loose from apron strings, fancy free – dependency on others during post-childhood years presents a radical contrast with this ideal. This can be the case both for elderly and disabled people.

Secondly, whilst there are many parallels in the social experiences and structural position of people who are dependent in some way, there is also unevenness in the way the classificatory process impinges on individual lives. Some people, for instance, manage to maintain their social and economic status, despite the actual or imminent onset of dependency. Indeed, they may find their social identities augmented rather than diminished, as they take on new roles as, for example, 'disabled athletes' or campaigners for pensioners' rights (see Chapter 6). In this respect, gender and social class may both play a decisive role in shaping the way in which structures of dependency constrain social experience. The reasons why the debilitating effects of age can sometimes be obviated, as well as accentuated, are therefore to be located in the structural patterning of status in Britain. This reflects Turner's observation of the persistence of 'ascriptive criteria in societies dominated by a formal doctrine of achievement and universalism' (1989: 594).

Thirdly, this cultural hegemony does not, of course, remain unchallenged. From tiny gestures of defiance and small acts of personal insurrection through to increasing politicization, elderly people, collectively and individually, often successfully resist and challenge this process of real and symbolic marginalization. Children and disabled people, too, find related forms through which to subvert the oppressive practices of adults. Discussion of the different ways in which this vicious circle has and may be broken are explored in more detail in the following chapter.

Despite this adversity, there remains, however, a clear pattern of parallels and convergences between the socio-economic positions of the young and elderly members of Western industrial societies. In noting these parallels it becomes possible to explore the socio-structural underpinnings of everyday interpersonal and professional practices such as infantilization and the more widespread metaphoric use of the category 'child'. In turn, these practices themselves may serve to legitimate and authenticate structural discriminations. Focusing on two spheres of life in contemporary British life – work and leisure – we will illustrate the shifting dynamics of this symbiotic relationship. Our aim is to show that the mode of thought which conceptually marginalizes many elderly people in their everyday interactions also finds a profound and disturbing resonance at a deep socio-structural level. Elderly people may have their access to social and economic resources restricted, their personal space made public and, like children, they may be denied effective participation in and membership of society. Striking parallels are to be found in the lives of many disabled people.

At issue, therefore, is a self-sustaining cultural and socio-structural system which gives shape to the experience of dependency in a Western industrial society such as Britain. It is encompassed by an ideology within which primarily independent adults wield effective social, economic and political power. Both young and old people are conceptually, and often practically, marginalized from central social processes and it is in sharing this position on society's boundaries that their status as metaphoric or real children is affirmed. Despite variation in the nature and extent of marginalization, there remain many recurring elements or motifs. In these is revealed the patterning of the structural marginalization of dependent people in contemporary British society.

Understanding marginality

To address these issues the body of anthropological literature concerned with ritual is particularly salient, for it is within ritual time and space that society's key metaphors take on a literal rather than figurative form. As Fernandez says, 'metaphors provide organizing images which ritual action puts into effect' (1977:

101).[2] A theoretical approach of this kind can, therefore, yield insights into those policies and practices through which metaphoric assertions about the nature of elderly people are made to take on literal substance.

Victor Turner's work on ritual symbolism and liminality (1974) develops Van Gennep's earlier account of rites of passage (1960 [1908]). In the light of the view that the experiences of childhood, old age and disability can often be an experience of liminality, it is this material which is now explored (Murphy et al., 1988). Van Gennep's tripartite model of a rite of passage suggested that change or movement occurs through shifts across boundaries which separate the everyday secular time and space of society's dominant structures from anti-structural or liminal time and space. Thus, for example, within rituals of initiation, neophytes will make a move out of their 'child-like' structural position – often expressed in their physical removal from the domestic space of the village – to the liminal world of 'nature' beyond. (See Richards's (1982) account of a girl's ritual of initiation, *Chisungu*, among the Bemba.) Kept in seclusion, separated from their former position within society's structure and made equal to one another, neophytes are exposed to the dominant metaphors of their society, now revealed in literal form. In this way they learn about structure during this period of anti-structure. Thus, while the liminal period will involve, for example, the simplification or levelling of dominant hierarchies and the inversion of customary rules, its focused intention is, ultimately, to reveal and explicate the dominant structures to which it stands in opposition. As a result of the creative processes which take place within liminal time and space, movement is established within ordinary time and space itself.

Alongside this notion of liminality as a context within which movement or change is created, can be set the concept of outsiderhood. Movement out of society's dominant structures places the neophyte betwixt and between society's structures and, for Turner, this experience is similar to that shared by outsiders such as pilgrims, mediums, priests or members of other sub-cultural groups such as hippies or New Age travellers (1974). They have all been either permanently or temporarily set apart. Marginals, by contrast, although sharing the experience of liminality, are 'simultaneously members . . . of two or more groups whose social definitions and cultural norms are distinct from, and often even opposed to, one another' (1974: 233). Marginal individuals use these groups in different ways: in one they seek unfettered emotional closeness (communitas), the other they use as a structural reference point. However, unlike ritual liminars, marginals have no 'cultural assurance of a final, stable resolution of their ambiguity' (Turner, 1974: 233).

This description of marginality fits well with the experiences of children and many elderly people. In contemporary British society, although distinctively different, their lives are none the less constructed in such a way that the dominant features of adulthood, from which they are both excluded, provide a continuous focus; Chapter 3, for example, showed how the body was a key site for the making of such comparisons.

Following Turner, it is in this time that is not a time, this liminal context, that root metaphors operate most powerfully, and move from being implicit and figurative to becoming explicit and literal. Turner's concept of marginality also allows us to see why it is that infantilizing practices seem so apt. Children, unlike those who are elderly, are assured their incorporation into adult society. They are unlike elderly people who are made to remain on the periphery of society's dominant structures, removed from its hierarchies and seemingly excused from its demands.

Moore and Myerhoff have noted that there is an inherent danger in presenting the implicit grounding of metaphoric thought for view in an open and deliberate fashion:

> beneath all rituals is an ultimate danger . . . the possibility that we will encounter ourselves making up our conceptions of the world, society, our very selves. We may slip in that fatal perspective of recognizing culture as our construct, arbitrary, conventional, invented by mortals. (1977: 18)

In that the made-up, arbitrary quality of metaphoric thought is susceptible to questioning in this way, the authenticity of meaning itself can become at risk. As a guard against this danger, then, the literal representation of society's root metaphors is often contained by the careful framing of ritual time and space: it is set apart, betwixt and between, controlled and contained by its own structures and rules, termed by Turner 'anti-structure'. In this way meaning, which might otherwise become contestable, is dramatized in carefully controlled ritual time and space. It is therefore unsurprising that figurative 'old girls' and 'old boys' become, as we have shown, *literally* infantilized in non-ordinary spaces, far removed from the familiar contexts of their adult lives: the nursing home, the geriatric hospital, the residential home. These spaces stand in a similar relationship to the mundane world of work and home life as that which links the sacred space of ritual practice with the secular world of everyday economic activity. But it is from this sacred, or non-ordinary space that a radical critique can emerge, for, as Turner noted, it is from their position on the interstices of structure, in some ways less bounded by its rules, that marginals have the opportunity to become its most radical critics. This process will be explored in the next chapter. Here, however, we map out the ways in which children and elderly people are effectively marginalized in social and economic terms. Through parallel illustrations we show that their experiences may be shared in a whole variety of ways by disabled people.

Life at work: to each according to their ability . . .

Definitions of work, as of leisure, are culturally specific and in addressing the first of two arenas of institutionalized marginalization – work – it is useful to follow Wallman's advice. In discussing 'work' in any culture, she argues that:

> we need not only ask what activities are called work and how their economic value is computed in that setting; we need also to know what forms of work are, in that setting, thought to be socially worthy and personally fulfilling. (1979: 2)

In taking up these questions we can begin to understand the way in which the cultural meanings of work in British society both sustain and are, in part, sustained by the exclusion of particular categories of people from particular spheres of work. The nature of 'work', and by association the nature of the 'workforce', is partly clarified as a result of boundaries which divide work from other activities and the worker from the schoolchild or the pensioner. Furthermore, the meanings which are attached to work can be shown to emanate from particular social groups or categories who occupy powerful positions in relation to that work. For example, Green, Hebron and Woodward (1990) have shown that conceptions of work and leisure have a gendered character. The definition of leisure as that which ensues once paid work is completed, represents an opposition which is intrinsic to men's work experience, but absent from women's less rigidly bounded experience of unpaid domestic work. In this chapter we shall show the way in which work in British society serves the interests of those currently in employment in that its associated meanings – to do with personhood and status (see Chapter 2) – are often manipulated to the disadvantage of those excluded from the adult workforce.

By unravelling these meanings it becomes apparent that definitions of 'work' in contemporary British society are ambiguous and that the distinction between 'work' and 'leisure' is often difficult to maintain. In certain contexts, for example, work has a 'leisure-like' aspect – the mother who takes her children swimming – whilst in others leisure may be hard work or be made to take on increasingly work-like characteristics – the DIY enthusiast, the dressmaker or the computer buff. This ambiguity finds other forms of expression. The misquote from Karl Marx's 'Critique of the Gotha Programme' (Marx, 1950 [1949]: 23) used as the heading for this section highlights another problematic relationship: the tension in contemporary British society between the competing moral and economic demands of the Welfare State and the labour market, between those who are seen as productive and those who are seen as not. The phrase 'to each according to their ability' exemplifies at one and the same time the ideology of a welfare system which gives to those who are not able, and the labour market which rewards those who are. Caught in the midst of these structural oppositions between work/leisure and work/benefits are many young and elderly people. Their ability to work may vary in relation to certain physical, temporal, spatial and moral constraints and it is this which both facilitates and prevents their access to particular forms of work and contributes to their social marginalization.

Contemporary Britain, like many Western industrial societies, can increasingly be described as a 'work society' (Kohli, 1988). This concept usefully evokes the way in which work, in Western industrial societies, shapes not only economic life but also cultural values. In the industrialized societies of the West, work does not simply provide the means of earning a living. It is a significant source of cultural meanings, shaping the structure of the individual's daily life and social encounters and providing a sense of self and social identity:

> the economy is a system that 'socializes' people by providing them with income and corresponding chances for consumption, but also by confronting them with systematic tasks and challenging their competence, by structuring their everyday routines, by integrating them into social relations – of co-operation as well as dependence and conflict – by locating them in the social world and shaping their identity. (Kohli, 1988: 370)

This cultural framing of work, as both a means of economic livelihood and of social and personal identity, has profound consequences for individuals who are not in employment. Not only does participation in work define who one is, in the way Kohli describes, but the economic rewards gained by working allow greater participation in 'the consumer society'. Here goods and taste may be used symbolically to make further statements about identity and social status (Bourdieu, 1984). It is therefore from both these sources that being unemployed in a Western industrial context gains its stigma.

Moreover, in the case of Britain, the recent domination of the 'market place mentality' has meant that access to and participation in work has assumed an increased importance as an index of social worth. Compare this with the persuasive power of the youth-initiated slogans of the 1960s such as, 'turn on, tune in, drop out'. The 'needy', for whose benefit the post-Second World War welfare reforms were primarily introduced, have increasingly had to compete for jobs alongside the 'well-off'. Whiteside (1991) notes the tension between the state's desire to save public money by integrating socially disadvantaged people into the labour market and the aim to improve efficient industrial performance. Statutory safeguards to protect the rights of women, disabled people and members of ethnic minorities can alienate employers, thereby losing their support for state training schemes.

In such an environment it is the resourceful, independent and striving individual – the hallmark of the successful competitor in the Thatcher era – who has prospered. The emergence of acro-nymic social identities – the YUPPY and the NIMBY – is consis-tent with an individualistic ethos, describing faceless individuals who serve as representatives of lifestyles gained through competi-tion rather than compassion. Would-be competitors, regardless of how determinedly they strive, are less likely to succeed, however, if they are members of a disadvantaged social category. For exam-ple, Whiteside (1991) shows that well-trained, qualified black people have fewer job opportunities than their white counterparts. White male unemployment between 1985 and 1987 averaged 11 per cent, whereas among Indians it was 15 per cent, among West Indians 24 per cent and among Pakistanis 28 per cent. The stress on competition in the 'work society' has meant that economic and personal success is largely achieved, therefore, on the bases of class, race, gender and able-bodiedness, social variables which make some more able to compete than others.

The paradoxical effect of such an ideology, intended to bring to an end dependence upon a 'nanny' state, is that those unable to participate competitively have become increasingly marginalized as dependent, and in many cases, infantilized. The rhetoric of competition has come to dominate the welfare ethos, displacing the earlier more democratic formulations of the relationship between the State and the individual which Beveridge envisaged (1942). Thus, the 'Victorian values' of self-sufficiency and rewards initiative have underpinned a process of systematically reducing state regulation of the labour market during the 1990s. Whiteside (1991) identifies a resulting 're-casualization' of employment, characterized by part-time, short-contract work. It comes as no surprise, given such a shift, that those who have become further marginalized as a result are those individuals whose 'ability' to work is already constrained: children and elderly people. The role of women as carers provides an interesting example of this marginalization. Finch and Groves (1983), for example, show that women have begun to recognize their position within society as a marginal one. Traditionally viewed as 'carers' – whether of children or of sick or elderly relatives – women's state provision of benefits has been limited and their work has gone unnoticed. Women's growing commitment to paid employment, however, represents a powerful challenge to social expectations of this kind.

Access to work

Whilst elderly people may be less dependent upon state benefits than other categories of dependent people, such as those who are disabled, members of all dependent categories may, none the less, experience parallel forms of discrimination with respect to access to work. Age discrimination, for example, marginalizes and excludes individuals from the world of work in an incremental fashion as they move through the life course, leaving elderly people with only very restricted access to work. Many of them encounter forced retirement prior to their statutory retirement ages. In Britain, for example, despite acute labour shortages in certain areas, a survey conducted by an employment agency in 1990 discovered that 'most employers felt that the only members of their staff over 50 should be the company chairman and the cleaner' and that almost 90 per cent of the employers surveyed regarded the under-35s as the 'most appropriate to meet their recruitment needs' (Sulaiman, 1990a). As individuals age, therefore, the conceptual links between work and identity may become increasingly problematic as employment opportunities begin to dwindle.

This is exacerbated by compulsory retirement at 65 for men and 60 for women. Introduced during the immediate post-war years, this set in motion the 'tradition of retirement for healthy men' (Harper, 1989: 13). In part, this was a response to the changes in working conditions; jobs traditionally done by older workers, such as light, rather than heavy work had disappeared. However, there was also 'no determined effort by industry to accommodate workers beyond the official pension age' (Harper, 1989: 12). Despite government support of re-training schemes, employers showed reluctance to employ older workers and 'the forties were clearly perceived as the age of transition from "young" to "old"' (1989: 11–12). Dex and Phillipson (1986) go further. They argue that attitudes to work in the later years of life are shaped by government employment strategies and the funding of policy-orientated research. Thus, the 1950s saw the emergence of industrial gerontology which addressed itself to the retention of older people within the workforce during a period when government was concerned about the imbalance between 'productive' and 'non-productive' members of society. By the mid-1960s, however, it had become apparent that a large workforce was not going to be needed and initiatives designed to promote a longer working life were rapidly brought to a halt. Whilst contemporaneous surveys revealed many men willing to exchange full-time for part-time work, this offer was rarely made available and older workers gradually withdrew from the labour market. The process has spiralled. Some 40 years later, the increasing trend to early retirement fosters and responds to a more entrenched ageist perception of the workforce. This lack of access to work may impose considerable financial hardship on elderly people, as can be seen in the account of an elderly couple who staged a raid on a building society to try to solve their desperate financial problems. Billed, humorously, as a 'Bonnie and Clyde' raid (*The Scotsman*, 25 May 1989), the account doubly marginalizes the elderly people. Through seemingly trivializing their attempt, however misguided, to accrue money, the report mockingly re-classifies the pensioners' marginal act of robbery.

The subtle process of marginalization, in terms of access to jobs, has clear parallels in the reluctance contemporarily shown by employers to make adjustments to accommodate disabled people. The requirement that job applicants must submit details of their age, gender, marital status, health and disabilities in writing, alongside their qualifications and experience, remains largely unquestioned. It is a testimony to the belief that recruitment strategies should quite legitimately take such aspects of the candidate's life into account. Whilst employers are reported to be continuing to ask married women questions about child care at interview, this practice has been officially outlawed by the Sex Discrimination Act of 1975 (Sulaiman, 1990b).

The perceived importance of youth and young/middle aged adulthood as the time of life when skills, fitness and aptitude are at their peak is highlighted, then, at the expense of the experience acquired through age. Most insidiously, where a woman's physical appearance contributes significantly to her employment opportunities in some segments of the labour market, an ageing appearance can begin to work against her. She becomes marginalized within the labour market. A recent report revealed that an airline company sacked a ticket agent for violating the company's rules for 'professional standards' which, for women, included wearing make-up. Her refusal to comply ended her employment (Maitland, 1991). Similarly, flight attendant Sherri Cappello was sacked by American Airlines after 25 years' service on the grounds that she had become 12 pounds overweight (Pennington, 1991).

At the opposite end of the life course age discrimination is also in evidence. Through their membership of an age class, children's access to work is restricted and, although theoretically in receipt of state benefit in Britain (Child Allowance), children themselves have no rights to direct access to this money. For many children, any income received is in the form of pocket money, allotted to them by adults, a situation which may persist until they leave the category 'child' and enter the world of work. Similarly, those who have grown old and then left the world of work may, on admission to residential care, be allotted the remaining portion of their state pension from the institution's matron in the form of pocket money (Hockey, 1990). Whilst for most, but not all children the basic necessities of life – food, shelter and clothing – are provided, (unlike elderly people who must finance these things for themselves), children's position as consumers parallels that of elderly people. Whilst those fit elderly people with occupational as well as state pensions may experience retirement as a time when they acquire freedom for themselves, for older, frail elderly people and those on a severely limited income, identity and selfhood may find a more limited form of expression. For both these categories of people – children and the elderly – the expression of self-identity through consumption may be restricted by a limited income. Hence tension is experienced in many families where children, who have no control over their own financial outgoings, none the less find their self-identity within peer groups to be at stake as the result of the effects of high pressure advertising for costly items such as training shoes.

Age discrimination also affects the opportunities open to children and elderly people to augment their incomes. As discussed earlier, nineteenth century legislation, introduced under a humanitarian banner, aimed to prevent the exploitation of children at work. The end result, however, has also been to lessen their access to work (Fyfe, 1989). There is an important distinction to be made here between labour and work: child labour is a subset of child work, an exploitative and damaging form. Child work, on the other hand, can 'be a positive experience and, in the best circumstances, children's work can prepare them for productive adult life' (Fyfe, 1989: 20–1). The legacy of nineteenth century reforms in Britain, however, has been to collapse this distinction and ironically to perpetuate some exploitative forms of child labour, whilst removing its positive dimensions. For example, legislation introduced through the Children and Young Persons' Act of 1933 limits the employment of children between 13 and 16 years of age, and also sets limits to the amount of work: 'no child may be employed before 7 a.m. or after 7 p.m. on any day, before the close of school, or for more than two hours on any day which he/she is required to attend school; for more than two hours on any Sunday, or to lift and carry or move anything so heavy as to be likely to cause injury' (Fyfe, 1989: 39–40). Work done outside these terms becomes, by definition, illegal and open to further and more exploitative conditions (see below). Hendrick, commenting on the exclusion of children from full-time paid work and the introduction of compulsory education, makes the following points:

> Children were removed from what has been called 'socially significant activity', with its 'major human values', which is essential 'for the development of a sense of individual worth' (Schnell, 1979: 10). Whatever the compensations, the school put these children into the servitude of a repressive innocence and ignorance. (1990: 47)

The obstacles which lie in the path of disabled people's access to work range from the subtleties of hidden prejudice, through to more overt forms of discrimination, to the practicalities of the working life itself. Lonsdale (1990) has recently documented these obstacles. In Britain only 35 per cent of men and 29 per cent of women with disabilities are in paid employment, compared with the figures for the general population of 78 per cent of men and 60 per cent of women. For those who do find employment, choice of work is often very restricted. Those who become, rather than being born disabled may also discover that, as Lonsdale argues, the onset of disability often leads to 'downward mobility and a drift into unemployment' (1990: 109). Rather than simply being a result of the gravity of an illness, this 'drift' reflects the attitudes and restrictive practices which hinder disabled people in their search for work.

The essentially practical problems of working can be the first barrier encountered by disabled people. Whilst their access to leisure facilities may have improved, recognition of access problems at work is less developed. As Tony Arber argues, unemployment could often be overcome through the simple provision of facilities for disabled people in the workplace. In his experience, however, there is a reluctance on the part of employers to make such changes, despite the availability of grants in Britain for this purpose:

> Any business can apply to do adaptations, to install a lift, or ramps or alter toilets, for example. The money is there from the government, it's controlled by local Job Centres through the Manpower Services Commission. But it's hardly ever touched, it's infuriating. (1991: 85)

Without such changes, job choice remains restricted. Had such practical problems been overcome in Arber's case, he would still have a job: 'I could have stayed at my job in a wheelchair. There was no reason why I couldn't, but because of my disability they sacked me' (1991: 85).

The apparent reluctance to enhance work opportunities for disabled people is not unrelated to the fact that in Britain 'good practice' remains a voluntary code rather than a legal requirement (Lonsdale, 1990). There is, for example, no equivalent in Britain of the anti-discrimination legislation introduced in 1988 in the United States under the banner of a civil rights issue. This state of affairs suggests that, in Britain, disabled people's employment is primarily conceptualized as a personal and not a socio-structural problem. As Lonsdale points out in her study, disabled women may be 'told that they cannot cope rather than being asked whether they can', which locates the problem 'within the woman with the disability, rather than in the environment in which they wish to work' (1990: 102). Using such distancing techniques to shift responsibility from social structure to human agent effectively prevents questioning of the status quo. It perpetuates the perspective that it is the individual, rather than society, that must change. More subtly, it bolsters the image of adulthood as a uniquely work-able condition, and not one which embraces the broader experiences of chronic illness or disability. As a result disabled people are increasingly marginalized from the world of work. A contributor to Campling (1981) describes this humiliating process as it occurred in a job interview: 'I actually felt like a freak. How many able bodied candidates are asked to explain how they would arrange their office furniture?' (1981: 78). For disabled women, the problem of employment may be further compounded by their gender. Despite sex discrimination legislation, women still find their access to jobs more restricted than men, their disability representing a double disadvantage (Lonsdale, 1990).

In addition to the obstacles already outlined, rigid working hours and restrictive legislation surrounding state benefits in Britain can act as other deterrents. Lonsdale points out that, unlike other countries, there is currently no provision of partial state benefits for those engaged in part-time work. Half-time work may not provide an economic wage with the result that many disabled people are deterred from seeking work at all.

Thus, restrictive state practices compound more practical obstacles to employment, with successive governments failing to legislate effectively on behalf of disabled people (Lonsdale, 1990). In this respect, the position of disabled people is considerably worse than that of elderly people. Although similarly in receipt of state benefit, in the form of a retirement pension, many elderly people may be less dependent upon it, having amassed savings through their working life or being in receipt of a pension from their former employer. However, even less well-off pensioners fare better in relation to the system of state benefits, their ceiling on earning being higher than that of disabled people before benefit is reduced (Lonsdale, 1990).

Types of work

The marginality and exclusion, the restrictions and controls of a socio-cultural nature encountered by young, elderly and disabled people shapes not only their access to work, but also the types of work they do and their working experiences. Thomas makes the following points:

> The similarities between the experiences of old age and/or disability are those of exclusion from the mainstream of life, a constriction of roles, limitations or opportunities and a progressive decline in self-directedness which gives way to a manner of life increasingly shaped by others. (1982: 90)

An attempt to retain the symbolic value of 'work' after retirement, as a means of maintaining their social identities may lie behind what Ekerdt (1986) describes as the 'busy' ethic common to the experience of many elderly people. Being 'busy' means that the leisure of retirement can take on some of the characteristics of work through which a person's previous identity was maintained. Ekerdt sees this positively, arguing that for many elderly people, being 'busy' may indeed soften the marginalizing experience which retirement can bring. However, in that it is but a pale reflection of the work ethic, it may also exacerbate rather than lessen their feelings of marginalization. It offers no challenge to the concept of a 'work' society and thus, effectively, helps sustain the dominance of 'work' as a primary source of social identity: 'the frequency of talk about being busy is an indication of the fragility and shallowness of the work ethic as a legitimating device for retirement' (Kohli, 1988: 382). In other words, 'being busy', although offered by elderly people themselves, may serve as a disguise for the marginalization which many feel when their participation in mainstream work is ended. In many ways, this concept of 'busyness' parallels the ideal of 'significant living without work' proposed for disabled people in the Warnock Report of 1978.[3]

Whilst not involved in full-time work, fit elderly people may therefore be engaging in work-like activities. Many of these lie on the fringes or at the interstices of the formal labour market. In this way, the kinds of jobs which elderly people do parallel those of disabled people. Often voluntary or low paid, much of this work is invisible, taking place informally in the domestic environment or outside mainstream labour markets. These contexts are also the places where children find work. In this way similar structural and ideological constraints help to sustain the marginal position of all three categories of dependent people in relation to the workforce.

Marginal work can take one of two forms. The first lies within the formal sector, but does not lend itself economically to full-time workers. In the case of children, this may involve doing milk or paper rounds, or babysitting; in the case of elderly people it may involve a night watchman's role, gardening or domestic cleaning. In each case, this kind of paid work is often temporally marginal to the 9-to-5 world of work, its economic rewards being insufficient to provide an even minimal wage. It represents an additional, rather than a main source of income. Low pay is, as we have seen, characteristic of much of the work done by dependent people and, in the case of children in particular, it is their willingness to work flexibly and for low pay which makes them attractive as workers. Agriculture, for example, provides a common source of work for children, but one which is often both illegal and exploitative. In a carrot-topping factory in East Anglia, investigated by a BBC television programme in 1985, it was found that children as young as nine worked an evening shift from 5 pm to 8 pm at a piece rate of 70p per hour. This was 16p below the minimum agricultural rate, which was at the time already thought to be set too low (reported in Fyfe, 1989). A recent survey of 1,700 school children found that 40 per cent of children between the ages of 11 and 16 were working in term time in jobs other than the usual ones such as babysitting. These ranged from newspaper rounds through to hotel and pub work, cleaning offices and street markets (Fyfe, 1989). Similarly the significance of elderly people's work, whether paid or unpaid, is also often disregarded. Paid work may be only a small part of 'being busy' with unpaid work forming the greater part of what fit elderly people do. Thane (1987) suggests that of the young elderly, those under 75, only about 5 per cent are in full-time employment and about 10 per cent are employed part-time. Much work-like activity is therefore taking place outside the economic system in the voluntary sector, a context where children and disabled people may also find a 'significant living without work'. Such work would include the care of grandchildren by grandparents, which enables many younger women to return to work, or charity work which increasingly involves either fund-raising or caring for those for whom the state no longer provides adequate support.

Disabled people within Western societies may similarly find work of only a very restricted kind, often unsuited to their ability and expressing subtle but far reaching prejudice: 'the expectations for girls in wheelchairs leaving school (unless they are intellectually high flyers) are set very low' (Campling, 1981: 79). Even for 'high flyers' it may be difficult (Sanders, 1991). Val Radford reflects on her experience:

> The real frustration for me has always been in employment. I'd like a job that satisfies me, where I feel as if I'm doing something worthwhile. Until I actually couldn't get jobs I applied for and wanted to do I didn't really think about not being able to see. (1991: 82)

The kind of work available for disabled people is characteristically located at the interstices of the economic structure. Effectively marginal work, it is often carried out within the home, or in sheltered workshops, a situation which both mirrors and exacerbates the social isolation that many disabled people may experience. It is often work which offers little satisfaction and training (Lonsdale, 1990). As Barnes notes:

> even when employment is offered it is often low-paid, demeaning work, and the match between abilities and occupations is frequently unbalanced. As well as unemployment many people with impairments have to contend with underemployment. (1990: 159)

A recent graduate with cerebral palsy echoes these feelings in a description of her own early work experience in a workshop: 'I had to do mundane jobs like counting squares and screwing up bits of newspaper into balls. Very stimulating' (*Times Higher Education Supplement*, 10 May 1991).

In institutional settings, employment opportunities may be worse still. Jones (1975) reveals that occupational therapy was envisaged in terms of literally occupying the patients, rather than training them for some occupation. Glueing paper bags and making trays, or 'all seated around tables with crayons' are some of the activities she describes. These infantile activities conceptually reinforced the other ways in which patients were treated as child-like by the staff, and were further marginalized as forms of 'work' by the methods of reward given to the patients: whilst the more able patients got 'pocket money', 'the severely subnormal got nothing but were provided with sweets in lieu' (1975: 28).

None the less, the domination of the ideology of 'work' – the devil finds work for idle hands – in an industrial society such as Britain means that those who are not in full-time employment must be found some kind of 'work' to do. Increasingly, this has come to be seen as not simply a way of passing time, but of finding rewarding and satisfying occupations. As Barnes notes, it is an idea mooted in the Warnock Report of 1978 through the introduction of the idea of 'significant living without work'. Whilst such a perspective is commendable, its implementation may be far from easy, given the socio-structural obstacles outlined above. For example, as Barnes (1990) comments, the suggestion in the Warnock Report that disabled people might take up voluntary work is decidedly unrealistic. Those capable of such activities would already be seeking employment in the open market.

However, such is the ethos of the work society that even mundane tasks may offer people with disabilities a release from the marginalization created by restrictive access to work. Deshen's study (1990) of disabled people in Tel Aviv, for example, describes how blind people are 'channelled into a very limited range of occupations' (1990: 269). Characterized by poor pay, this routine and undemanding work is often both alienating and frustrating. But the significance of work as a symbol of independence means that even such conditions of underemployment may be accepted by disabled people. In his study, Deshen shows how, through creatively restructuring their work in terms of its practices and meanings, blind employees managed to derive personal satisfaction and enhanced self-respect from their work, despite its menial aspect. A contributor to Campling (1981) outlines a similar predicament, after an attack of polio left her 80 per cent disabled: 'I did the only thing I could do lying down and that was to work as a telephone canvasser. The work was boring and after a long period of it, became soul destroying but I didn't care, I was so thrilled to be working at all' (1981: 108). The ethos of the labour market in a Western 'work' society thus shapes both the form and content of disabled people's employment opportunities. As Thomas argues, 'in a society dominated by the morality of the market place, the disabled would appear to be among the most vulnerable sections of the workforce' (1982: 180).

Throughout all the examples described, it has become apparent that young, elderly and disabled people are conceptually placed outside the labour force whilst, *at the same time*, making a very significant contribution to the wider economy. Being unpaid, their labour increasingly props up that economic system. For example, as Thane notes, many elderly people 'provide a wide range of formal and informal voluntary services. Often, indeed, the fit young elderly are the carers for very old parents, friends and neighbours or for younger sick and disabled people' (1987: 12–13).

The extent of this work remains unacknowledged and elderly people continue to be seen as a potential burden on the state rather than as a resource, their work being regarded primarily as of benefit to them as individuals (Thane, 1987). In that the kinds of work being described are often invisible, their contribution to the wider economy also remains unacknowledged. In her account of the lives of Traveller Gypsies, members of another marginal category, Okely (1983) reports their significant but unrecognized contribution to the scrap metal industry. Similarly, Rogers (1980) describes the invisibility of women's economic contributions in Third World countries when examined from the Western perspective which informed thinking at the United Nations during the 1970s. Women's unpaid seasonal agricultural work may not be detected by the researcher who visits only briefly. Similarly, Western measures such as 'man hours' may also be inappropriately applied to women's flexible working patterns, organized to incorporate the needs of children and elderly people. Again women's contributions remain invisible as a result.

The structural marginality of young, elderly and disabled people is thus reflected in the kinds of 'work' they do. Conceptually, their work is seen as 'marginal' in that it occupies a liminal position, halfway between the spheres of work and leisure. And it is this attribute which enables such work to be seen as beneficial for the person, rather than for society as a whole, individualizing their marginality. Just as disabled people are thought to need employment to make them 'feel useful', such work is said to allow elderly people to have 'a role in society' and to be given a 'chance to get out and about'. Children are similarly encouraged to undertake voluntary work in order to 'widen their horizons', 'think about others', 'learn to give'. A parallel can be seen here with the meaning of married women's incomes, often trivialized as personal 'pin money', rather than being recognized as an important contribution to the family budget (Martin and Roberts, 1984). Such opportunities for work are conceptualized as primarily 'good' for the individual rather than the world at large, paralleling the way in which the reasons for restricted access to mainstream work are also located within the person, that is, in their age or their disability.

Work and status

The primacy of the work ethic in Western industrialized societies means that in various ways, as we have shown, social status is conceptually tied to the ability to participate in the labour market (see Chapter 2). Elderly people, like children, are accorded low social status through their marginal involvement in the work society, whether that marginality is actual or imagined. In other cultures, where work and leisure do not form opposed categories, but rather can be situated along a continuum, this may not occur. For example, in mid-eighteenth century Britain industries were predominantly rural and job specialization was virtually non-existent (Quadagno, 1982). In this kind of environment, industrial and agricultural work was pursued with flexibility in accordance with the seasons, and leisure, in the form of religious holidays, was similarly fluid. Basham (1976) describes the life course of the traditional Hindu as one in which the Western polarization of work and leisure holds no sway. Instead a working life leads on to a yet more demanding life, but of a spiritual rather than a materially productive nature. By sacred law, men will leave the village and move into the forest when their hair turns white. There they subsist on gathered food or alms, seeking out suffering and hardship. Known as Vanaprastha, they devote themselves to the study of religious texts. For the dedicated a further stage awaits, where all material goods and shelter are abandoned and men become Sannyasin, or holy beggars.

Whilst age may prevent everyday participation in work activities, such as agriculture or cattle herding, in these traditional societies, there may not be an accompanying loss of status. For example, as Fortes noted amongst the Tallensi, even an old man who is blind or mentally incompetent and has effectively relinquished control of everyday affairs to his son is not a social outcast. Remaining as the head of the family and acting as an intermediary between them and the ancestors, such an old man would be told of events and his consent sought before plans could be enacted (reported by Foner, 1984). In such communities, even though elderly people may 'do' very little, they may 'still occupy supervisory positions and be respected for their expertise' (Foner, 1984: 105). Loss of social status does not necessarily accompany the end of active participation in work.

In addition to a changing level of participation, the onset of old age may bring with it a change in the nature of work in some cultures. For example, it may involve a move from status as agricultural worker or farmer to ritual specialist. It may also involve a change of spheres: from the primarily economic to the domestic sphere, as Lepowsky (1985) describes for the Vanatinai of south-east Papua New Guinea. Here, even if an old person is too infirm to engage in garden cultivation they will still be regarded as having an important contribution to make. This may involve looking after young children while adults are away in the fields, or tending fires to keep away evil spirits. In other cultures a move may be made in the opposite direction. Among the New Zealand Maoris, status and prestige increases rather than declines with old age. As men and women are relieved of their domestic responsibilities they become more active in public affairs (Sinclair, 1985). Indeed, contrary to expectations, the post-colonial era has witnessed an increase, rather than a decline in the activities of elderly Maoris. Older women in particular have become successful mediators between the two cultural traditions, for their knowledge of contemporary problems, gained through the experience of child-rearing in such a context, has enabled them to augment their social position during old age. Whilst the elderly, rural members of many non-Western societies continue to be incorporated into the working life of the family, in the manner described, their experiences are not shared by those living in urban settings within the same societies. With little state care or provision for elderly people, in these contexts old people may be increasingly marginalized like their Western counterparts (Fleming, 1990).

In a similar vein, both children and disabled people in other cultures may participate in 'work' alongside able-bodied adults, carrying out tasks appropriate to their abilities. In these examples, then, it is possible to see alternative approaches to childhood, old age and disability which are neither marginalizing nor alienating. However, the structural conditions of contemporary Western industrial societies, with the strict separation between work and leisure, actively excludes such possibilities.

A social life

Enshrined in the concept of 'busyness', introduced earlier, is the ethos of the labour market, so central to a Western work society. Indeed, although, as has been suggested, the spheres of work and leisure mutually define one another – leisure is a respite from work – in contemporary British society for example, 'work' remains the dominant conceptual category. For those who are marginal to the main labour force, however, maintaining this distinction may be difficult. Those who are not 'working' may not have earned their leisure and therefore leisure may become work-like. For women in full-time domestic care work their exclusion from paid work means that their right to leisure is not seen to be comparable with that of paid workers (Green et al., 1990). Their 'work' may extend into 24-hour child care responsibilities, which means that their 'leisure' activities are confined to the home. Often, then, 'leisure', such as watching television, becomes combined with the 'work' of ironing or knitting clothes for the family.

This conceptual confusion is aptly illustrated in another example. In her work on the transfer of mentally handicapped adults from long stay hospitals into community homes, Christine McCourt Perring describes how, although many residents did paid work at a day centre, the rate of pay was nominal, seen as pocket money rather than wages. Residents found the work boring and unrewarding, with many arguing, quite logically, that being of retirement age they should be entitled to retire like other people. This posed a problem for the managers of the home who believed that 'psychiatric patients if allowed to be inactive will relapse into symptoms such as hearing voices' and who, in organizational terms, need 'to have residents provided with structured activity during the day' (McCourt Perring, 1992: 321). Moreover, as we have shown, the logic of the conceptual system within which such work takes place admits no such possibility: not 'working' in terms of mainstream economic activity, how could they ever retire from it?

What this example reveals is the figurative nature of 'work' which is often allocated to mentally handicapped people. Literally, it is a lower status form of activity, something which 'keeps them busy' and avoids 'idle hands'. Thus, similarly, their leisure may also be differently valued. As McCourt Perring continues, it was ironic that, 'considering the homes' emphasis on rehabilitation, those residents who wished to pursue more independent activities were repeatedly reported as problems' and 'an unwillingness to fit with the official ideal was regarded as evidence of problems within the person' (1992: 321).

Given the conceptual interdependence of work and leisure, it is not surprising therefore to find that the economic marginality of young, elderly and disabled people is echoed in their social marginality. Just as in the case of work, so leisure too is often experienced in terms of discrimination, whether in the area of access or of opportunities. Hendricks and Cutler underline the importance of this in their suggestion that leisure, like work, might be 'identity-affirming' (1990: 85). Thus, if access to leisure and

kinds of leisure are restricted, then the marginalization imposed
through the work sphere will be exacerbated in the sphere of
leisure. Indeed both these forms of discrimination may be intensified, for often work itself provides access to social life and
friendships. Lonsdale suggests that one byproduct of the lack of
participation in work is precisely the social isolation which it brings
with it (1990).

In the case of age discrimination Britain, among European countries, is particularly noted for its adult-oriented public social life.
Whether in church or restaurant, the social organization of space
rests upon the assumption that children will be neither seen nor
heard. For example, although many public houses now admit
children to their premises, they are confined to 'family' rooms,
marginal spaces, separated off from the main bar and adult drinking areas. Often decorated and furnished in 'kids' style', with
children's menus provided, such rooms serve to reinforce, rather
than diminish children's exclusion from adult life. This can be
compared with the inclusion of children of all ages at adult meals
in restaurants in European countries such as France and Sweden. In
a similar way the eventual shift out of coupledom and into widowhood is overlooked within adult social life. As interloper or odd-
one-out at the dinner table or on the dance floor, the elderly widow
or widower find themselves at least unwelcome, if not excluded.

An age-based social life is the alternative offered to young and
elderly people. Tweedie (1990) humorously describes how, as
children, we are forced to mix

> with whatever other children our parents and our schools [produce].
> The selection [is] often random and often frightening . . . [in old age]
> we're dumped back into exactly the same situation. Come along, dear,
> meet Maude and Gladys and Janet and Hilda, you're all over eighty.
> And if we don't get on, we're difficult, a nuisance, selfish, withdrawn.

As in the case of voluntary work, such a social life is often framed
by an adult sense of 'worthy' activity or self-improvement. In
effect, it represents the extension of the work ethic into leisure for
those who are excluded. Adults, to maintain their self-respect and
identity, must be seen to be usefully occupied, as Dawson's study
of clubs for the elderly in Britain poignantly demonstrates (1991).
In one of many examples, a parallel with the example cited by
Jones (1975) earlier, Dawson shows how it is through the activities
of carers – usually able-bodied adults – that such a world view is
promulgated.

Dawson describes how two younger women came to assist at the
elderly people's clubs and, alarmed by what they considered to be

the old people's inefficiency and inactivity, took it upon themselves to rectify the situation:

> They planned to 'ease the strain' and 'inject a bit of life' into the place. They also explained, quoting from an Age Concern leaflet, that they hoped to make the participants aware of their potential value to the community. They could show them that their dying knowledge of handicraft skills could be passed on to younger members of the community, and thus used as an educational asset. They intended to make a start on this at the next day centre meeting. The following week they returned, armed with scissors, glue, old greetings cards, cotton wool and used toilet rolls . . . the elderly participants were going to make some pretty collages to decorate the hall in time for the visit of local school children. (1991: 10–11)

As Dawson describes, further 'infantile' pursuits followed, leading to progressive discontentment amongst the elderly people and to later acts of insurrection, resulting in the removal of the helpers.

For many elderly and young people, age discrimination therefore shapes their access to leisure, much as it does to work, and an age-based social life is common. With the exception of the Club Méditerranée – a safe annexe for the otherwise dangerous 'teen 'n twenties' sexuality – it is children and elderly people who are confined to 'play', alongside their peers. Children are sent off on pony trekking holidays, outward bound courses or educative play schemes. Elderly people are offered quasi-educational or gently sportive holidays through SAGA or the Holiday Fellowship. Cubs, Brownies, Woodcraft Folk, youth clubs, Darby and Joan clubs, luncheon clubs, over-sixties clubs and Evergreen clubs are all made available as places of social contact for the young and old. In each case, adults willingly accept *their* social exclusion. They have no need for such leisure provision.

Many of these activities are organized by adults, rather than by young or elderly people themselves. As we have seen, clubs for elderly people may be just that: not their clubs, but run for them. Similarly, youth clubs are run by youth leaders and may not allow children much participation or decision-making. As Bernard argues:

> It is high time that policy makers, planners and professionals began a proper dialogue with older people concerning their needs and wants for leisure as well as with other areas of their lives. It is no longer sufficient to go on adopting a 'we know best' attitude. If nothing else, the demographic changes alone mean that older people are part of mainstream life and can no longer be confined to the backwaters of late twentieth century society. (1991: 12)

The controlled and orderly nature of such leisure activities is perceived to be appropriate for young and elderly people. For the young, it gives them opportunities to socialize and to learn to mix in a controlled environment; for the elderly, clubs are seen to provide a solution to the social isolation presumed to accompany the ageing process and much leisure provision is, as Bernard notes, 'geared to their incompetencies and limitations rather than being designed to build on existing skills and abilities' (1991: 11). As Hazan writes, there is 'intensive effort spent on promoting recreational activities amongst the aged' directed to getting people together to pass their time away:

> There is also the assumption that elderly people seek social contact for its own sake and participate in occupational therapy, discussion groups and the like first and foremost for the companionship they may offer . . . and is probably the rudimentary motivation upon which day care for the elderly is devised. (1980: 32–3)

Such a view assumes 'that members would attend these establishments for the simple pleasure of meeting other people, regardless of other benefits which might be gained by such encounters, and with no other purpose in mind' (1980: 33). Contemporary child-rearing practices for the under-fives stress, in a comparable way, the importance of the social contact which playgroups can provide. In both cases, the age-based nature of clubs for the elderly and playgroups for the young ensures that they will mix and socialize as a group apart, and not part of the wider community.

'Disordered' activity is seen as inappropriate among both young and elderly people. Not only spatial restrictions, which serve to isolate both groups in 'clubs', but temporal limits may be used to control them. A newspaper report humorously entitled 'Pensioners are told rock around the clock must stop' exemplifies this process. It tells how, in an old people's home in Birmingham, pensioners 'simply won't act their age'. They were holding parties until well into the early hours of the morning and, that such was their disruptive influence, the social services stepped in to impose a time limit: a 10.30 pm finish was proposed as reasonable, with occasional late extensions to 11.30 pm (*Guardian*, 18 September 1987). The time limits imposed by parents to curb their children's activities serve to control the amount of time children may be absent from home, or stipulate the amount of sleep they have. That both these temporal limits are frequently a source of friction between parents and children indicates the powerful controlling function which they have. In residential homes, meal times, bath times and bed times are similarly regulated by staff and, at times, resisted by residents. Whilst the parents of very young children strive desperately to stop them getting up 'too early' in the morning, very elderly people may yearn to stay in bed, but are required by care staff to maintain 'adult' waking hours (Hockey, 1990). In both cases an adult control system is operating in opposition to the desires of the social category in question.

Having control over time and how time is spent is a key aspect of leisure in Western industrial societies. Leisure represents freedom from the 'rat race' or the '9-to-5' job, from clocking in and out, from shift work and piece work. But it is precisely this freedom to control the timing of one's leisure which is taken away from young, elderly and disabled people. Barnes, for example, reports a young disabled woman's complaint about a day centre which insisted she clock in and out at lunch time. She felt she was 'being treated like a little kid' (1990: 149). In a comparable example, Dawson tells of one man's experience of living with his family:

> he told me that he had had to cut out late night rendezvous with his mates in the local working men's clubs because the son and daughter-in-law with whom he lived worried about him being out after dark. (1991: 5)

Whilst age is the basis upon which access to social life is ordered and shaped for young and elderly people, disability too may serve as a parallel discriminatory barrier to leisure. Thus restrictions on 'access' may be in terms of physical impediments, as well as those more subtle limits to access engendered by prejudicial attitudes. For example, although it is now far more common for there to be toilets, ramps and lifts for disabled people in public buildings and leisure facilities, problems may still crop up. Barnes details the practical difficulties entailed by a trip to a shopping mall, newly built in 1983. In its design the mall made few concessions to the needs of disabled people:

> the only access from the car park, which was in the basement of the complex, for people unable to walk, was via the loading bay. Once inside, getting in and out of some of the shops and boutiques was almost impossible for individuals with mobility problems. Moreover, although the entire precinct spanned three storeys, there was only one lift which could hold only two wheelchair users and their helpers at once. Ambulatory shoppers, in contrast, were well catered for by escalators and staircases . . . The restaurants in this structure are all self-service and again inaccessible to individuals confined to a chair. All the menus are located high above the self-service counters and are virtually unreadable to anyone with visual problems or reading difficulties. (1990: 164)

Paralleling the way in which older and younger people may find their social lives constructed around similarities of age, disabled people may be forced to find a social life through the shared experience of disability.[4]

A theme which connects many of the issues discussed so far is the gloss placed over such social stratifications as class or gender, for example in spheres such as leisure. It is assumed that the commonality of age or disability will provide a shared point of contact. In this way, young, elderly and disabled people are further marginalized from society. In their 'liminal' position, such structural constraints as class, gender or race are deemed to be absent and yet, as ethnographic work reveals, it is precisely these differences which elderly or disabled people may cling to in order to preserve a social identity and sense of self which their experience of marginality is gradually eroding. For example, Okely (1990) reports hidden tensions within an old people's club in Northern France where elitist, middle class values were allowed to dominate among a clientele in part made up of retired farmers and smallholders. Culturally prestigious activities such as choral singing were pursued, angering those who, as a result, were excluded by virtue of their illiteracy. In a residential home in the north-east of England (Hockey, 1990), differences of social class similarly provoked tensions:

> Sissy Crowther, a middle class woman in her eighties, had come to Highfield House to try to be 'independent' and 'make her home' in the institution. Sharing a room with Ada Brown, a mentally handicapped, working class woman, Sissy remarked, 'Do you know, I pay eighty-six pounds a week to stay here. And I have to share a room with her!' Ada objected to Sissy's use of a heater, saying, 'Have you got that bloody heater on again!' Sissy said afterwards, 'Well, I'm not used to that sort of thing. Language like that. I don't know what my nephews and nieces would say if they knew. Well, I wouldn't tell them.'

Barnes, in another example, shows how fashion and youth culture were continually made use of by a group of young people attending a day centre for physically handicapped people in their attempts to assert their independence from its values. Unlike the very dependent members of the day centre who 'had obviously been "got ready" by someone else, they were clearly concerned about the way they looked and wore clothes and make-up similar to those worn by their able-bodied peers' (1990: 120).

What has been traced out through the examples presented in this chapter is, then, a sequence of structural constraints, each of which carries implications that result in the negative intermeshing of exclusions of all kinds. Thus the economic dependency created through compulsory schooling, compulsory retirement and inflexible working practice produces forms of social marginality or isolation which become recognized as 'social problems'. Difficulty is thus located within the agent rather than the structure. Whether in Scout camp, Darby and Joan club or geriatric hospital, those who find themselves excluded from forms of adult work and leisure are drawn into forms of institutionalized marginality. Not only their economic independence but also their personhood and self-identity comes under threat, as is shown in the final examples. As Keith argues:

> the fact that ethnographers are able to report roles for old people in many societies emphasizes by contrast a peculiar constraint on older members of some industrial societies: the 'roleless' role or the lack of clear social expectations – constraining or otherwise. (1980: 350)

In summary, this chapter has highlighted structural parallels in the way in which young, elderly and disabled people are positioned in Western societies, making comparisons with more fluid sets of arrangements which pattern the social and working lives of members of non-Western societies. A commonality of experience across all three social categories is both a reflection as well as a reinforcement of metaphoric strategies that blur the boundaries between dependent children and adults who are elderly or disabled. When explored in detail, however, a shared experience of marginality may take on different qualities or varying meanings depending upon whether that marginality is transitory, as in the case of children, whether other social identities are being submerged within an overarching marginality, or whether forms of resistance, collective or individual, can be mustered against the persistent undercutting of adulthood. The following chapter develops the third of these variations, the mustering of resistance, thereby revealing the negotiable nature of social power.

Notes

1 Chapter 4 offers discussion of the variety of meanings which the term 'dependency' can have.
2 Drawing on the example of the native Americans of the North Pacific coast, Fernandez refers to Boas's work on *potlatch* (1965 [1911]). Discussing this practice, the ritual consumption/destruction of material wealth, Boas refers to 'the use of metaphorical terms in poetry, which in rituals are taken literally', going on to suggest that the ritual of *potlatch* is 'closely related' to the metaphor 'devouring of wealth'.
3 Blau (1973) and Reichard et al. (1962) feature among the more strenuous critics of disengagement theory, which was developed by authors such as Havighurst (Havighurst and Albrecht, 1953) and Cumming (Cumming and Henry, 1961; Cumming, 1963). Disengagement theory describes a universal withdrawal of elderly people from active life within every society, and argues that this is an

adaptive or functional response to declining physical and mental abilities. Critics such as Blau and Reichard saw disengagement theory as an attempt to legitimate practices that systematically disempower elderly people. In response, they marshalled evidence of elderly people's 'busyness', thereby failing to acknowledge the descriptive value of disengagement theory as an account of the way in which many elderly people in the West do respond to retirement. They also failed to provide a critique of 'busyness' as a reflection of the dominant cultural values which have worked to disadvantage elderly people.

4 The existence of PHAB (Physically Handicapped and Able Bodied) clubs and day centres can underline the gulf between the social experiences of disabled and able-bodied people and, rather than dispelling discriminatory attitudes, such clubs may contribute to their persistence. By contrast, those groups for disabled people which are focused on a shared activity, such as sport, rather than simply the common experience of disability, represent a more positive facility. Like the clubs of the able-bodied – squash and tennis clubs – it is the activity which unites people rather than the body which excludes.

6

WEAKNESS AND POWER

The theme of power and marginality has been implicit in the preceding chapters. A view of adult power as something that rarely manifests itself as an overt process of oppression exerted by adults upon elderly and disabled people has been developed through arguing that, instead, the metaphor of the child is frequently and subtly used to mediate the relationship between the worlds of independent adulthood and dependency.

To what extent, however, is this abstract schema applicable to all those who are dependent? Are they equal in their vulnerability to adult power, or, as Chapter 5 indicated, is there variation in its effects? This chapter develops a perspective which allows us to ask whether some categories of very young or elderly people have ways either of exercising power themselves, or of resisting the imposition of unwelcome cultural and social constraints. Is the same true for disabled people? In answering these questions, this chapter explores power exercised and power resisted, from the perspective of the less powerful and indeed of the weak. Again, it is Britain and America which provide the sources of our examples.

Taking account of the diverse social identities of those whose individuality can become blurred within all-encompassing social categories such as 'kids', 'the disabled' or 'the elderly', this chapter develops discussion of the contradictory manifestation of dependency within a society powerfully orientated towards individualism (see Chapter 4). It shows how personhood is both threatened and defended as a result and in doing so therefore questions any simplistic notion of their disempowerment.

The power of the margins

Here, then, we highlight differences of gender, age, ethnicity and class which fracture the apparent uniformity of marginalized social categories such as children, elderly and disabled people. We also identify other, additional forms of differentiation which can divide marginalized people from one another through showing that some individuals, despite cultural and structural threats to their personhood, may draw on and mobilize one or more of three rather different sources of power, depending upon their social positioning. These sources of power can be distinguished as follows:

1 Alternative sources of wealth and/or social status, grounded in the social variables of class, gender, age or ethnicity.
2 Resistance to the imposition of category membership perceived as damaging to one's social identity.
3 Visible membership of a disadvantaged social category.

1 Alternative sources of social power

The first category embraces all those whose social class position, in the broad Weberian sense of income, occupation and lifestyle, is sufficiently elevated as to transcend the deprivations brought about as a result of ageing or disability. Here, elderly people and those who are dependent mobilize and capitalize on sources of power within the dominant adult world. Elderly people may endeavour to resist relinquishing their *past*, using its key symbolic aspects – such as gender or class – to retain vestiges of power in old age. These may be both literal and figurative, ranging from the Lord of the Manor who maintains his estates and power till death, to the middle class lady who, despite physical dependency, maintains a semblance of control over those who 'service' her as 'tradesmen', 'little men' or as 'carers'. Social class position, while in most cases failing to compensate entirely for the loss of status associated with ageing, none the less remains a viable alternative source of positive social identity which can be drawn upon, provided the physical manifestations of ageing remain relatively unobtrusive. With sufficient income, even these manifestations can be masked by private nursing at home, rather than visibility within an institution.

As well as the advantage conferred through social class, there is that made available through gender, as Evers (1981) describes. Despite advancing age, masculine identity remains resilient. Retirement, marked as it has been traditionally with ceremony and gift giving, validates the right of the man to leisure and relaxation, having successfully fulfilled his role as employee. Women, by contrast, find new meaning in the adage, 'a woman's work is never done'. Women's commitment to domestic work continues as long as independent living is sustained, their efficacy none the less diminishing as age advances. Signs of failed domesticity threaten a woman's social identity within the community; they also threaten her independence in that they may invite the intervention of medical or welfare professionals. Within residential care, gender differences make themselves felt in a similar fashion (Evers, 1981). For men, traditionally, the provision of domestic care by women is an entirely familiar experience – only the personnel are different. For women, however, the handing over of cooking, cleaning and washing to female staff can seriously undermine their social identity. Evers suggests that it is only upper class women who find it appropriate to accept care from other women.

Research within a residential home (Hockey, 1990) supports this point, revealing how the stigmatizing role of age may be tempered by gender and social class. Women from a middle or upper class background clearly found the receipt of services from care staff far less threatening than did those from a working class background. Working class women either found frequent fault with the quality of food or bedmaking, comparing it unfavourably with the way they would have done it, or else strove to express their gratitude. This expressed their wish to create a reciprocal relationship of some kind, rather than one in which they were rendered powerless through obligation (Mauss, 1966 [1925]). Fieldnotes describe the contrasting behaviour of one middle class resident:

> Mrs Crowther was lying in bed wearing some sort of frilly cap. She got me to arrange her bedside table and her bed. Somehow she transforms the bleakness of the home. Behaving like a 'lady' she renders me a lady's maid. When Brian, the porter/handyman, helped her go through her 'boxes' last week he immediately appeared to take on the role of valet.

Social class and gender here, thus, ameliorate or even transcend the disadvantages associated with old age in Western society. Sissy Crowther draws on her previous life's experience to ease her passage into the margins.

This situation has its converse in the forms of oppression which have been sustained throughout life, again grounded in differences of class, gender, ethnicity, disability and sexuality, which can make themselves felt even more keenly, once ageing ensues. Examples include the way in which ageing women's changed physical appearance disadvantages them in a way that men escape (Sontag, 1978). Similarly, the effects of disability are gendered. Disabled women often find themselves invisible in that their social, economic and sexual needs are overlooked, precisely because passivity and dependence are understood to be in some way 'natural' to women (Lonsdale, 1990). Berry's study of elderly West Indians highlights the effects of race and ethnicity on the experience of old age, drawing on interview material:

> The problem is they don't look on us as people, they look on us as black pensioners. They don't realize that we know we are black, and we are proud to be black. White people my age group is very selfish. They

don't think we should even have a bus pass. I hear black people complain about some of the white pensioners who think black people should not have the things that are provided for pensioners.

. . .

I didn't know about 'pensioners' until I came here . . . we don't call people old. We don't throw people on the scrap heap. (Berry, 1981, cited in Fennell et al., 1988: 125)

Similarly, with respect to class-based differences, Fennell et al. (1988) describe 'the absence of an "active concept of retirement" (Stearns, 1977)' among working class men and women. He cites Featherstone's work (1987) on the leisure-orientated lifestyle of middle class retired people, well placed to participate in 'an expanding consumer market and culture' by virtue of their hefty occupational pensions.

2 Resisting adult power

Among the second group of people who resist the imposition of undesired category membership are those who fabricate an identity which places them within the more dominant group. Here direct resistance is the most straightforward response to the imposition of negatively perceived category membership. It is, however, often the least successful.

Ethnographic accounts of English children's cultures (James, 1986, 1993), show the ways in which children resist the limiting nature of the category 'childhood' and how this resistance is quite literally manifested through 'acting up', through acting as if they were adults. In other words, it shows how children continually anticipate the numerical growth, predicated upon years passed, which will make them eligible for membership of the more powerful social category, 'adult'. In this sense, the passage of calendrical time can be experienced as a control system which defines them as members of a marginal category separated off as a group apart:

the standard question which adults ask of children is: what do you want to be when you are grown up? This questioning thus denies time present in the life of the child, focusing as it does on the interrelationship between time past and time future. (James and Prout, 1990a: 221)

Even little children, of three or four years old, see themselves as restricted by their lack of age and show an awareness of this implicit patterning of their lives:

In the last few weeks at nursery school, children talked of their move to 'big school' when they would themselves become 'big': a 'big boy' or a 'big girl'. Later, during their first weeks at primary school, they looked back on the time they had passed in the nursery as the time when they were at the 'little school' for little children. This was safe in the knowledge that this time had passed. As one boy put it: 'I'm big now, aren't I'. (James and Prout, 1990a: 233)

In this example is reflected the structural patterning of childhood through the institution of schooling which, as argued in Chapter 2, can be seen as integral to the progressive marginalization of Western children in social life. Therefore, although adults may look back on school days as the happiest days of their lives, children and young people who are passing through the experience of schooling may have a different perception. Often their experience is of being restricted and controlled for both time and space – to the extent that they are constructed by adults such as teachers and parents who shape the experiences of young people. Thus, the passage of calendrical time is experienced as a control system which defines them as members of a marginal social category, separated off as a group apart. For example, their lack of age may, for some children, become something to circumvent (James, 1986). Controlled and constrained through the adult ordering of time, children none the less discover forms of resistance. As James's ethnographic research among British school children reveals, older children when asked their age, will usually reply with an exactitude beyond the requirements of the question. They often give their age in years and months or fractions of years – as 15 and three-quarters or 12 years and seven months – for, implicit within the question, they perceive another: eligibility? Integral to the concept of being 'old enough' to perform certain activities, is the adult granting of access to particular social spaces. The question is never phrased as 'how young are you?'. The positive value placed by adults on maturity, upon being 'grown up' and hence socialized, negates children's perception of their own age. Life, for many of them, is the endurance of years until they are 'old enough'. Hence, as field material shows, they endeavour to maximize their age through arguing that they are 'nearly 15' or '16 next October'. Thus, the authenticity of Sue Townsend's humorous diary of a teenage boy is enhanced by the maximizing of it's 'author's' age in the title, *The Secret Diary of Adrian Mole, aged 13¾* (1983). When Adrian first meets his future girlfriend, Pandora, his diary entry reads, 'I might fall in love with her. It's time I fell in love, after all I am 13 years old' (1983: 17).

For children, the power of calendrical time to restrict their access to social space is a daily experience. They feel themselves marginalized through legal prohibitions on their activities based on the quantification of age. Age becomes something to circumvent and disguise. To short-circuit calendrical time through verbal mystification of numerical age is just one of the many strategies employed to gain an earlier entry to these forbidden zones.

Again, ethnographic research shows that, when asked their age, children may avoid using numbers. Without figures, definitive classifications cannot be placed upon them. They reply, instead, with standard formulae drawn from the verbal culture of childhood. 'I'm as young as my tongue but older than my teeth.' As one girl explained, 'you are born with your tongue but not with your teeth'. In this manner children detail their age correctly but elude the restrictions which a numerical answer might place upon them. Changes in category status, then, are understood by children in relation to time. The numerical magic which quantification of age works for the child reveals itself particularly at certain transitional points when activities such as drinking, smoking and sex finally become 'legal'.

Although children might have been drinking in 'safe' pubs and smoking cigarettes for some time before the ages of 18 and 16 respectively, reaching 'the age' signals eligibility to perform previously restricted activities in previously restricted spaces. Reaching 'the age' is a form of life course transition registering movement from a marginal to a more central social position. Examples of children's resistance represent subtle manipulations of adult control systems. In a youth club where fieldwork was carried out, children were forbidden to smoke under the age of 16. Those who were 'under–age' at 10 or 11 years circumvented this restriction by hanging out of the window to smoke or going outside the walls of the club. In being outside rather than inside the club, they argued, this adult rule could not be applied. Similarly, within the school 'Cancer Corner' and 'Lung Tree' were known to the children as places where they could smoke without being caught. Related forms of resistance can be found in children's linguistic strategies. Certain knowledge, particularly that pertaining to sexual matters, or the use of swear words, is considered to be inappropriate for children and to be 'adult' knowledge. Not surprisingly, it is precisely this kind of knowledge that children are keen to obtain as they resist the myth of childhood innocence: 11- and 12-year-old boys conspiratorially pooled knowledge they had managed to obtain, competing with each other with 'rude' foreign terms or smutty rhymes and jokes. These illustrations underline further that the infantilizing of elderly people is an adult myth of childhood against which children themselves are constantly fighting. 'Child' is a category from which many children wish to escape (Holt, 1975).

Conversely, resistance amongst children may take the form of *retreating* from adult status in defiance of adults' attempts to 'socialize' children. Young children of seven or eight years may 'infantilize' themselves linguistically, using the pronoun 'me' instead of 'I' ('me want', 'me can't'). Returning to the babytalk of early childhood may be a strategy used by children to thwart adults' claims that they are 'capable', in contexts where children do not wish to comply.

The child's flight from childhood is paralleled by the disabled or elderly person's desire to transcend the boundary which separates them from the able-bodied world. This is less successful, however. Morris (1991) provides the examples of the disabled person who feels pride in her able-bodied lover, or her able-bodied child, her inclusion in 'mainstream' schooling, or her job, proffering each one to an external, able-bodied world as tokens of her 'normality'. These are the examples cited in the media, held up for our admiration. But however successful this strategy might be, Morris (1991) criticizes it from a radical perspective. She sees it as a form of 'passing' (Goffman, 1968), in that the disabled person feigns the characteristics of a social category to which they do not belong. For Morris, resistance to the negatively perceived category 'disabled', in the form of refusal, is ultimately self-destructive in that it renders the reality of lost sight, hearing or mobility invisible. As in the case of some categories of elderly people, the disabled person who 'passes' as 'normal' never becomes a full member of 'normal' society. Thus, the elderly person who marries late in life – a normal act of adulthood – is held up by their peers as both unusual and, often, amusing (Dawson, 1991). In Morris's view an important aspect of the disempowering implications of the category 'disabled' is the felt need to deny the reality of one's physical or mental condition, thereby exacerbating rather than diminishing the powerlessness of disabled people through incomplete solidarity with one another.

Resistance in the form of refusal to comply with the categories of identity is a strategy which many elderly people also embrace. Again, it is rarely totally successful. Matthews's study (1979) of the social world of old women drew on participant observation at a senior citizen's centre in America, as well as interviews with elderly women. She describes the uncertainties of her informants' lives, in that they lacked a clear sense of identity. Whilst wishing to exclude themselves from the category 'elderly', they were none the less experiencing the vulnerability of old age in terms of a lack of control over their futures and a sense of the imminence of death. In response to this they had developed a range of strategies to enable them to 'pass' as members of the social category 'adult' and to preserve their 'adult' identity in an attempt to mask the reality of physical and social changes which had ensued as a result of time passing. Thus women avoided saying their age; they described their aged external appearance as misleading and stressed that they were unchanged on the inside; they avoided hectic or demanding situations which they could not manage without revealing their frailty; they avoided speaking their minds for fear of sounding old-fashioned; they rationalized their self doubts, dismissing their frailties as no different from those of younger people; they rationalized their isolation from their families in terms of their children's busy success; and they reciprocated gifts and service, avoiding any suspicion of one-way dependency.

MacDonald and Rich's account of women's experience of ageing and ageism highlights the invisibility of later life, an emphasis which is reflected in the title of their work, *Look Me in the Eye* (1984), Objects of the 'male gaze' when young (Mulvey, 1975), women progressively lose their passive power to attract the attention of members of the more powerful social category, 'adult men', as the years pass. In order to become visible, women must hide or deny those bodily attributes which render them invisible in the sense of being unworthy of male attention. What they offer in order to re-create a fictive social identity is a visual fabrication which masks their new, literal identity as 'elderly'. Rich argues that:

> Passing – except as a consciously political tactic for carefully limited purposes – is one of the most serious threats to selfhood. We attempt, of course, to avoid the oppressor's hateful distortion of our identity and the real menace of our survival of his hatred. But meanwhile, our true identity, never acted out, can lose its substance, its meaning, even for ourselves. Denial to the outside world and relief at its success ('Very few people think of me as old as I am. They don't. People can't tell how old I am') blurs into denial of self (I'm always surprised when I look down and see all that gray hair, because I don't feel gray headed). (MacDonald and Rich, 1982, cited in Morris, 1991: 36)

Research among elderly people living in residential care (Hockey, 1990) reveals that this is a strategy which is not limited to the 'young' elderly, those whose physical appearance might allow them some scope for 'passing' as someone still in their prime. Unambiguously 'old' individuals in their eighties may none the less continue to resist imposition of the category 'old' in speech and in action.

Sissy Crowther, for example, a widow in her eighties without children, had made a conscious decision to come into a residential home after an unsuccessful attempt to live with a nephew and his wife. Eight months later she felt she was deteriorating. Every day it got worse. Around her she witnessed elderly people who had experienced up to 10 or 11 years of frailty. Feeling she had little to look forward to she none the less asserted that she would have to make herself happy. Despite increasing mobility problems, she took on the role of visitor to frailer residents with whom she felt she had a shared class background. Minutes after asserting that she would have to make herself happy she appeared in the room of another resident, Elsie Hall, who was ill in bed. Fieldnotes described the following interaction:

> Elsie was in bed, curtains drawn, looking and feeling very unwell. Sissy came in to 'visit', and played the sensitive, caring, middle-class sick visitor role to perfection. It was an impressive effort on Sissy's part. Elsie Hall was very pleased to be visited and rose to the occasion with a great show of emotion and pained feebleness.

That Sissy's visit was something more than a mere 'dropping in' was borne out in the way other female residents took opportunities to assert themselves as 'carers', thereby distancing themselves from the role of 'cared for'. In this way they recreated a fictive 'adulthood', not in terms of their appearance, but rather, in terms of their actions. Carefully, residents avoided contact with others whose confusion or deterioration was particularly marked. Rather, they chose those whose frailty was sufficiently evident as to highlight their own, relative robustness, yet not so advanced as either to stigmatize their carer through association, or reveal the fitter resident's limitations as a carer.

Ethel Carr, a resident in her mid-eighties, recounted how a very confused resident, Alice Hepple, was calling for her continuously. Drawing on a familial metaphor, Ethel refused Alice's demands, saying: 'Alice's not one of mine! Gran Robson's a different case. I could adopt her. She's such a character.' And indeed Gran Robson was strong-minded and alert, if a little unsteady on her feet. Leading Gran from lounge to dining-room, or on walks in the grounds, Ethel was able to identify herself publicly as an able, kindly carer. In her fictive adulthood she was able to distance the literal dependency of her old age spent in the care of others (Hockey, 1990: 139–41).

These examples illustrate a relatively straightforward strategy of resistance, one which to varying extents grants the disadvantaged person a fragile and transitory membership of the more powerful social category 'able-bodied adult'. Wagnild and Young reveal how elderly women may also resist the loneliness and structural marginality of old age by reinterpreting their past lives in such a way as to challenge the negative stereotypes of old age: they quote a 91-year-old woman as saying:

> Old age seems not so bad when you have been through other sadnesses that are even greater. I wake up each morning and say, 'Well, another day!' I'm getting on in years and each day is an extra gift. I'm happy. I look around at some of the other old people and notice that I'm not doing too badly myself. (1990: 254)

Fieldwork amongst children in an English primary school revealed a parallel process of distancing. Six- and seven-year-old girls took great pleasure in describing how they 'cared for' and 'looked after' the little ones in the playground. Through positioning themselves as care-givers, rather than receivers of care, these girls elaborated their own 'bigness' in contrast to the 'littleness' of those but a year younger than themselves (James, 1993).

3 The power of the weak

The third category is the most complex and elaborate of the three. Whilst the first two strategies chart escapes of some kind from a disempowering form of categorization, the third demonstrates the power which can arise out of membership of a disadvantaged social category. However, it is important to be clear about the kinds of power being referred to. Turner's work on liminars addresses the nature of social power, making an important distinction between secular and sacred power. He notes, 'how often the term "sacred" may be translated as "set apart" or "on one side" in various societies' (Turner, 1974: 241), and, in drawing on Van Gennep's account of the central, transitional phase of rite of passage, the liminal period, Turner develops a theoretical understanding of the relationship between secular and sacred power. It is within the liminal phase of a rite of passage that Van Gennep, and later Turner, see forms of sacred power emerging through the experience of movement or change. For Turner, this power arises out of the juxtaposition of the central, transitional phase and the twin periods of separation and reintegration which provide its boundaries. He sees this relationship as oppositional. For example, he describes an opposition between the enduring rule-bound hierarchies of the familiar social world and the transitory unbounded nature of liminal time and space. As individuals enter into a rite of passage, whether in the transition from youth to adulthood, from sickness to health, or from one year's end to another's beginning, they submit to a temporary loss of their social power and position during its central phase. In temporarily setting aside secular power within sacred time and space they are then able to return to society empowered.

Turner argues that the relationship between the three phases of a rite of passage is not confined to a ritual context. Instead he identifies certain areas or roles within society as a whole which, in his view, are permanently 'sacred' or 'set apart'. Albeit of an enduring nature, they none the less display the 'sacred power' characteristic of the transitory, liminal phase of a rite of passage. They may be categories of experience such as holidays, leisure, political campaigns or higher education; social categories such as New Age travellers or football hooligans; or individuals such as Gandhi or Bob Geldof. Each of these examples displays the forms of power that Turner describes as transcendent, in that society's customary hierarchies are, in every case, being refused or subverted. None the less, each example, both in terms of its content and in terms of its actors, stands in a slightly different relationship to society's dominant order or structure. Turner identifies three forms which, in some way, reflect the characteristics of liminality, the central phase of a rite of passage. They are (a) marginality, (b) outsiderhood and (c) structural inferiority.

Marginality, the term often used to describe the social positioning of disabled or elderly people, in many ways resembles liminality. That is to say, the marginal individual is separated from his/her previous position within society, and experiences a loss of worldly power. This can be clearly seen in Morris's personal history of 'disability': 'by becoming paralysed I had become fundamentally different and set apart from the non-disabled world' (1991: 3). The reactions of those around her she describes as 'defence mechanisms' which 'all took the form of people separating themselves off from me' (1991: 2). This suggests, then, that the socially constructed separateness of disabled people might be understood in terms of the sacred and as possessing an inherent power. However, unlike the participant in a rite of passage (the liminar), the marginal individual remains betwixt and between social roles, 'simultaneously members . . . of two or more groups whose social definitions and cultural norms are distinct from, and often even opposed to, one another' (Turner, 1974: 233). The material which follows shows older adults discovering themselves betwixt and between the stable, powerful world of adulthood and the shifting, vulnerability of old age.

Turner makes a distinction between the marginal's membership of more than one group and the outsider's exclusion from any or all structural arrangements. He also contrasts the outsider's position with that of the structurally inferior individual, 'the outcast, the unskilled worker, the harijan, and the poor' (1974: 234). In some instances, age or impairment can lead to the severance of all ties between the individual and society's dominant structures. As a result, the individual may choose to exploit this situation, feeling that there is nothing further to lose by indulging in 'anti-social' behaviour. To the list of the structurally inferior might be added the category 'child'. For our purposes these are useful distinctions.

Thus, whilst the members of these three distinctive social categories stand in a different relationship to society's dominant structures, each, in their ambiguity, their exclusion or their inferiority has attributes of the liminal or transitional phase of a rite of passage. They therefore might be considered to have potential access to power associated with the sacred, the set apart or the weak.

Using this theoretical perspective we go on to explore the exercise of power by those excluded from the social power intrinsic to adulthood. In Turner's view, marginal individuals are often those who provide a critique of society, particularly of its dominant relations of power. Among outsiders, Turner identifies groups that stand on the periphery, yet represent sources of mystical, unfathomable or disruptive power from the perspective of those at the centre. In many ways these groups resemble the structurally inferior, who also represent alternative forms of power, such as the mystical or the affectional. The structurally inferior are 'the model of an undifferentiated whole whose units are total human beings' (1974: 234). Theirs is a powerful role by virtue of its symbolizing capacity, a role into which children often find themselves placed (see Chapter 2; Hendrick, 1990). In that the structurally inferior are not pinned within the ranks and hierarchies of the powerful, their attributes remain open to interpretation, potentially manipulable by those who find themselves in this role.[1]

In summary, Turner offers a fruitful account of forms of power which might be described as sacred and which can certainly be seen as the potential property of those whom society sets apart, either temporarily or permanently. Within this diverse set of responses to society's dominant order, two key strands can be identified. These are the capacity to offer a critique of the dominant order, and the capacity to confront society's adult members with forms of ultimate knowledge, in relation, for example, to the limits of life, of human ability and meaning itself. Turner's ideas and his development of Van Gennep's work have been influential in anthropological analyses. Here we add to this growing body of literature about marginality.

First, we can consider the varying forms through which critiques of the dominant order manifest themselves. Morris (1991) argues it is only when disabled people acknowledge their difference and acknowledge each other in their difference, that the beginnings of solidarity become possible. The same could be said of elderly people and children. Power derives from asserting their position on the margins, a position from which to challenge the negative stereotypes through which they are perceived (see Chapters 1 and 3). Morris describes her anger when receiving praise for the way she lives with her disability, arguing that such praise is patronizing and that, moreover, it is grounded in the belief that her physically paralysed body is tragically inferior to 'normal' able bodies. Thus she is being praised for heroically making the best of what is seen as a potentially worthless life. Thomas (1982) similarly identifies what he calls 'super heroes', those who are applauded for being 'super' human in their achievement – for example, Douglas Bader and Helen Keller. By contrast, those, like Morris, who insist on being seen as *differently* abled rather than disabled, point out, in their radical critique, that *all* human beings have limits to their abilities. Thus they celebrate that difference. Clearly this response to being categorized as disabled is one that draws on the power of being set apart, indeed the power to shock. When politically active disabled people demonstrate outside television studios against charity 'telethons' the effect is powerfully dramatic, challenging the value society places upon giving and upon gratefully receiving (Eayrs and Ellis, 1990). Morris describes her feelings:

> Being part of a group of obviously disabled people shouting our anger across the road at those who think all that they are doing is being kind to us, is a unique experience. Most importantly, it feels very powerful, much more powerful than I ever felt on a trade union, Labour Party or women's movement march back in the days when I could walk. (1991: 190)

Chris Davies, who describes himself as a 'disabled journalist', similarly draws on both his professional role and his self-acknowledged disability to reveal to society's members their disabling attitudes and behaviours. In his foreword to *What the Papers Say and Don't Say about Disability* (Smith and Jordan, 1991), he points up the role of the press in reinforcing these attitudes. He argues for the recruitment of disabled journalists to write, in clearly identifiable sections of newspapers, on disability issues. As such, his recommended strategy would make visible the critique's source, namely disabled people themselves.

The politicizing which is taking place among disabled people finds parallels among elderly people. In America the 29 million members of the American Association of Retired People represent a powerful lobby, with its own mail-order drugs company and its own television programme, *Modern Maturity*. Since 1987 it has been illegal in America for private companies to set a compulsory retirement age (Mardell, 1988: 18). The Association's campaign now extends to Britain, seeking to 'put an end to the use of age restrictions in job advertisements. In France, Canada and America such discrimination is banned by law' (Rose, cited in Sulaiman, 1990a). Similarly, the retired people who produce the newsletter *British Pensioner*, rather than 'passing' as 'young at heart', boldly include within its headline their goal of 'uniting pensioners throughout Great Britain in the cause of a dignified retirement'. Their campaigning role is evident in the winter issue of 1991 which confronts the reader with the question 'HOW MANY WILL DIE THIS TIME?' in heavy black type, boxed within equally heavy black lines. Inside are listed the deaths from cold among elderly people over the past 25 years: 3,500 pensioners died of cold in two weeks in February 1991. Like those campaigning around disability, the British Pensioners and Trade Union Action Association demand equal rights and not charity. At the end of 1991 they drew up a charter which demanded improvements in pension, health, heating, travel, housing and community service provision for pensioners. The charter was to be presented to the prime minister, together with a petition.

Elderly people, too, may, like disabled people, reject the primacy of the body/mind split in defining their personhood. Members of the University of the Third Age offer a vigorous challenge to allegations that age, of itself, is an indication of declining intellect. Established in 1982, the University of the Third Age had developed its membership to 14,000 by 1990. In its internal structures it adheres to many of the features seen by Turner to characterize liminality. For example, study groups set their own agendas on the basis of common interests, working collectively and in a non-hierarchical way.

In all these examples, the groups who are offering a challenge or critique to society are clearly asserting membership of a negatively perceived category and demanding that both the perception and the treatment of members of that category be altered. They can be described as marginals in that they find themselves betwixt and between full membership of the category 'adult' and confinement within a peripheral social category which confers a child-like status upon its members. Their critique of the oppressive attitudes and policies of the dominant adult order emanates from their position as oppressed, and is coupled with the demand that they too be seen as full adults and share the same rights.

Alongside these critiques, which draw power from unequivocal self-assertion, can be placed more subtle forms of critique, also from those who find themselves in a marginal position in relation to society. Field material gathered among elderly people living in residential care indicates ways in which those whose adulthood has been called into question, who find themselves subject to a range of infantilizing practices, are able to make powerful, critical statements by manipulating the metaphors through which they are being positioned (Hockey, 1990).

Very elderly people, positioned in a twilight marginal zone may be those who, free from structural constraints, can offer a critique of dominant social forms. Despite physical dependency, from this position, elderly people can and often do provide potent and perceptive social comment. In this sense they manage to retain both dignity and control of the self in the face of the process of infantilization. The following words from a male resident ironically register his physical dependency: 'Well, we are but little children, frail and helpless all . . .' Having been dropped on to his chair by care staff after his bath he complained about their carelessness. He acknowledges his own dependency through pointed reference to his now child-like status. Other residents were more obvious in their resistance. They found ways to both subvert and exploit the second childhood imposed upon them and to adjust the balance of power.

For example, one elderly woman, who had been well educated and had driven ambulances during the First World War, found herself confined behind bed bars. She was a poor sleeper, confused and unable to walk unsupported. Being tucked up in preparation for another night's fitful sleep, she was urged by the Matron to settle down. This bedtime ritual was ended with a blown kiss from the Matron as she left the room. Though physically constrained and slow to speak, the resident was able to express her feelings of resentment at this childish gesture by offering a stuck-out tongue in exchange. Using a 'child's' response to her infantilized position, she offered symbolic resistance in the way she challenged the imposition of metaphors of childhood. More passive, but none the less effective, were those residents who were able to turn their 'child-like' dependency on care staff to their own advantage. A slumped body and a deaf ear could be put to powerful effect when resisting the repeated demands of busy staff endeavouring to assemble the entire company in the dining-room for their thrice-daily meals. Manipulating the temporal order by refusing to 'hurry' upset the regimented flow of work within the home. On another occasion, a new and very overweight resident demanded without success to be given a wheelchair. When staff made her stand up in the corridor she slid down the wall, two or more care assistants being required to return her to her feet. When they put her commode on the other side of the room to make her walk across to it she infuriated them by urinating in her coffee mug. Another scarcely mobile woman invariably set off on her long journey to the toilets whenever the lunch bell was rung, thus disrupting the ordered flow of lunch-time routine. Endeavouring to circumvent her late arrival in the dining-room, a care aide asked her some 15 minutes before lunch if she needed the toilet. Managing not to hear the question until it had been shouted repeatedly, the resident held up her hand and replied: 'Please teacher. I don't. Not yet.' By dramatizing the adult-to-child relationship set up by the care aide she revealed its inappropriateness. She thus, effectively, asserted her adult right to choose when *she* wanted to go to the toilet.

The pervasive cultural strategy of infantilization was therefore being resisted by residents in a variety of ways. In taking on the child-like characteristics which were imputed to them, residents were able, like children, to 'disobey' the demands of younger adults, and indeed to cause child-like scenes of chaos or conflict. Thus some women assumed tiny girlish voices to suggest to staff that they might be unwell and should be allowed to lie in bed. Others resorted freely and rapidly to verbal and physical violence in conflicts with other residents. As well as name-calling or explicit rebuffs to unwelcome residents who dared to venture into one of the lounges – 'we're not having her here. She doesn't belong here' – there was surreptitious kicking under the dining table and impatient banging on toilet doors with walking sticks.

That the effect upon staff is powerful is evidenced in the following extract from fieldnotes. It demonstrates how a participant observer role allowed the researcher to be drawn into a parent-child relationship by residents. It was a role which left her powerless and exasperated and which made her unequivocally aware of the oppressive nature of the system she was participating in:

A care assistant asked me to strip beds downstairs before breakfast. Ethel Carr was sitting on her bed and when I said I'd come to strip it, she replied, 'You never get a minute's peace in this place. You can't sit down for five minutes before breakfast. And they start clearing tables before you've finished your meal!' Nellie, another resident, was shouting and I said I'd be back later to strip Ethel's bed. I put my head round Nellie's door and watched her silently as she sat, head back, eyes closed, face screwed up, shouting, 'Jan! Jan! Jan! [a care assistant]. I went in and Nellie said she wanted a paper – I shouted in her ear – she'd get her paper after breakfast. She continued to demand a paper, agitatedly, calming briefly when I rubbed her arm. However, the shouting for a paper was repeated and the care assistant and I went in and out over and over again.

I went into Mabel Johnson's room where Eileen Bavister, Mary Brown and Ethel Carr [residents] were gathered, chatting. Was I Jennifer, Jenny or Jen, they asked. Eileen began calling me 'Ginny', cackling at her joke. Mabel groaned to herself about Eileen. As I left the room Eileen continued to call me Ginny, almost tauntingly, and slapped me forcefully on the shoulder as I passed.

Over breakfast residents complained, as if insulted, that they hadn't got their grapefruit [the home had run out], their tea-spoons, and so on. Eileen shouted for me – she wanted more cornflakes. Suddenly, with a vengeance, I shared the staff's exasperation with the residents. I felt really harassed by them, all being so difficult while I was exhausting myself looking after them. It made me think about the way the home breeds childishness and selfishness in the residents. Stripped of all responsibility and privacy, they become assertive in a child-like, grasping fashion. (Hockey, unpublished data)

One final episode from this particular field setting reveals the intersubjective nature of power within the home. Not only was it exercised subtly, but also seldom in a unidirectional fashion:

Winnie Elliott, a resident of Highfield House, had been in sick bay for more than four months, categorized by staff as 'frail', 'likely to pop off soon'. When Jan, a care assistant of about twenty, entered the room Winnie said, 'I'm fed up'. 'Well I am too, Winnie,' replied Jan. 'Well, you took the job on, I didn't,' answered Winnie. Jan held a clenched fist to Winnie's face and Winnie laughed. (Hockey, 1990: 179)

This fleeting exchange of joke and counter-joke exemplifies a gentle wrangling over power which characterizes much staff–resident interaction at Highfield House. Winnie is bedbound and alone, excluded even from the marginal world of a residential home. She is fed up. Jan is a member of the more powerful institutional category, 'staff'. Whilst paid to maintain the well-being of those in her care, she can do little to alleviate Winnie's boredom, other than claiming to share it. Thus she figuratively sets herself up as Winnie's equal, which in reality she is not. Yet time may eventually collapse the structural distance between them, Jan too becoming dependent upon others. Winnie accuses Jan of bringing her gloom upon herself by taking on the job, yet Winnie is utterly dependent upon Jan's labour. And Winnie also suffers at Jan's hands, in that they confine her, 'for her own good', behind bed bars. Finally Jan, powerless to alleviate Winnie's suffering, offers a clenched fist, mockingly asserting a physical power which she has and yet cannot use, in the face of Winnie's joking rudeness. And

Winnie laughs in the face of this mock aggression, just as the dependent child laughs when tickled by its more powerful mother. In the end nothing has changed. They have played with the forms which constitute their situation and their relationship, but the episode has amended neither the constraints of Winnie's physical helplessness, nor their shared experiences of the institution's limitations. Winnie has claimed a little attention and Jan has made her laugh. Their mutual rudeness expresses the intimacy of their complex, extended relationship. Power cannot be said to lie exclusively with one or the other of these two women (Hockey, 1990).

As this incident reveals, elderly and disabled people are extremely vulnerable to the power associated with adults. It is also evident, however, that the exercise of adult power often operates in a complex, negotiated fashion. Age and impairment can therefore best be understood as sites of struggle rather than scenes of defeat. By approaching questions of power from this perspective it becomes possible not only to develop a more accurate and subtle appreciation of its mode of operating, but also to consider ways in which the balance of power is, or might be, amenable to change.

Sites of struggle

Whilst adult power is often expressed through metaphoric strategies which position elderly or disabled people as children, they, in turn, as ethnographic material reveals, can act out that re-positioning in ways that not only reveal its humiliating absurdity, but also directly undermine the power of the adult as metaphoric 'parent'. These skills and devices are, as children themselves are aware, effective within power struggles with the adult world. Refusing to walk while out shopping and sitting on the pavement is a common tactic used by little children to disrupt the flow of adult activity. The power of bodily wastes to mess up adult order is similarly recognized and wielded by angry young children who urinate on the carpet and choose to need the toilet as soon as a long car journey is under way. Elderly people, being treated by adults as children, thus empower themselves in a child-like manner in their rejection of the process of infantilization.

Representations of children and elderly people in the media and in popular literature, when examined carefully, show similar strategies in operation. There are the examples of children who are positioned in adult roles – for example, Dougie Hawser in the American television series, the boy takes on a crusading role as a member of the medical profession in early adolescence; in the past the Famous Five, Enid Blyton's group of children, played a similar role in defying adult wrong-doers of every kind. There are also examples of elderly people who are positioned as 'adults' in the sense that they display adult behaviours such as active sexuality – *The Golden Girls* and *Last of the Summer Wine* offer examples. The characters within each of these forms of popular literature or media stand as marginals, betwixt and between adulthood and childhood or old age. Among the forms that feature 'adult' children, a critique of adulthood is offered in that what is represented is the child as *hero*. As noted earlier, those who are structurally inferior, such as children, are often seen to embody highly valued, transcendent human qualities such as purity, innocence or wisdom. Popular representations of children often place them alongside adults in a way that highlights the qualities of corruptibility or short-sightedness within the adults. Children are there to save the day, a dramatic device which is all the more effective in that it counters everyday wisdom which assumes the mischievousness and foolhardiness of children. What lends authenticity to television series such as *Dougie Hawser, MD*, or book series such as the *Famous Five* is that they confirm adult fears about their own natures and those of other adults. By contrast, a television series such as *Grange Hill*, set in a modern British comprehensive school, provokes fearful reaction in adults too, as children powerfully debunk the 'innocence' of childhood and the myth of happiness. *Grange Hill* reveals children as people with 'adult' problems.

Those television series which feature elderly people such as *The Golden Girls* and *Last of the Summer Wine* also create their dramatic effect by countering assumptions, in these instances the assumption that old age is a time of asexual prudence. By transgressing the boundaries of their social category through overt sexual interest and activity a critique of adult assumptions is offered. Among the cast of the BBC series *Last of the Summer Wine*, discussed in Chapter 3, characters who are marginal, in that they are elderly, are brought together with a central character who takes on the role of outsider. With a storyline which revolves almost entirely around elderly people living in rural Yorkshire, the series finds its humour in the contrast between its central character, Compo, an elderly man who flouts all social convention, and his 'respectable' elderly peers. Compo enjoys a powerful, central position as an outsider, an old man who exploits the child-like status imposed upon him. Bold, dirty and dishevelled, Compo subverts the metaphoric constraints of child-like old age and displays an adult interest in any possible sexual opportunities. Running riot, he provides humorous comparison with his marginal peers who seek to maintain a fading 'adult' sense of dignity which fixes them, passively, on the fringes of the adult world.

Thus far marginals, those individuals who find themselves betwixt and between two social categories, have been the main focus in exploring forms of power which lie at society's peripheries. In watching *Last of the Summer Wine*, however, we experience the difference between marginality and outsiderhood. Outsiderhood is paradoxical. It encompasses both the all-powerful and the downtrodden and lies at the end of the continuum which exists between outsiderhood and marginality. Thus, when we speak of the 'marginalizing' of children, elderly or disabled people we are describing a process which may realize itself only gradually, but may also eventually lead to unequivocal outsiderhood. For example, among the category 'elderly', there are newly retired people who, whilst marginalized in that they are dispossessed of the power associated with their previous adult role of 'employee', none the less, in many respects, retain membership of the category 'adult', albeit from a less powerful position. Similarly, in Chapter 1 the term 'infantilization' describes a continuum of social practices which range from the mild but insidious, 'Let me help you with that, dear' as the older person manages their shopping, through to the childish pastimes and spoon-feeding common in residential homes. Outsiderhood itself can stem from a variety of sources, with the result that there are those whose outsiderhood is positively perceived, and those whose outsiderhood is negatively perceived. In the first category can be placed leaders of the church and the state, or artists, musicians and writers. For them the limitations imposed through ageing or impairment are waived. Their pronouncements are heeded in that they emanate from sources of power above and beyond the everyday dictates of those adults whose power derives from society's dominant hierarchies – minor government officials, middle management or dominant members of the immediate family. For example, Jane Bown's photographic record of 90-year-olds sets out to give 'the lie to the notion that you're past it at 90' (Gwyther, 1990). However, six out of the seven portraits are of individuals whose former social role carried some kind of prestigious association, in many cases grounded in social class position. Bown's selection encompasses the oldest surviving member of the Bloomsbury group, whose memoirs had recently been published; a former electrician at a famous public school; the retired principal of Salisbury Theological College; an actor ('I'm certainly not retired. An actor never retires'); a former actress and singer who spends four hours a day writing children's stories; and an actress who still performs occasionally. Whilst focused on their age, their media prominence quite clearly derives from factors additional to their being in their nineties. In the second category of outsiders can be placed tramps and down-and-outs, 'disruptive' geriatric patients and frail, confused or impaired residents of institutions. They too occupy structural positions which lie outside society's internal hierarchies. Lying 'beyond the pale', rather than '*above* and beyond', such individuals may experience none of the privileges of social membership. Equally, however, they may discover the freedom to disrupt, subvert and threaten existing structures.

In her poem *Warning*, Jenny Joseph (1974, cited in Martin, 1979) foresees the subversive possibilities of an old age lived as an outsider:

> When I am an old woman I shall wear purple
> With a red hat which doesn't go, and doesn't suit me.
> And I shall spend my pension on brandy and summer gloves
> And satin sandals, and say we've no money for butter.
> I shall sit down on the pavement when I'm tired
> And gobble up samples in shops and press alarm bells
> And run my stick along the public railings
> And make up for the sobriety of my youth.
> I shall go out in my slippers in the rain
> And pick the flowers in other people's gardens
> And learn to spit.
>
> You can wear terrible shirts and grow more fat
> And eat three pounds of sausages at a go
> Or only bread and pickle for a week
> And hoard pens and pencils and beermats and things in boxes.
>
> But now we must have clothes that keep us dry
> And pay our rent and not swear in the street
> And set a good example for the children.
> We must have friends to dinner and read the papers.
>
> But maybe I ought to practise a little now?
> So people who know me are not too shocked and surprised
> When suddenly I am old, and start to wear purple.

For Joseph, then, old age can be a time of wilful eccentricity. In the role of outsider she will be society's scourge rather than its victim.

Martin (1979) provides another example of an elderly woman who can be seen as an outsider. She has been diagnosed as 'manic-depressive', yet this psychiatric label seems ineffective as a form of social control. Neither ill nor dependent, Mrs T was described by the community psychiatric nurse as a 'bloody nuisance' and ineligible for institutional care. Lacking a social role of any kind, Mrs T was well placed to wreak havoc upon a world which had rejected her. Throughout her 'rampage of anti-social behaviour' she delivers pithy criticisms of the adult world, ranging from members of her own family through to the local council:

> at 4 am she set off the fire alarm in the flats because she wanted a cup of tea and couldn't find the lead to her kettle. Later she burst into her grandson's school waving an ice lolly for him. At lunch time her daughter rang hysterically saying that she had seen her mother 'covered in blood' and that 'she ought to be put away'. (When asked about this the next day Mrs T, grinning wickedly, said 'Oh that was tomato ketchup . . . silly cow . . . she ought to know the difference.') Come five o'clock she was busy digging up plants from a tub in the lobby of the town hall, oblivious of the astonished staff who streamed past her on their way home. When rebuked she said, 'Oh, do leave off . . . there are plenty more . . . we paid for them anyway.' She then went into the staff cloakroom, stripped off her clothes, turned on all the taps and had a 'bath'. (Martin, 1979: 8)

Outsiderhood, as this example indicates, can represent a powerful position from which to resist institutionalized forms of care and control. It can also be costly to the individual as the following example reveals. When one woman's proposed marriage failed at the altar, it represented the beginning of an aberrant domestic life. The *Guardian* reports (3 February 1992) that 'her strange life was invisible from the surrounding homes. "The house was completely enclosed in undergrowth" said police.' It was, then, her reclusiveness which saved her from the medical or social work intervention that might otherwise have ensued if her age and domestic 'inadequacy' had become visible. Her very marginal social position, however, constituted an effective form of resistance and at the age of 70 she died in the 'nest-like lean-to of twigs and umbrellas' which she built in her garden. Thus those who are positioned outside dominant social structures – queens and bag ladies, clowns and criminals – are free to comment on, to critique and to subvert the givens of everyday life. Sun City, Arizona, offers another example. Here an entire community is composed of elderly people, 80,000–90,000 residents, living together permanently in a space set apart. As Bernard (1990: 10) describes, the group of Hells Angels she meets, 'clad in black leather jackets, gloves, sturdy boots, black and red helmets and mirror-lensed sunglasses' are all old people:

> Beneath the blazing skies of the Arizona desert, a diametric alternative is being put to the test. This is Sun City, a place where, in the words of one resident: 'You get up in the morning with nothing to do, and you go to bed at night with about half of it done!' (Bernard, 1990: 10)

In this marginal desert zone, this group of outsiders offers a radical critique to the dominant perception of the ageing process. In contrast with the power of the negatively perceived outsider can be set members of the social category 'child' who, rather than resisting adult power by striving for shifts across boundaries between categories, have created for themselves a fictive social identity which is none the less that of a child. These are the child stars. Thus, among children, the limitations intrinsic to the category 'childhood', which amount to what Turner describes as structural inferiority, can be overcome, not by a flight from childhood but rather as the result of an objectification of the category 'child' through performance. Whilst legislation excludes children from regular paid work (see Chapter 2), 11-year-old Macaulay Culkin earned $250,000 for his leading role in the film *Home Alone*. In playing themselves, in the sense of acting the part of a child, child stars also transcend the limits of the category. Indeed Charlie Korsmo, the child star of Spielberg's film *Hook*, based on the story of Peter Pan, announced his retirement because, as a star, he could no longer be a 'regular kid'. That the screen 'child' represents a fictional identity for the real child is also evidenced in the difficulties faced by casting agents who discover, in the words of 15-year-old child star Rees Witherspoon, 'there's a real problem with Hollywood kids; they don't act like kids, they act like little adults. It's a lot easier if somebody actually possesses that innocence, that naivety'. That adults need to believe in the authenticity of the screen 'child', rather than to acknowledge that child as a fiction skilfully created by the child actor, extends into a concern expressed about the *unchild-like* lifestyle of child actors who reap adult financial rewards for their skill. The Screen Actor's Guild therefore limits the exposure of children to the cameras and recently a therapy group for 'derailed child stars' has been established, significantly called 'A Minor Consideration'. Thus the categorical anomaly of Culkin's earnings is expressed in terms of his age – 'well over £700 for every day he's spent on this earth' – and in relation to adult actors – 'his salary for the sequel, which he is currently shooting is around $4.5 million plus profits, well above even Julia Roberts' (*Observer Magazine*, 2 February 1992; *Weekend Guardian*, 1/2 February 1992).

Children can therefore transcend the subordinate role of 'child' by creating a fictive identity, rather in the way disabled or elderly people can also transcend the limitations of their own social role. However, in the case of the child star it is by re-creating the identity believed to characterize the category of which they are already a member – and not that of the members of the dominant social category. In placing themselves outside social hierarchies in this way, child stars are powerful and ambiguous figures, a constant focus for adult control, a constant challenge to adult notions of the vulnerability and dependency which is believed to be intrinsic to childhood. They can be set alongside the 'whizz kids' and 'infant prodigies' discussed in Chapter 3. In both cases, adult concern is evoked in response to aspects of adulthood such as dramatic, musical, mathematical or money-making skills which manifest themselves, literally, in certain children. Child stars must therefore ensure that their fictive, on-screen 'child' identity is sustained within their private lives.

Death of the 'child'

By exploring an extensive range of ethnographic examples, from the acts of resistance instigated within residential homes for elderly people and within private homes where children are growing up, through to a variety of media representations, a pattern of critiques of the dominant world of adulthood can be traced. The second strand identified within the forms of power which Turner describes as accessible to those occupying 'weak' positions in relationship to a society's dominant order is the capacity to confront society's adult members with forms of ultimate knowledge (1974: 231–71). It is a capacity most strongly associated with those occupying the position of either outsiderhood or structural inferiority.

The following material from research within a residential home for elderly people provides an example of how positions of outsiderhood or structural marginality can be used to highlight forms of 'ultimate knowledge' which the dominant order is committed to disguising or distancing (Hockey, 1990).

Throughout this volume it has been argued that the practice of infantilization is not merely an inevitable response to the physical depredations of the ageing process. Rather, it can be understood, in part, as an aspect of a prevailing cultural strategy through which metaphors of life, symbolized in the image of the child, are used to mask the approach of death. In the following material, gathered by Hockey during fieldwork in the north-east of England, elderly people subvert processes of infantilization in such a way as to reveal the immanent nature of human mortality.

Mabel Walkenshaw, a female resident in her early eighties, drew on the metaphor of childhood when resisting the institutional system of doling out medicines, regardless of residents' wishes. Having managed to refuse her pills, Mabel smiled winningly and said, 'I'm a naughty girl.' The officer-in-charge urged her, 'You take notice of me. They do you good!' But Mabel held her ground, replying 'If I'm going to die, then I'll die.'

In these statements, Mabel both exploits and subverts the figurative social category 'child' through which staff seek to control her. She begins by making metaphoric use of the wilfulness which is attributed by adults to children in defiance of their authority: 'I'm a naughty girl.' She then goes on to further subvert its implicit purpose of masking the approach of death by making *explicit* reference to her own death. She boldly declares herself to be prepared and unafraid.

Mabel's provocative reference to her own death was a far from unique occurrence. Although elderly residents played with the controlling metaphoric category 'child', they also gave many subversive nods in the direction of death itself. Many conversations would end with a parting shot such as:

> 'I won't live much longer. I'm 84. All my friends are dead.'
> 'If I live till next December I'll be 95.'
> 'You can be struck down in a moment.'
> 'What can you expect. I won't live much longer.'

Even death itself is mimicked. On one occasion a care aide took early morning tea to a resident to find him, with his arms crossed on his chest, corpse-fashion. He then opened his eyes and grinned at her.

Explicit references to death and dying thus subvert the very process which infantilization is attempting to control. Naked after her bath, a female resident told care staff of a dream where she saw her body laid out in its coffin. She had removed her wedding ring, lest it fall into the hands of the undertakers. Staff exchanged shocked glances. They were lost for words through which to deflect this resident's dangerous revelation of the incipient fate of the body they were drying and dressing. When another resident was asked by a care aide when she was next due for a bath, the woman replied, 'Push me under when I have my next one. I'm 95, that's old enough.'

That elderly people are aware of and not taken in by the metaphors imposed upon them by the dominant adult world finds expression in other ways. When staff in the home empty rubbish into black plastic sacks or sweep remnants of food from the dining-room floor, residents make barbed jokes such as, 'You can put me in there too', or 'Sweep me up too. You might as well. I'm not important any more. I'm not important to anyone.' And in every case of this kind, staff struggle weakly for another joke through which to counter and diffuse the power of such embarrassing honesty.

Through the style and timing of explicit statements about their own mortality, these elderly people, in common with other marginal social groups, therefore lay claim to some final acts of self-control in their vulnerability. They are able, from their liminal position, to expose the naked truth which the dominant group seeks to mute or distance. From their position of liminal power, they can very effectively reveal its weaknesses, thereby highlighting the contested nature of power.

The examples assembled in this final chapter confirm the negotiated, context-specific nature of the conceptual system which has been explored throughout this volume. Infantilization in any of its extensive range of manifestations is a process which may be resisted by a very young or an elderly person, may be submitted to, or may be embraced in ways that attract to the infantilized person the 'power of the weak' – to disrupt, subvert or reveal the power associated with the members of the dominant social category, 'adult'. In that the system is 'lived', in that it involves the participation of the infantilized as well as their 'carers', it is a system which is amenable to change and development. This volume charts a growing awareness of the effects of infantilization and the pressing need for change.

Its additional purpose has been to unravel the sources of the metaphoric forms through which dependency is currently made manageable. To this end the construction of the child, both historically and within the family, and the embodiedness of the child's social identity have been key themes. What has been highlighted too is the structural as well as cultural nature of the social processes described. Not only at the level of personal interaction or cultural representation, but also within the sphere of economic policy, dependent people may find themselves sharing a child-like status. As argued, good intentions require firm foundations, and this volume is offered as a theoretical underpinning to strategies for change. It ends with accounts that highlight existing scope for power among dependent people, scope which at times may be used at some cost to the individual. None the less, in the fluid nature of the episodes discussed in this chapter lies the prerequisite for change. It is change which, to be consolidated, must find expression both in the spheres of personal interaction and state policy. In the redefining of childhood, old age and disability lie the seeds of an expanded adulthood, one which admits and indeed values vulnerability as an essential prerequisite for human growth and development.

Note

1 For example, Okely (1983) gives an account of female travellers' success in drawing upon the dominant society's stereotypes of the 'gypsy woman' in ways that work to their advantage.

REFERENCES

Ablon, J. (1990) 'Ambiguity and Difference: Families with Dwarf Children', *Social Science and Medicine*, 30(8): 879–87.

Abramovitz, M. (1991) 'Putting an End to Doublespeak about Race, Gender, and Poverty: an Annotated Glossary for Social Workers', *Social Work*, 36(5): 380–4.

Allan, G. (1985) *Family Life: Domestic Roles and Social Organization*. Oxford: Basil Blackwell.

Arber, S. and Ginn, J. (1991) *Gender and Later Life*. London: Sage.

Arber, T. (1991) 'The First Day of the Rest of my Life', in Labelled Disabled Collective, *Labelled Disabled*. Sheffield: The Labelled Disabled Collective.

Ardener, E. (1975) 'Belief and the Problem of Women', in S. Ardener (ed.), *Perceiving Women*. London: Dent.

Ariès, P. (1979 [1962]) *Centuries of Childhood*. Harmondsworth: Penguin.

Arluke, A. and Levin, J. (1984) 'Another Stereotype: Old Age as a Second Stereotype', *Aging*, August/September, 7–11.

Armstrong, D. (1983) *Political Anatomy of the Body: Medical Knowledge in Britain in the Twentieth Century*. Cambridge: Cambridge University Press.

Ashley, J. (1973) *Journey into Silence*. London: Bodley Head.

Axon, W.E.A. (ed.) (1902) 'The Wonderful Child', *Chetham Miscellanies*. N.S., 1.

Barnes, C. (1990) *'Cabbage Syndrome' – The Social Construction of Dependence*. Basingstoke: Falmer Press.

Barrett, M. and McIntosh, M. (1982) *The Anti-Social Family*. London: Verso.

Barthes, R. (1973 [1957]) *Mythologies*. London: Granada.

Basham, A.L. (1967) *The Wonder that was India*. London: Fontana/Collins.

Bauman, Z. (1990) 'Modernity and Ambivalence', *Theory, Culture and Society*, 7(2): 143–69.

Baxter, P.T.W. and Almagor, V. (eds) (1978) *Age, Generation and Time*. London: Hurst.

Benedict, R. (1955) 'Continuities and Discontinuities in Cultural Conditioning', in M. Mead and M. Wolfenstein (eds), *Childhood in Contemporary Cultures*. Chicago: University of Chicago Press.

Bennett, T. (1981) 'Christmas and Ideology', *Popular Culture, Themes and Issues 1*, Open University U203, Block 1, Units 1/II. Milton Keynes: Open University Press.

Bernard, M. (1990) 'Leisure and Lifestyle in Later Life', *Nursing the Elderly*, September/October: 10–12.

Bernard, M. (1991) 'Vision for the Future', *Nursing the Elderly*, January/February: 10–12.

Bernardes, J. (1985) '"Family Ideology": Identification and Exploration', *The Sociological Review*, 33(2): 275–97.

Berndt, R. and Berndt, C. (1964) *The World of the First Australians*. London: Angus and Robertson.

Berry, S., Lee, M. and Griffiths, S. (1981) *Report on a Survey of West Indian*

Pensioners in Nottingham. Nottingham Social Services Department, Research Section.

Beveridge, W. (1942) *Social Insurance and Allied Services.* Cmnd 6404. London: HMSO.

Billig, M. (1992) *Talking of the Royal Family.* London: Routledge.

Black, M. (1962) *Models and Metaphors: Studies in Language and Philosophy.* Ithaca, NY: Cornell University Press.

Blacking, J. (1990) 'Growing Old Gracefully: Physical, Social and Spiritual Transformations in Venda Society, 1956–66', in P. Spencer (ed.), *Anthropology and the Riddle of the Sphinx, ASA Monographs 28.* London: Routledge.

Blau, Z. (1973) *Old Age in a Changing Society.* New York: New Viewpoints.

Bloch, M. (1985) 'From Cognition to Ideology', in R. Fardon (ed.), *Power and Knowledge.* Edinburgh: Scottish Academic Press.

Bloch, M. and Parry, J. (eds) (1982) *Death and the Regeneration of Life.* Cambridge: Cambridge University Press.

Boas, F. (1965 [1911]) *The Mind of Primitive Man.* New York: Free Press Paperback.

Boas, G. (1966) *The Cult of Childhood.* London: Warburg Institute.

Booth, T.A. (1978) 'From Normal Baby to Handicapped Child: Unravelling the Idea of Subnormality in Families of Mentally Handicapped Children', *Sociology,* 12(2): 203–21.

Bourdieu, P. (1977 [1972]) *Outline of a Theory of Practice.* Cambridge: Cambridge University Press.

Bourdieu, P. (1984) *Distinction.* London: Routledge and Kegan Paul.

Boyden, J. (1990) 'Childhood and the Policy Makers: a Comparative Perspective on the Globalization of Childhood', in A. James and A. Prout (eds), *Constructing and Reconstructing Childhood.* Basingstoke: Falmer Press.

Bradley, B. (1986) *Visions of Infancy.* Cambridge: Polity Press.

Brewster, B. (1979) *Sociology and Psychology: Essays by Marcel Mauss.* London: Routledge and Kegan Paul.

Briggs, J. (1990) 'Playwork as a Tool in the Socialisation of an Inuit Child', *Arctic Medical Research,* 49: 34–8.

Brooks, D.H.M. (1990) 'The Route to Home Ventilation: a Patient's Perspective', *Care of the Critically Ill,* 6(3): 96–7.

Brown, C. (1990) *My Left Foot.* London: Mandarin.

Brown, R. (1977) *A Poetics for Sociology.* Cambridge: Cambridge University Press.

Bryman, A., Bytheway, B., Allatt, P. and Keil, T. (eds) (1987) *Rethinking the Life Cycle.* London: Methuen.

Campbell, J. (ed.) (1971) *The Portable Jung.* New York: Viking Press.

Campling, J. (ed.) (1981) *Images of Ourselves: Women with Disabilities Talking.* London: Routledge and Kegan Paul.

Carroll, L. (1960 [1865]) *Alice's Adventures in Wonderland.* Harmondsworth: Penguin.

Carver, V. and Liddiard, P. (1978) *An Ageing Population.* Milton Keynes: Open University Press.

Cheaney, M. (1990) 'Body Blow', *Guardian,* 27 March.

Cohen, A. (ed.) (1986) *Symbolising Boundaries.* Manchester: Manchester University Press.

Collier, J.F. and Rosaldo, M.Z. (1981) 'Politics and Gender in Simple Societies', in S. Ortner and H. Whitehead (eds), *Sexual Meanings*. Cambridge: Cambridge University Press.

Community Care: Agenda for Action (1988) London: HMSO.

Coote, A. (1990) 'Mother and Father of a Battle', *Guardian*, 26 September.

Coote, A., Harman, H. and Hewitt, P. (1990) *The Family Way: a New Approach to Policy-Making*. London: Institute for Public Policy Research.

Counts, D.A. and Counts, D.R. (1985) 'I'm not Dead Yet! Aging and Death: Process and Experience', in D.A. Counts and D.R. Counts, *Aging and its Transformations: Moving Toward Death in Pacific Societies*. Lanham, MD: University Press of America.

Coupland, N. (1991) *Language, Society and the Elderly: Discourse, Identity and Ageing*. Oxford: Basil Blackwell.

Cousins, M. and Hussain, A. (1984) *Michel Foucault*. London: Macmillan.

Coveney, P. (1957) *Poor Monkey: The Child in Literature*. London: Rockcliff.

Coward, R. (1984) *Female Desire*. London: Paladin.

Crick, M. (1976) *Explorations in Language and Meaning: Towards a Semantic Anthropology*. London: Malaby Press.

Crump, A. (1991) 'Promoting Self Esteem', *Nursing the Elderly*, March/April: 19–20.

Cumming, E. (1963) 'Further Thoughts on the Theory of Disengagement', *International Social Science Journal*, 15(3).

Cumming, E. and Henry, W.E. (1961) *Growing Old, the Process of Disengagement*. New York: Basic Books.

Dahl, R. (1981) *George's Marvellous Medicine*. London: Puffin Books.

Dalley, G. (1988) *Ideologies of Caring. Rethinking Community and Collectivism*. Basingstoke: Macmillan Education.

Davidoff, L., L'Esperance, J. and Newby, H. (1976) 'Landscape with Figures: Home and Community in English Society', in J. Mitchell and A. Oakley (eds), *The Rights and Wrongs of Women*. London: Penguin.

Dawson, A. (1991) '"Ageing Well": The Construction of Perceptions and Responses to Physiological Ageing in Clubs for Elderly', Paper presented to the British Sociological Association Conference, Health and Society, Manchester.

Demos, J. (1971) 'Developmental Perspectives on the History of Childhood', in T.K. Rabb and R. Rutberg (eds), *The Family in History*. London: Harper Row.

Deshen, S. (1990) 'The Performance of Blind Israelis at Work', *Disability, Handicap and Society*, 5(3): 269–80.

Dex, S. and Phillipson, C. (1986) 'Social Policy and the Older Worker', in C. Phillipson and A. Walker (eds), *Ageing and Social Policy*. Aldershot: Gower.

Dobash, R.E. and Dobash, R.P. (1992) *Women, Violence and Social Change*. London: Routledge.

Dolinsky, E.H. (1984) 'Infantilization of the Elderly: an Area for Nursing Research', *Journal of Gerontological Nursing*, 10(9): 12–19.

Donzelot, J. (1980) *The Policing of Families*. London: Hutchinson.

Douglas, M. (1966) *Purity and Danger*. Harmondsworth: Penguin.

Douglas, M. (1975) 'Animals in Lele Religious Symbolism', in M. Douglas, *Implicit Meanings*. London: Routledge and Kegan Paul.

Eagleton, T. (1991) *Ideology*, London: Verso.

Eastman, M. (1984) *Old Age Abuse*. Mitcham: Age Concern England.

Eayrs, C.B. and Ellis, N. (1990) 'Charity Advertising: For and Against People with Mental Handicaps', *Journal of Social Psychology*, 29: 349–60.

Ehrenreich, B. and English, D. (1979) *For Her Own Good: 150 Years of the Experts' Advice to Women*. London: Pluto Press.

Ekerdt, D.J. (1986) 'The Busy Ethic. Moral Continuity between Work and Retirement', *The Gerontologist*, 26(3): 239–44.

Elder, G. (1977) *The Alienated*. London: Writers and Readers Publishing Cooperative.

Elias, N. (1982) *The Civilizing Process*. Volume 2: *State Formation and Civilization*. Oxford: Basil Blackwell.

Elshtain, J.B. (1981) *Public Man, Private Woman: Woman in Social and Political Thought*. Princeton, NJ: Princeton University Press.

Ennew, J. (1986) *The Sexual Exploitation of Children*. Cambridge: Polity Press.

Evans-Pritchard, E. (1951) *Kinship and Marriage among the Nuer*. Oxford: Clarendon Press.

Evers, H. (1981) 'Care or Custody? The Experiences of Women Patients in Longstay Geriatric Wards', in B. Hutter and G. Williams (eds), *Controlling Women: the Normal and the Deviant*. London: Croom Helm.

Fallon, K. (1990) 'An Involuntary Workforce', *Community Care*, 4 January.

Farrant, W. (1979) 'Who's Deprived?', in M. Hoyles (ed.), *Changing Childhood*. London: Readers and Writers Publishing Cooperative.

Featherstone, M. (1982) 'The Body in Consumer Culture', *Theory, Culture and Society*, 1: 18–33.

Featherstone, M. (1987) 'Leisure, Symbolic Power and the Life Course', in J. Horne, D. Jary and A. Tomlinson (eds), *Sport, Leisure and Social Relations*. Keele: Sociological Review Monograph No. 33.

Featherstone, M. and Hepworth, M. (1986) 'New Lifestyles for Old Age?', in C. Phillipson, M. Bernard and P. Strang (eds), *Dependency and Interdependency*. London: Croom Helm.

Featherstone, M. and Hepworth, M. (1990) 'Images of Ageing', in J. Bond and P.G. Coleman (eds), *Ageing in Society: an Introduction to Social Gerontology*. London: Sage.

Fennell, G., Phillipson, C. and Evers, H. (1988) *The Sociology of Old Age*. Milton Keynes: Open University Press.

Fernandez, J.W. (1970) 'Persuasions and Performances: Of the Beast in Every Body . . . and the Metaphors of Everyman', in C. Geertz (ed.), *Myth, Symbol and Culture*. London: Hutchinson.

Fernandez, J.W. (1977) 'The Performance of Ritual Metaphors', in J.D. Sapir and J.C. Crocker (eds), *The Social Use of Metaphor*. Philadelphia: University of Pennsylvania Press.

Finch, J. and Groves, D. (1983) *A Labour of Love: Women, Work and Caring*. London: Routledge and Kegan Paul.

Finnegan, R. (1981) 'Celebrating Christmas', *Popular Culture, Themes and Issues 1*. Open University U203, Block 1, Units 1/II. Milton Keynes: Open University Press.

Firestone, S. (1971) *The Dialectics of Sex*. London: Paladin.

Fleming, J. (1990) 'Growing Old in Kenya', *Nursing the Elderly*, November/December: 34–5.

Foly, W. (1986) *A Child in the Forest*. London: Ariel Books, British Broadcasting Corporation.

Foner, N. (1984) *Ages in Conflict: a Cross Cultural Perspective on Inequality between Old and Young*. New York: Columbia University Press.

Ford, P. (1991) 'Room for Choice', *Nursing the Elderly*, January/February: 16.

Foucault, M. (1977) *Discipline and Punish*. London: Allen Lane.

Foucault, M. (1979) *The History of Sexuality*, Vol. 1. London: Allen Lane.

Fraser, M. (1973) *Children in Conflict*. Harmondsworth: Penguin.

Freeman, J. (1979) *Gifted Children*. Lancaster: MTP Press.

Friedan, B. (1981) *The Second Stage*. New York: Summit Books.

Fyfe, A. (1989) *Child Labour*. Cambridge: Polity Press.

Gamble, R. (1979) *Chelsea Child*. London: BBC.

Garvey, A. (1991) 'Will You Still Love Me Tomorrow?' *Guardian*, 5 June.

Geertz, C. (1975) *The Interpretation of Culture*. London: Hutchinson.

Geertz, C. (1977) 'From the Native's Point of View', in J.L. Dolgin, D.S. Kemnitzer and D.M. Schneider (eds), *Symbolic Anthropology*. New York: Columbia University Press.

Glendinning, C. (1988) 'The Invisible Carers', *New Society*, 13 May.

Goffman, E. (1968) *Stigma*. Harmondsworth: Penguin.

Grant, L. (1991) 'The Shock of the Old Hits Adland', *Independent*, 30 June.

Green, E., Hebron, S. and Woodward, D. (1990) *Women's Leisure, What Leisure?* London: Macmillan Education.

Greer, G. (1984) *Sex and Destiny: The Politics of Human Fertility*. New York: Harper and Row.

Gresham, M.L. (1976) 'The Infantilization of the Elderly', *Nursing Forum*, 15(2): 195–210.

Gwyther, M. (1990) 'Portraits of the 90s', *Observer Magazine*, 18 November.

Hadley, R.G. and Brodwin, M.G. (1988) 'Language about People with Disabilities', *Journal of Counselling and Development*, 67: 147–9.

Hall, S., Clarke, J., Jefferson, T. and Roberts, B. (eds) (1976) *Resistance through Rituals*. London: Hutchinson.

Hanmer, J. and Maynard, M. (1987) *Women, Violence and Social Control*. London: Macmillan.

Hardman, C. (1973) 'Can there be an Anthropology of Children?', *Journal of the Anthropology Society of Oxford*, 4(1): 85–99.

Harper, S. (1989) 'The Older Male in Post-War Britain', *Generations*, 10: 10–14.

Harris, C. (1987) 'The Individual and Society: a Processual Approach', in A. Bryman, B. Bytheway, P. Allatt and T. Keil (eds), *Rethinking the Life Cycle*. London: Macmillan.

Havighurst, R.J. and Albrecht, R. (1953) *Older People*. London: Longmans, Green.

Hazan, H. (1980) *The Limbo People*. London: Routledge and Kegan Paul.

Hebdige, D. (1979) *Subculture: the Meaning of Style*. London: Methuen.

Helman, C. (1988) 'Dr Frankenstein and the Industrial Body', *Anthropology Today*, 4(3).

Hendrick, H. (1990) 'Constructions and Reconstructions of British Childhood: an Interpretive Survey, 1800 to the present', in A. James and A. Prout (eds), *Constructing and Reconstructing Childhood*. Basingstoke: Falmer Press.

Hendricks, J. and Cutler, S.J. (1990) 'Leisure and the Structuring of our Life Worlds', *Ageing and Society*, 10: 85–94.

Hendry, J. (1986) *Becoming Japanese*. Manchester: Manchester University Press.

Hertz, R. (1960 [1907]) *Death and the Right Hand*. New York: Free Press.

Hirschon, R. (1984) *Women and Property: Women as Property*. London: Croom Helm.

Hockey, J. (1990) *Experiences of Death: an Anthropological Account*. Edinburgh: Edinburgh University Press.

Hockey, J. and James, A. (1988) 'Growing Up and Growing Old: Metaphors of Ageing in Contemporary Britain', Paper presented to the Association of Social Anthropologists Conference, 1988, The Social Construction of Youth, Maturation and Ageing, London.

Holt, J. (1975) *Escape from Childhood*. Harmondsworth: Penguin.

Holy, L. (1987) *Comparative Anthropology*. Oxford: Basil Blackwell.

Howell, S. (1987) 'From Child to Human: Chewong Concepts of Self', in G. Jahoda and I.M. Lewis (eds), *Acquiring Culture*. London: Croom Helm.

Hutchings, V. (1988) 'Sex and the Over Seventies', *New Statesman and Society*, 15 July: 29.

James, A. (1986) 'Learning to Belong: the Boundaries of Adolescence', in A. Cohen (ed.), *Symbolising Boundaries*. Manchester: Manchester University Press.

James, A. (1993) *Personifying Children: Identities and Social Relationships in the Experience of the Child*. Edinburgh: Edinburgh University Press.

James, A. and Prout, A. (1990a) 'Re-presenting Childhood: Time and Transition in the Study of Childhood', in A. James and A. Prout (eds), *Constructing and Reconstructing Childhood*. Basingstoke: Falmer Press.

James, A. and Prout, A. (1990b) *Constructing and Reconstructing Childhood*. Basingstoke: Falmer Press.

Jenkins, R. (1990) 'Dimensions of Adulthood in Britain: Long Term Unemployment and Mental Handicap', in P. Spencer (ed.), *Anthropology and the Riddle of the Sphinx*. ASA Monographs 28. London: Routledge.

Jones, K. (1975) *Opening the Door: A Study of New Policies for the Mentally Handicapped*. London: Routledge and Kegan Paul.

Joseph, J. (1974) 'Warning', in J. Joseph, *Rose in the Afternoon*. London: Dent.

Keith, J. (1980) 'The Best is Yet to Be: Toward an Anthropology of Age', *Annual Review of Anthropology*, 9: 339–64.

Kitching, N., Low, L. and Evers, C. (1990) 'Entitled to Respect', *Nursing the Elderly*, November/December: 9.

Kitzinger, J. (1990) 'Who are you Kidding? Children, Power and the Struggle against Sexual Abuse', in A. James and A. Prout (eds), *Constructing and Reconstructing Childhood*. Basingstoke: Falmer Press.

Knowles, R. (1987) 'Who's a Pretty Girl Then?', *Nursing Times*, 83(27): 58–9.

Kohli, M. (1988) 'Ageing as a Challenge for Sociological Theory', *Ageing and Society*, 8: 367–94.

La Fontaine, J. (ed.) (1978) *Sex and Age as Principles of Social Differentiation*. London: Academic Press.

La Fontaine, J. (1985) 'Person and Individual: Some Anthropological Reflections', in M. Carruthers, S. Collins and S. Lukes (eds), *The Category of the Person*. Cambridge: Cambridge University Press.

Lakoff, G. (1987) *Women, Fire and Dangerous Things*. Chicago: University of Chicago Press.

Lakoff, G. and Johnson, M. (1980) *Metaphors We Live By*. Chicago: University of Chicago Press.

Laurance, J. (1988) 'The Myths of Old Age', *New Society*, 18 March: 19–21.

Leach, E. (1966) 'Two Essays concerning the Symbolic Representation of Time', in E.R. Leach, *Rethinking Anthropology*. London: Athlone Press.

Leach, P. (1977) *Baby and Child*. London: Michael Joseph.

Lepowsky, M. (1985) 'Gender, Ageing and Dying in an Egalitarian Society', in D.A. Counts and D.R. Counts (eds), *Aging and its Transformations: Moving Toward Death in Pacific Societies*. Lanham, MD: University Press of America.

Levi-Strauss, C. (1973) *Tristes Tropiques*. London: Jonathan Cape.

Lewis, J. and Meredith, B. (1988) *Daughters who Care: Daughters Caring for Mothers at Home*. London: Routledge.

Longmore, P.K. (1985) 'Screening Stereotypes: Images of Disabled People', *Social Policy*, 16(1): 31–7.

Lonsdale, S. (1990) *Women and Disability*. London: Macmillan.

MacCormack, C. (1985) 'Dying as Transformation to Ancestorhood: the Sherbro Coast of Sierra Leone', *Curare*, Sonderband 4: 117–26.

McCormack, J. (1991) 'A Hostage in His Own Home', *Guardian*, 27 November.

McCourt Perring, C. (1992) 'The Experience and Perspectives of Patients and Care Staff', in S. Ramon (ed.), *Psychiatric Hospital Closure: Exploring Myths and Realities*. London: Chapman and Hall.

MacDonald, B. with Rich, C. (1984) *Look Me in the Eye: Old Women, Ageing and Ageism*. London: The Women's Press.

MacFarlane, A. (1978) *The Origins of English Individualism*. Oxford: Basil Blackwell.

Macpherson, C.B. (1962) *The Political Theory of Possessive Individualism*. Oxford: Oxford University Press.

Maitland, S. (1991) 'Lipstick Traces, Egg on Their Faces', *Observer*, 19 May.

Malinowski, B. (1922) *Argonauts of the Western Pacific*. London: Routledge.

Mardell, M. (1988) 'Glad to be Grey', *The Listener*, 24 March.

Martin, J. and Roberts, C. (1984) *Women and Employment: A Lifetime Perspective*, London: HMSO.

Martin, P. (1979) *I Shall Wear Purple*. Occasional Paper 7. Mitcham: Age Concern England.

Martin, W.C., Bengston, V.L. and Acok, A.C. (1974) 'Alienation and Age: a Context-specific Approach', *Social Forces*, 53(2): 266–74.

Marx, K. (1950 [1949]) 'Critique of the Gotha Programme', in Karl Marx and Frederick Engels, *Selected Works, VII*. London: Lawrence and Wishart.

Matthews, S. (1979) *The Social World of Old Women*. London: Sage.

de Mause, L. (ed.) (1976) *The History of Childhood*. London: Souvenir Press.

Mauss, M. (1966 [1925]) *The Gift*. London: Routledge and Kegan Paul.

Mead, M. (1955) 'Children and Ritual in Bali', in M. Mead and M. Wolfenstein (eds), *Childhood in Contemporary Cultures*. Chicago: University of Chicago Press.

Milner, D. (1983) *Children and Race: Ten Years On*. London: Ward Lock Educational.

Moore, S.F. and Myerhoff, B.G. (eds) (1977) *Secular Ritual*. Assen: Van Gorcum.

Morris, J. (1991) *Pride Against Prejudice: a Personal Politics of Disability*. London: The Women's Press.

Moyo, E. (1973) *Big Mother and Little Mother in Matabeleland*. History Workshop Pamphlets, 3.

Mulvey, L. (1975) 'Visual Pleasure and Narrative Cinema', *Screen*, 16(3): 6–18.

Murcott, A. (1980) 'The Social Construction of Teenage Pregnancy', *Sociology of Health and Illness*, 2(1): 1–23.

Murdock, G.P. (1949) *Social Structure*. London: Macmillan.

Murphy, R.F. (1987) *The Body Silent*. London: Dent.

Murphy, R.F., Scheer, J., Murphy, Y. and Mack, R. (1988) 'Physical Disability and Social Liminality: a Study in the Rituals of Adversity', *Social Science and Medicine*, 26(2): 235–42.

Musgrove, F. (1964) *Youth and the Social Order*. London: Routledge and Kegan Paul.

Myerhoff, B.G. (1984) 'Rites and Signs and Ripening: the Intertwining of Ritual, Time and Growing Older', in D.I. Kertzer and J. Keith (eds), *Age and Anthropological Theory*. Ithaca, NY: Cornell University Press.

Newton, E. (1980) *This Bed my Centre*. London: Virago.

Nissel, M. and Bonnerjea, L. (1982) *Family Care of the Elderly: Who Pays?* London: Policy Studies Institute.

Oakley, A. (1974) *The Sociology of Housework*. London: Martin Robertson.

Okely, J. (1983) *The Traveller Gypsies*. Cambridge: Cambridge University Press.

Okely, J. (1990) 'Clubs for le Troisieme Age', in P. Spencer (ed.), *Anthropology and the Riddle of the Sphinx*. ASA Monographs 28. London: Routledge.

Oliver, M. (1989) 'Disability and Dependency: a Creation of Industrial Societies', in L. Barton (ed.), *Disability and Dependency*. Lewes: Falmer Press.

Oliver, M. (1990) *The Politics of Disablement*. London: Macmillan.

Parsons, T. (1964) *Essays in Sociological Theory*. New York: Free Press.

Pennington, S. (1991) 'Chewing Out the Fat', *Guardian*, 23 May.

Perring, C. (1989) 'Ordinary People? The Question of Deinstitutionalization in Community Care' (unpublished).

Phillipson, C. (1982) *Capitalism and the Construction of Old Age*. London: Macmillan.

Phillipson, C. and Walker, A. (1986) *Ageing and Social Policy*. Aldershot: Gower.

Pinchbeck, I. and Hewitt, M. (1969) *Children in English Society*, Vol. I. London: Routledge and Kegan Paul.

Pinchbeck, I. and Hewitt, M. (1973) *Children in English Society*, Vol. II. London: Routledge and Kegan Paul.

Pizzey, E. (1974) *Scream Quietly or the Neighbours Will Hear*. Harmondsworth: Penguin.

Plumb, J.H. (1975) 'The New World of Children in Eighteenth Century England', *Past and Present*, 67: 64–95.

Polhemus, T. (ed.) (1978) *Social Aspects of the Human body*. Harmondsworth: Penguin.

Pollitt, P.A., O'Connor, D.W. and Anderson, I. (1989) 'Mild Dementia: Perceptions and Problems', *Ageing and Society*, 9: 261–75.

Pollock, L. (1983) *Forgotten Children: Parent–Child Relations 1500–1900*. Cambridge: Cambridge University Press.

Powell, L.A. and Williamson, J.B. (1985) 'The Mass Media and the Aged', *Social Policy*, 16(1): 38–49.

Prout, A. and James, A. (1990) 'A New Paradigm for the Sociology of Childhood? Provenance, Promise and Problems', in A. James and A. Prout (eds), *Constructing and Reconstructing Childhood*. Basingstoke: Falmer Press.

Quadagno, J.S. (1982) *Ageing in Early Industrial Society: Work, Family and Social Policy in Nineteenth Century England*. New York: Academic Press.

Qureshi, H. and Walker, A. (1989) *The Caring Relationship*. London: Macmillan.

Qvortrup, J. (1990) 'A Voice for Children in Statistical and Social Accounting: a Plea for Children's Rights to be Heard', in A. James and A. Prout (eds), *Constructing and Reconstructing Childhood*. Basingstoke: Falmer Press.

Radford, V. (1991) 'You Can Change the Future', in Labelled Disabled Collective, *Labelled Disabled*. Sheffield: The Labelled Disabled Collective.

Reichard, R., Livson, F. and Peterson, P.G. (1962) *Ageing and Personality*. New York: John Wiley.

Reynolds-Whyte, S. (1990) 'Problems in Cross-cultural Research on Disability', in F.J. Brown and B. Ingstad (eds), *Disability in a Cross-Cultural Perspective*. Working Paper No. 4, Department of Social Anthropology, University of Oslo.

Richards, A. (1982) *Chisungu: a Girl's Initiation among the Bemba of Zambia*. London: Tavistock.

Richards, M. and Light, P. (eds) (1986) *Children of Social Worlds*. Cambridge: Polity Press.

Ricoeur, P. (1978 [1975]) *The Rule of Metaphor*. London: Routledge and Kegan Paul.

Rinehart, J.W. (1972) 'Affluence and the Embourgeoisement of the Working Class: a Critical Look', in G. Ritzer (ed.), *Issues, Debates and Controversies: an Introduction to Sociology*. Boston: Allyn and Bacon.

Roebuck, J. (1978) 'When Does Old Age Begin? The Evolution of the English Definition', *Journal of Social History*, 12: 416–28.

Rogers, B. (1980) *The Domestication of Women*. London: Tavistock Publications.

Rose, J. (1984) *The Case of Peter Pan or the Impossibility of Children's Fiction*. London: Macmillan.

Rousseau, J.J. (1969 [1762]) *Emile*. London: Dent.

Samuel, R. (ed.) (1981) *People's History and Socialist Theory*. London: Routledge and Kegan Paul.

Sanders, C. (1991) 'Some Smart Moves', *Times Higher Education Supplement*, 10 May.

Sankar, A. (1984) ' "It's just Old Age": Old Age as a Diagnosis in American and Chinese Medicine', in D.I. Kertzer and J. Keith (eds), *Age and Anthropological Theory*. Ithaca, NY: Cornell University Press.

Schildkrout, E. (1978) 'Roles of Children in Urban Kano', in J. La Fontaine (ed.), *Age and Sex as Principles of Social Differentiation*. London: Academic Press.

Schnell, R.L. (1979) 'Childhood as Ideology: a Reinterpretation of the Common School', *British Journal of Educational Studies*, 27(1): 7–28.

Schottman, W. (1988) 'Participant, Observer and Mother', *Anthropology Today*, 4(2): 10–12.

Segal, L. (1983) *What Is to Be Done about the Family?* Harmondsworth: Penguin.

Sharp, H.S. (1981) 'Old Age among the Chipewyan', in P.T. Amoss and S. Harrell (eds), *Other Ways of Growing Old. Anthropological Perspectives*. Stanford, CA: Stanford University Press.

Shearer, A. (1981) *Disability – Whose Handicap?* Oxford: Basil Blackwell.

Shostak, M. (1976) 'A !Kung Woman's Memories of Childhood', in R. Lee and I. DeVore (eds), *Kalahari Hunter–Gatherers*. Cambridge, MA: Harvard University Press.

Sinclair, P. (1985) 'Koro and Kuia: Aging and Gender among the Maori of New Zealand', in D.A. Counts and D.R. Counts (eds), *Aging and its Transformations: Moving Toward Death in Pacific Societies*. Lanham, MD: University Press of America.

Smith, S. and Jordan, A. (1991) *What the Papers Say and Don't Say about Disability*. London: The Spastics Society.

Social Trends (1988) No. 18. London: HMSO.

Social Trends (1992) No. 22. London: HMSO.

Söder, M. (1990) 'Prejudice or Ambivalence? Attitudes towards Persons with Disabilities', *Disability, Handicap and Society*, 4(3): 227–41.

Sontag, S. (1978) 'The Double Standard of Ageing', in V. Carver and P. Liddiard (eds), *An Ageing Population*. Milton Keynes: Open University Press.

Sontag, S. (1983) *Illness as Metaphor*. Harmondsworth: Penguin.

Sontag, S. (1990) *Aids and its Metaphors*. London: Penguin.

Spencer, P. (ed.) (1990) *Anthropology and the Riddle of the Sphinx*. ASA Monographs 28. London: Routledge.

Spender, D. (1980) *Man Made Language*. London: Routledge and Kegan Paul.

Sperber, D. (1986) *Symbols that Stand for Themselves*. Chicago: University of Chicago Press.

Stacey, J. (1987) 'Are Feminists Afraid to Leave Home? The Challenge of Conservative Pro-family Feminism', in J. Mitchell and A. Oakley (eds), *What is Feminism?* Oxford: Basil Blackwell.

Steadman, C. (1990) *Childhood, Culture and Class in Britain: Margaret McMillan, 1860–1931*. London: Virago.

Stearns, P. (1977) *Old Age in European Society: The Case of France*. London: Croom Helm.

Stedeford, A. (1984) *Facing Death*. London: Heinemann Medical Books.

Steinmetz, S. (1988) *Duty Bound: Elder Abuse and Family Care*. London: Sage.

Stone, L. (1979) *The Family, Sex and Marriage in England, 1500–1800*. Harmondsworth: Penguin.

Strathern, A. (1971) *The Rope of Moka*. Cambridge: Cambridge University Press.

Sulaiman, S. (1990a) 'Age Concern', *Guardian*, 16 August.

Sulaiman, S. (1990b) 'Why Can't a Woman be Treated More Like a Man?', *Guardian*, 9 October.

Sutherland, A.T. (1981) *Disabled We Stand*. London: Souvenir Press.

Tambiah, S.J. (1973) 'Classification of Animals in Thailand', in M. Douglas (ed.), *Rules and Meanings*. Harmondsworth: Penguin.

Thane, P. (1983) 'The History of Provision for the Elderly to 1929', in D. Jerrome (ed.), *Ageing in Modern Society*. London: Croom Helm.

Thane, P. (1987) 'Golden Oldies', *New Society*, 13 November: 11–13.

Thomas, D. (1954) *Under Milk Wood*. London: Dent.

Thomas, D. (1982) *The Experience of Handicap*. London: Methuen.

Thomas, K. (1973) *Religion and the Decline of Magic*. Harmondsworth: Penguin.

Thompson, E.P. (1968) *The Making of the English Working Class*. Harmondsworth: Penguin.

Thompson, F. (1979) *Lark Rise to Candleford*. London: Penguin.

Thompson, J.B. (1984) *Studies in the Theory of Ideology*. Cambridge: Polity Press.

Tinker, A. (1990) 'Who Cares about Old Women . . . and their Carers', *Guardian*, 25 September.

Townsend, S. (1983) *The Secret Diary of Adrian Mole, aged 13¾*. London: Methuen.

Tucker, N. (1977) *What is a Child?* London: Fontana.

Turner, B. (1984) *The Body and Society: Explorations in Social Theory*. Oxford: Basil Blackwell.

Turner, B. (1987) *Medical Power and Social Knowledge*. London: Sage.

Turner, B. (1989) 'Ageing, Status and Sociological Theory', *British Journal of Sociology*, 40(4): 588–607.

Turner, V. (1974) *Dramas, Fields and Metaphors. Symbolic Action in Human Society*. Ithaca, NY: Cornell University Press.

Tweedie, J. (1990) 'Home Where the Elderly Heart Aches', *Guardian*, 1 October.

Ungerson, C. (1987) *Policy is Personal: Sex, Gender and Informal Care*. London: Tavistock.

Van Gennep, A. (1960 [1908]) *The Rites of Passage*. London: Routledge and Kegan Paul.

Vesperi, M.D. (1985) *City of Green Benches: Growing Old in a New Down-town*. Ithaca, NY: Cornell University Press.

Wagnild, G. and Young, H.M. (1990) 'Resilience Among Older Women', *Image*, 22(4): 252–5.

Walker, A. (1982) 'Dependency and Old Age', *Social Policy Administration*, 16(2): 115–35.

Wallman, S. (1979) *Social Anthropology of Work*. London: Academic Press.

Walvin, J. (1982) *A Child's World: a Social History of English Childhood. 1800–1914*. Harmondsworth: Penguin.

Wardle, D. (1974) *The Rise of the Schooled Society*. London: Routledge and Kegan Paul.

Warnock Report (1978) *Special Educational Needs*. London: HMSO.

Welford, H. (1990) 'Face Values', *Guardian*, 21 March.

Whiteside, N. (1991) *Bad Times*. London: Faber and Faber.

Williams, D. (1975) 'The Brides of Christ', in S. Ardener (ed.), *Perceiving Women*. London: Dent.

Williamson, W. (1982) *Class, Culture and Community*. London: Routledge and Kegan Paul.

Wilson, A. (1980) 'The Infancy of the History of Childhood: an Appraisal of Phillipe Aries', *History and Theory*, 19(2): 132–54.

Wollstonecraft, M. (1967 [1792]) *The Vindication of the Rights of Women*. New York: Norton.

Woodhead, M. (1990) 'Psychology and the Cultural Construction of Children's Needs', in A. James and A. Prout (eds), *Constructing and Reconstructing Childhood*. Basingstoke: Falmer Press.

Woodward, K. (1988) 'Youthfulness as Masquerade', *Discourse*, 11(1): 119–42.

Woodward, K. (1991) *Aging and its Discontents*. Bloomington: Indiana University Press.

Wright, P. (1987) 'The Social Construction of Babyhood: the Definition of Infant Care as a Medical Problem', in A. Bryman, B. Bytheway, P. Allatt and T. Keil (eds), *Rethinking the Life Cycle*. London: Macmillan.

Young, M. and Willmott, P. (1973) *The Symmetrical Family*. London: Routledge and Kegan Paul.

Young, P. (1990) 'As I was Saying', *Nursing the Elderly*, November/December: 28.

INDEX